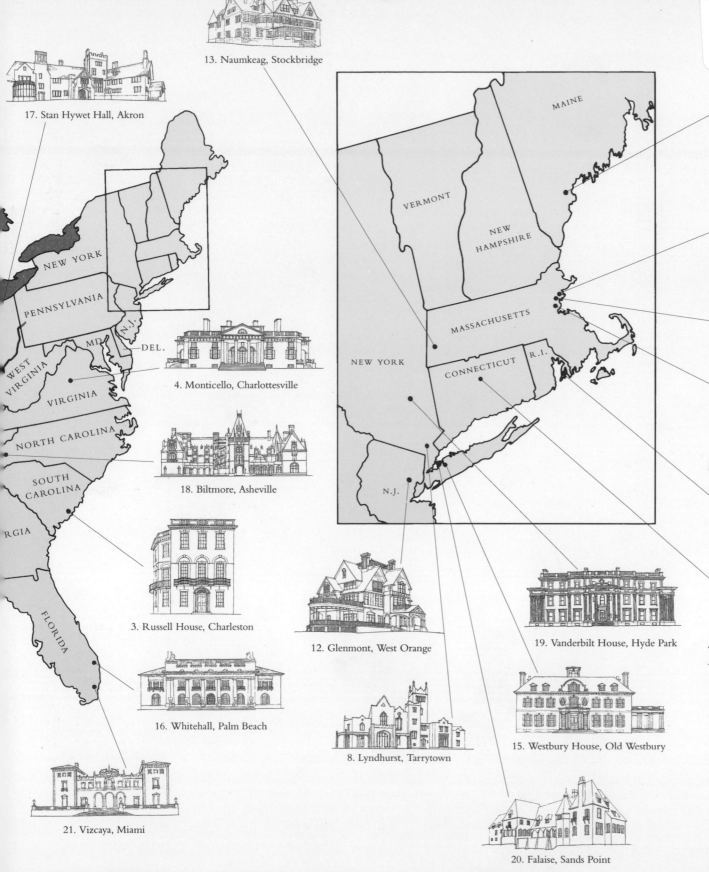

13. Naumkeag, Stockbridge

17. Stan Hywet Hall, Akron

9. Morse-Libby House, Portland

2. Lee House, Marblehead

1. Iron Works House, Saugus

25. Gropius House, Lincoln

10. Château-sur-Mer, Newport

11. Mark Twain House, Hartford

4. Monticello, Charlottesville

18. Biltmore, Asheville

3. Russell House, Charleston

16. Whitehall, Palm Beach

12. Glenmont, West Orange

8. Lyndhurst, Tarrytown

19. Vanderbilt House, Hyde Park

15. Westbury House, Old Westbury

21. Vizcaya, Miami

20. Falaise, Sands Point

Great American Houses

AND THEIR ARCHITECTURAL STYLES

Great American Houses

AND THEIR ARCHITECTURAL STYLES

VIRGINIA AND LEE MCALESTER

PHOTOGRAPHS BY
ALEX MCLEAN

DRAWINGS BY
LARRY BOERDER

FLOOR PLANS BY
CAROL BOERDER-SNYDER

ABBEVILLE PRESS   PUBLISHERS
NEW YORK   LONDON   PARIS

FRONT COVER:
Westbury House garden façade (see page 195).
BACK COVER:
The conservatory at Glenmont, Thomas Edison's house (see page 163).
FRONTISPIECE:
The grand staircase at Château-sur-Mer, designed by Richard Morris Hunt (see pages 132–33).

EDITOR: Jacqueline Decter
DESIGNER: Nai Y. Chang
PRODUCTION EDITOR: Owen Dugan
PRODUCTION MANAGER: Simone René
MAP: Jerry Guthrie

Text copyright © 1994 VEL Corporation
Photographs copyright © 1994 Alex McLean
Illustrations copyright © 1994 Larry Boerder

Compilation, including selection, order, and placement of text and images,
copyright © 1994 Abbeville Press.

Photographs on page 50 (RIGHT), 51, 52, 53 (BOTTOM), 54, and 55 copyright © Robert C. Lautman.

Library of Congress Cataloging-in-Publication Data

McAlester, Virginia
　　Great American houses and their architectural styles /
Virginia and Lee McAlester ; photographs by Alex McLean ;
drawings by Larry Boerder and Carol Boerder-Snyder.
　　　　p.　cm.
　　Includes bibliographical references (p.) and index.
　　ISBN 1-55859-750-6
　　1. Architecture, Domestic—United States—Themes,
motives.　2. Interior decoration—United States—Themes,
motives.　I. McAlester, A. Lee (Arcie Lee), 1933– .
II. McLean, Alex.　III. Title
NA7205.M36　1994
728.8'0973—dc20　　　　　　　　　　　　　　94-11055

Contents

ECLECTIC HOUSES · 190

Preface

This book is an outgrowth of, and in many respects a supplement to, our *Field Guide to American Houses* (1984). In that work we attempted to treat "the entire spectrum of American domestic building, from the most modest folk houses to the grandest mansions, but with a heavy emphasis on the smaller dwellings that lie between these extremes." Here the focus is shifted to the grand mansions themselves and to the story they tell of our country's changing tastes in housing design over the past three hundred years.

Each of the twenty-five landmark dwellings treated was chosen to illustrate one of the principal styles of American houses built during the long period from the first European colonies until about 1940. As in the *Field Guide,* the houses are presented chronologically. Six illustrate the dominant styles of the Colonial era (c. 1600–1820); three represent the Romantic era (c. 1820–1880); five the Victorian era (c. 1860–1900); and eleven the Eclectic era (c. 1880–1940), which was a high point in the diversity of American housing styles.

Choosing a single representative landmark for each style was a difficult task made only slightly easier by adhering to three criteria we felt were essential:

1. An exterior design typical of the style and, when at all possible, designed by a leading proponent of that style.

2. Interior design and furnishings, again when possible, appropriate to the period and style of the house. (We usually opted for houses with original fixtures and furnishings over those that are primarily restorations.)

3. Open to the public so that the interrelations between interior and exterior design can be viewed firsthand by all.

These restrictions, particularly the second and third, eliminated many potential choices. Some landmarks retain their original exteriors but the interiors have been extensively updated to reflect later fashions. Likewise, many superb houses are still private residences whose interiors can seldom, if ever, be visited. This is especially true for Victorian- and Eclectic-era landmarks, relatively few of which have been converted into museum-houses.

Even with these restrictions numerous difficult choices remained. The final selections must thus be considered only as our personal preferences among the many hundreds of superbly preserved and appropriately furnished American museum-houses available today for all to enjoy.

VIRGINIA AND LEE MCALESTER

Colonial Houses

(1600–1820)

For the first half of its history our country was not an independent nation but a group of scattered colonies belonging to England, Spain, or France. England controlled the Atlantic seaboard, which had the most direct access to Europe. Its thirteen colonies were by far the most populous. The vast center of the continent, drained by the Mississippi River and its tributaries, was a sparsely settled colony of France. The area that is now the southwestern United States was the remote northern outpost of a huge Spanish empire that stretched southward through Mexico and Central America into northern South America. All of the European colonists in these New World possessions brought with them the distinctive house-building traditions of their native countries. These styles persisted into the early decades of the nineteenth century, well after the colonies had become the independent United States.

The prosperous English colonies most closely mirrored the changing housing fashions of their mother country. During the seventeenth century their houses were built in what is now called the First-Period English style (pages 18–19), based on the venerable building practices of late medieval Britain. After 1700 the English colonies began a shift to the Renaissance-based Georgian style (pages 30–31), which had recently become fashionable in Britain (Colonial styles tended to lag behind those of the mother country by at least fifty years). By the time of the American Revolution, Colonial taste had begun changing to a related, but more delicate and refined, architectural fashion known in Britain as the Adam style but called the Federal style (pages 44–45) in the newly independent United States. This persisted until about 1820.

A fourth housing fashion of the English colonies was based not on medieval or Renaissance precedents but on a return to the architecture of ancient Rome that had originally inspired the Renaissance. Called the Early Classical Revival style (pages 58–59), it was far less common than the contemporaneous Federal style and was almost single-handedly popularized among wealthy southerners by Thomas Jefferson, our only architect-president.

Farther west, in the former French colony of Louisiana, only a small handful of houses in the French Colonial style (pages 70–71) survive. Most are in New Orleans or upriver along the Mississippi for about a hundred miles. Houses in the Spanish Colonial style (pages 82–83) are equally rare in the southwest, but scattered examples can still be found in parts of Texas, New Mexico, Arizona, and California.

The American Colonial styles are familiar today, thanks not to the rare original examples but to a later fashion for "reviving" Colonial designs (see the Colonial Revival style, pages 204–5, and the Spanish Eclectic style, pages 292–93). This trend began with the 1876 Philadelphia Exposition, which celebrated the centennial of American independence, and continues to this day.

Jane Braddick Peticolas (1791–1852), View of West Front of Monticello and Garden *(detail), 1825, watercolor on paper, 13⅝ × 18⅛ in.*

1

Iron Works House

First-Period English Style

*T*he phrase "Colonial New England" calls up visions of tidy, whitewashed villages with comfortable Georgian houses surrounding a pastoral square graced by a tall-spired church of elegant simplicity. This image is not incorrect but merely incomplete, for it applies only to the newly prosperous English colonies from about 1700 until the outbreak of the American Revolution in 1776. Before this came a longer period—beginning with the first permanent English settlement at Jamestown, Virginia, in 1607—during which the early colonists slowly replaced hardship and privation with a dependable supply of food, shelter, and clothing. Only half jokingly, some old-time New Englanders still refer to the seventeenth century as their ancestors' "struggle period."

Most houses of that time were simple, one- to four-room structures built for basic shelter rather than stylish living. These looked quite unlike the Renaissance-based Georgian dwellings that were then just becoming fashionable in England. Instead, these First-Period, or Postmedieval, English houses still used medieval building traditions that had been evolving in Britain for hundreds of years.

Only a small handful—probably less than two hundred—of these early structures have survived three centuries under threat of fire, decay, or demolition. Among the most complete and typical of these survivors is the handsome dwelling now known as the Iron Works House, located on the northeastern outskirts of Boston in Saugus, Massachusetts. The house's modern name derives from its proximity to the first major industrial enterprise in the New World, the Iron Works at Lyn, now the Saugus Iron Works National Historic Site, administered by the U.S. National Park Service.

The early New England colonies rather quickly became self-sufficient in most of the everyday necessities of life. The virgin continent's fertile soils and abundant game and fish assured a bountiful supply of food, while its vast forests and swift streams provided logs and sawmill sites for a limitless supply of lumber. Two essentials, however, had to be imported from England: cloth and iron goods.

A distinctive chimney dominates the rear view of the Iron Works House today. The left side shows the typical one-room depth of the style. The partial lean-to extension on the right and the secondary house beyond were added during the 1915–17 restoration. The original house probably had a full-width lean-to extension.

PAGE 10 *The restored rear parlor door features the wrought-iron hardware and decorative nail heads that were typical of the period.*

Wishing to maintain a monopoly on supplying cloth to its expanding colonies, England forbade the colonists to build textile mills. But because timber for smelting iron ore was becoming increasingly scarce in seventeenth-century England, Colonial iron manufacturing came to be encouraged. The New England enterprise, supported by both local entrepreneurs and English investors, was the first large-scale attempt to produce iron in North America. When completed in 1646, it was also one of the dozen or so most technologically advanced iron works in the world. Unfortunately, this ambitiously large enterprise soon suffered from mismanagement as well as from the artificially low price for its iron mandated by the English authorities. By 1675 the unprofitable works were abandoned and falling to ruin, and by 1700 the industrial structures had vanished. In the 1950s they were painstakingly restored to their original configuration through the efforts of the American Iron and Steel Institute.

Local tradition long maintained that a continuously occupied seventeenth-century house adjacent to the iron works had been part of the early industrial site—perhaps the residence of one or a series of iron masters who oversaw the complex operation. Modern historical, architectural, and archaeological research indicates that the house was more likely built about 1680 after the works were abandoned. Its first recorded owner was a local aristocrat named Samuel Appleton, Jr., who acquired the site to establish a farming enterprise in 1676. It is easy to imagine, however, that Appleton's large house is just the sort of dwelling the Company of Undertakers of the Iron Works in New England might have built for their agent-in-charge had the industrial enterprise still been prosperous thirty years after its founding.

None of our country's few surviving First-Period English houses persisted into this century in anything like their original appearance. All had been variously remodeled, expanded, and "modernized" so that their original structural elements lay hidden beneath later modifications. These changes usually served the dual purpose of increasing the living space and updating the style of the house's exterior appearance. The photograph below shows the Iron Works House as it looked about 1900, after more than two centuries of alterations. The appearance is generally Georgian, the dominant style of the English colonies in the 1700s, which featured whitewashed walls, balanced placement of double-sash windows, and elaborated front-door surrounds. To the practiced eye, however, there are several discordant notes, including Post-Georgian features, such as the large, six-per-sash window panes typical of the Federal style, which followed the Georgian, and a Romantic-era porch, probably added in the mid-1800s. Still more revealing are the steep front-roof pitch and the massive, multi-unit chimney, both of which suggest that an older First-Period house lies buried within.

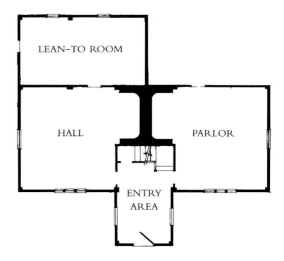

Original floor plan (as restored in 1915).

The Iron Works House about 1900, before restoration. An enormous rear extension, replaced windows and doors, and an added front porch all but obscured the original house. The massive chimney, steeply pitched roof, and partially obscured overhang provide the only exterior clues that this was originally a First-Period house.

Leaded-glass casement windows (ABOVE) and decorative pendants (BELOW) were added in the 1915–17 restoration.

RIGHT *The restored front façade.*

The original Massachusetts colonists came mostly from eastern England, an area that lacked local building stone and where, even in a timber-scarce country, houses were still built with heavy timber frames and sheathed with wooden clapboards. New England's vast forests allowed these colonists to duplicate closely the dwellings they had left behind. A problem arose, however, with roofing materials. In the milder and less stormy English climate roof timbers were typically covered with bundles of coarse straw called thatch, which must be applied at a steep angle to shed water properly. This tradition accounts for the original steep roof pitch of First-Period New England houses. These were initially covered with thatch, as in England, but after a few harsh, blustery New England winters with deep accumulations of rooftop ice and snow, it became clear that some other roofing material was essential. Soon thatch was replaced by thick, overlapping wooden "shakes," crudely split shingles that made a much stronger roof. The tradition of steeply pitched roof framing, though unnecessary for shake roofs, persisted for many decades. Note the rear half of the roof in the photograph on page 13, which shows the gentler roof pitch typical of Georgian houses of the 1700s. In this case the rear roof has been elongated to create a saltbox shape that accommodates larger rooms at the rear of the original plan.

The photo's second clue to the older house within is the massive, decorated chimney. Through much of the medieval period English houses, with the exception of grand palaces, lacked chimneys altogether. Instead, a fire for cooking and heating was located in the center of an all-purpose room, or "hall." The smoke wafted upward into the tall, open attic space, where it escaped, most inefficiently, through small roof openings. By late

LEFT *The central projection, with its high-pitched gabled roof, contains an entry area below and a small private room for the master of the house above. Historically this projection would have been called a "porch."*

RIGHT *The front door is made of thick vertical boards; the iron knocker is a twentieth-century copy of a seventeenth-century design.*

medieval times even modest English houses had begun to employ central chimneys, which not only removed smoke from the living area but also permitted the formerly open attic to be floored for second-floor sleeping rooms. These early chimneys had very large fireplace openings for cooking and heating, just like their unenclosed predecessors. Our earliest English colonists brought with them this late medieval fireplace and chimney tradition. Not until the 1700s did smaller and more efficient designs take their place.

Most larger First-Period houses, like their English counterparts, were two rooms wide and two stories high but only one room deep. Thus each floor had only two main rooms: a formal parlor and an all-purpose hall on the first and two bedrooms, or chambers, on the second. Additional space, when needed, was provided in three ways: 1) an enclosed central projection (called a porch in England, where American-style outdoor porches are known as verandas); this allowed a first-floor entry area and a small additional second-floor room; 2) third-floor attic rooms beneath the steep roof, lighted by tall gables; and 3) one-story lean-to projections extending to the rear. Appleton's large dwelling originally had all three of these features, which makes it an unusually complete example of seventeenth-century design.

Visitors to the Iron Works House often assume that the restoration to its 1600s appearance took place in the 1950s, at the same time as the reconstruction of the adjacent iron-making facilities—furnace, forge, mill, and storehouse. In fact the house was restored as a private dwelling much earlier—in 1915—as part of an early twentieth-century movement to identify and restore the best surviving examples of our country's

Colonial architecture. When carefully done, as is the case with the Iron Works House, these restorations approach the appearance of the originals. Modern research has shown, however, that many early restorations were based on erroneous conjectures about the houses' original designs.

Even the most elaborate surviving First-Period houses seem simple and austere when compared with the Georgian dwellings that replaced them (see Lee House, pages 20–31). The Iron Works House is no exception. Today three of its principal rooms are furnished with sturdy "Pilgrim-style" furniture that dates from the period of the house's construction.

The first-floor parlor was used both for receiving callers and for special-occasion dining. In more modest dwellings of the period it also had a curtained bed and served as a private master bedroom away from the upstairs bed chambers. This is understandable, given that the average family in those days numbered more than a dozen people, including not only many children but often grandparents and unmarried uncles and aunts as well. The second principal downstairs room, or hall, was the all-purpose cooking, eating, working, and "living" area. The hall in the Iron Works House now serves as a small museum of seventeenth-century hardware and building practices.

The principal second-floor bedroom is furnished as a formal parlor chamber, a French-style master bedroom that was also used for receiving close friends. Such rooms were then the latest fashion in England and the colonies. The other second-floor bedroom is now devoted to exhibits featuring the work of photographer and antiquarian Wallace Nutting (1861–1941), who was responsible for the house's 1915 restoration, which remains essentially unaltered today. A smaller second-floor room in the projecting porch is now furnished to resemble a seventeenth-century office or private room for the master of the house. Together the splendidly evocative Iron Works House and the adjacent reconstruction of America's first major industrial enterprise offer a unique glimpse into the life and times of our country's pioneering English colonists.

LEFT *The second-story parlor chamber was used for receiving honored visitors. The hand-woven wool cloth is dyed green, the most popular decorative color of the day.*

RIGHT *Attic view showing its heavy timber construction and the sculptural form of the multi-unit chimney.*

First-Period English Style
(1600–1700)

The English colonists who first settled our Atlantic seaboard in the 1600s brought with them what was to be the final phase of British medieval building practice. Typical houses of this first period of English colonization had just one or two ground-floor rooms with either a full sec-

ond story or smaller attic rooms above. Windows were small and irregularly spaced and were typically closed by wooden shutters. Only the wealthy could afford glass windows, then made of very small panes joined together with thin strips of lead. The most distinctive feature of these

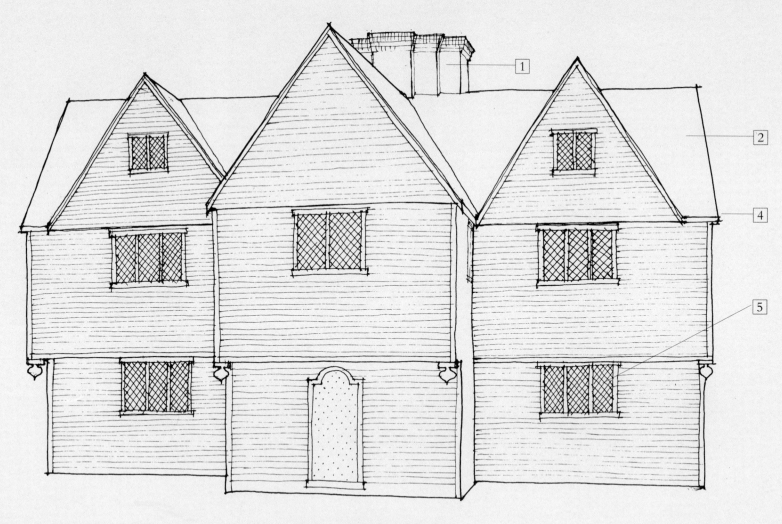

IRON WORKS HOUSE

18

First-Period houses was a steep and massively framed roof designed to be covered by bundles of stout straw called thatch. The steep pitch was necessary because thatch sheds water properly only when applied at very acute angles. Flatter applications soon become waterlogged and rot away. Such houses were built in the early 1600s by the first colonists at Plymouth, Boston, and elsewhere in coastal New England, and around Jamestown, Virginia, the first center of settlement in the southern colonies.

Throughout the 1600s, as the colonists prospered and new immigrants arrived, many more First-Period dwellings were built, and by 1700 these housed a total population of 220,000. During the first decades of the 1700s these medieval dwellings, already obsolete in England, lost popularity in the colonies as well. As in the homeland, they were replaced by houses in the Renaissance-inspired Georgian style, which featured flatter roofs, smaller chimneys, larger glass-paned windows, and formal, balanced façades centered around a prominent doorway emphasized with a decorative crown and moldings. This new fashion persisted with only slight modifications for the next 120 years of American expansion and growth. By the mid-1800s our country's First-Period English dwellings had all but disappeared; most were either destroyed by fire or demolished. A few, however, were remodeled into a more fashionable style. About 1900, antiquarians began to locate and restore, with varying degrees of accuracy, the few surviving First-Period houses. One of the most tireless of such workers was New England's Wallace Nutting, through whose efforts we can today enjoy the Iron Works House in an approximation of its original appearance three centuries ago.

IDENTIFYING FEATURES

1 MASSIVE CHIMNEY

2 STEEPLY PITCHED ROOF

3 ONE-ROOM DEPTH

4 NO EAVE OVERHANG OR CORNICE DETAILING

5 SMALL CASEMENT WINDOWS WITH MANY SMALL PANES

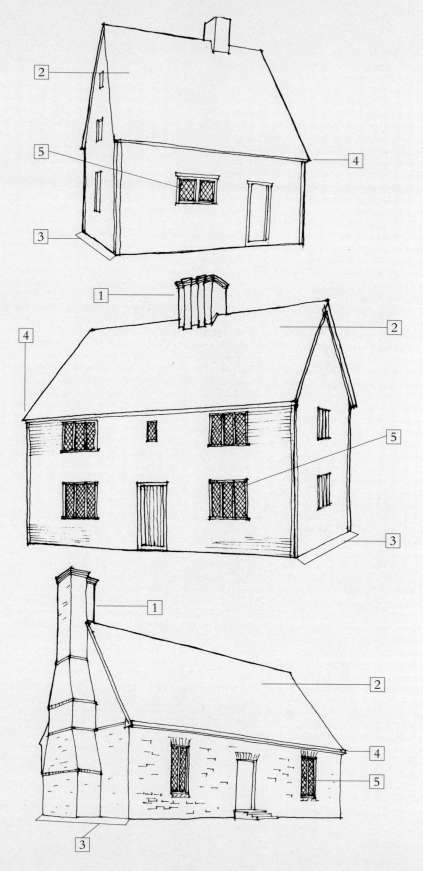

John O. J. Frost (1852–1928),
Marblehead Harbor, c. 1925, oil on board, 46½ × 71 in.
Collection of the Jeremiah Lee Mansion,
Marblehead Historical Society.

2
Lee House

MARBLEHEAD, MASSACHUSETTS

Georgian Style

Among the rarest of American Colonial houses are those that have survived for more than two centuries without being modified or "modernized." One of these is the large and elegant home built by merchant Jeremiah Lee (1721–1775) in Marblehead, north of Boston. The house has never had plumbing, is electrified only in one small area, has never been heated by anything but the original fireplaces, and still retains much of its original interior decoration.

The house has survived with so little change in part because it has had only three principal owners—Lee and his heirs from its completion in 1768 until 1804; the Marblehead Bank from 1804 to 1909; and the Marblehead Historic Society since 1909. The century-long stewardship of the Marblehead Bank was particularly important to the house's preservation. Today institutions utilizing older buildings routinely make extensive interior changes even when they are dedicated to preserving historic exteriors. Not so in this case. The bank's business was conducted in the two front rooms while the rest of the house was occupied by the chief cashier and his family. Such dual uses were then a common practice. The Marblehead Bank must have been an unusually thrifty and conservative New England institution, for not only did its owners never install any newfangled mechanical systems in the house, but they also left most of the original interior finishes intact throughout a hundred years of occupancy.

When the Lee House was put up for auction in 1909, the Marblehead Historic Society had the foresight to purchase the splendidly pristine house as a headquarters and museum. At that time techniques for preserving historic buildings were still in their infancy, yet the group practiced what has only in the past twenty years become a cardinal rule of the preservation movement—change as little as possible. Thus the members of the society did not add heating or cooling systems or plumbing; they did not "early up" any part of the house (that is, make changes to conform with one's picturesque notion of how an old house should look); they decided not to replace any original wallpapers, even those that looked a bit tattered in places. They simply

A nineteenth-century Chinese ivory fan with hand-painted scenes on each side and its original lacquer box; it is a typical example of the intricate products brought back to North America via the China trade routes.

maintained the house as it was, and in so doing presented future generations with a unique American landmark.

Marblehead is one of America's earliest towns, settled in 1629, only nine years after the Pilgrims arrived at Plymouth. At first it was under the jurisdiction of nearby Salem, but in 1649 it was incorporated as an independent town. Like other villages that grew up along Massachusetts's north shore during the Colonial era, Marblehead's fortune was tied to the sea. Its own special niche in the local maritime economy was fishing and not, for example, whaling, lobstering, or shipbuilding. Many of the town's first residents were fishermen from the south coast of England and the Channel islands. By 1660 their skills prompted a royal agent to report to the king that Marblehead was "the greatest Town for fishing in New England."

For more than a century Marblehead's fishing fleet brought the town great prosperity. By the outbreak of the American Revolution in 1776 it was the sixth-largest town in the American colonies, and second only to Boston in New England. Marbleheaders were ardent patriots and generously supported the revolutionary cause with men, ships, and money. It was, for example, Marblehead seamen who transported Washington and his army across the Delaware. And during the War of 1812, most of the crew members of the famous frigate *Constitution* were Marbleheaders.

Despite its citizens' heroism, Marblehead's economy never fully recovered from wartime losses. The final blow came in 1846, when much of the town's fishing fleet went down in a raging gale, leaving many fatherless families behind. This tragedy effectively put an end to the town's already ailing fishing industry.

Shoemaking, which had been the traditional winter occupation of Marblehead's fishermen, became the primary local industry for a time, but it, too, came to an end in 1888, when two disastrous fires destroyed the principal shoe factories. Then, in the late nineteenth century, Boston-area pleasure boats started gravitating to the old town's fine natural harbor. Local yacht clubs were formed, and designers, sail makers, and builders of recreation craft began to thrive. Marblehead thus developed a new tie with the sea and regained its prosperity as a center for pleasure sailing and yachting.

Today, with its narrow, winding streets and houses set close to one another on irregular sites, Marblehead still retains the charm of the medieval-style village it once was. The town's earliest houses were of medieval design (see Iron Works House, pages 10–19), but most of these were replaced during the 1700s by the more fashionable Georgian dwellings that continue to dominate the oldest part of the town.

In Marblehead's heyday as a Colonial fishing port, the town's wealthiest men were merchants whose vessels traveled the high seas seeking markets for the town's catch, which was preserved by salting, as well as for supplemental cargos of local lumber, grain, and rum. Jeremiah Lee was one of those who made his fortune in this very complex and risky business of overseas trade.

Successful traders balanced their cargos shrewdly, making sure never to carry too much of any one item, so as to avoid flooding the market and depressing prices. The ports a merchant chose to visit had to offer goods suitable for becoming his new cargo and at a price that would allow him to make a profit at the next port of call. Indeed, it was an unwritten rule of sea-trade economics that a captain bought his new cargo at the port where the old had been sold—long voyages with an empty vessel were a sure path to financial ruin. After several such stops, the trading ships returned to their home ports—hopefully with profits and valuable goods for local sale—only to start the cycle all over again.

While the bulk of New England's exports were salt fish and timber products (most commonly barrel staves) from local forests, a favorite return cargo was West Indian molasses, which was distilled into rum to become another valuable product for export. Typically, shorter trading voyages between New England, other Colonial ports, and the islands of the West Indies provided the cash for less frequent and longer voyages to Europe, where the merchants would buy expensive manufactured goods. Despite these preliminary runs, most New England traders were constantly in debt to English merchants, for they lacked enough cash crops to cover the purchase of all the English manufactured goods needed by the prosperous colonies. Furthermore English law sought to maintain this imbalance by forbidding most manufacturing in the colonies.

To help solve the problem of low-value exports, Jeremiah Lee and other Marblehead merchants took part in what was called the Iberian trade. The Catholic Spanish and Portuguese inhabitants of the Iberian Peninsula would pay premium prices for the very best of New England's salt fish. When caught, the fish were divided into three classes: "merchantable," "middling," and "refuse." It was the merchantable category that appealed to the Iberians and that Lee and others obligingly carried to them in large sailing vessels. The sale of the prized fish permitted the merchants to purchase high-value manufactured goods in England without making the tedious multiport coastal voyages.

Lee accumulated a substantial fortune from this Iberian trade and in 1768, when he was forty-seven years old, he completed his magnificent Marblehead house, then and now one of the largest and finest in all of New England. He was to enjoy it for only seven years.

Lee was a fourth-generation American, a descendant of one of the first Colonial families. He was also an ardent patriot and a member of the revolutionary Committee of Safety and Supplies for Massachusetts. In 1775 he attended a meeting of the committee in what is now Arlington, Massachusetts. Later that night British soldiers came to search the inn where Lee and two friends were staying. The three hastily escaped and, clad only in nightclothes, hid through the night in a freezing cornfield. It is reported that the chill Lee caught that night led to his death, probably from pneumonia, just a few weeks later. His widow continued to occupy the grand house until 1790, shortly before her death in 1791.

Located near the center of Marblehead, the Lee House is large and spacious even by later standards, and its interior finishes are unusually elegant. The earliest American examples of such large Georgian dwellings are the gracious plantation houses of Virginia built in the first decades of the 1700s. Generous land grants and the export of high-value tobacco made fashionable dwellings possible in Virginia at an early date. In contrast, New

A historical pedestal supporting a sundial is surrounded by a formal garden of octagonal design. The shape was chosen to echo the house's octagonal cupola.

ABOVE *Front façade of the Lee House.*

RIGHT *The subtly asymmetrical rear façade of the Lee House reveals the basic organization of the interior: smaller family rooms to the left, broad stair hall in the slightly projecting central section, and large formal rooms to the right.*

OPPOSITE TOP *The ten-paneled front door of the Lee House is accentuated by a classical entry porch, a design feature found on only a few Georgian houses.*

OPPOSITE BOTTOM *An early-nineteenth-century bronze door knocker in the shape of a dolphin.*

England, with its Puritan roots and large middle class, did not have the concentrated wealth needed for large and high-style dwellings until several decades later.

The exterior of the Lee House features a centered pavilion, a section of the façade that is thrust slightly forward and crowned by a triangular gable. Whereas the typical New England house of the period was two stories high with five vertical columns of windows on the front façade, the Lee House is three stories high with two additional columns of windows to offset the extra height. The house is actually larger than it appears because the shape is well balanced and mimics the proportions of smaller houses.

The exterior wall surfaces are made of wood crafted to look like rusticated stone, a favorite device of high-style Georgian designs. Even the corners of the house have wooden quoins, and the windows are topped by wooden lintels and keystones that also simulate stone.

The front entrance of the house has one of the earliest surviving American entry porches, or porticoes. These were rare for American Georgian houses but became a common feature of the Federal style that followed. A side entry of the Lee House has a more typical Georgian doorway.

Visitors entering the house find themselves in the central main hall and are immediately struck by its imposing size. The hall is sixteen feet wide, forty-two feet long, and twenty-two feet high. A grand seven-foot-wide stairway that ascends at a low angle dominates the hall. The stairway's handrail and balusters, as well as the hall's decorative dado, are made of handsomely carved Santo Domingan mahogany, possibly brought to Marblehead in Lee's own ships. The finely carved balusters accentuate the stairway's gentle slope. There are three balusters of different designs on each step. The outside edge of each riser is decorated with an inset panel and a carved leaf and rosette design.

The English-made wallpaper of the main hall, the upstairs hallway, and the two front rooms on the second floor is one of the great treasures of the house. It is original—hand painted in tempera especially for this house—and has remained in place for well over two hundred years. Similar wallpaper survives from only two other eighteenth-century houses, one English and the other American. The American example was in the now-demolished Van Rensselaer House in Albany, but the wallpaper is preserved in New York's Metropolitan Museum of Art.

With their painted scenes surrounded by elaborate trompe l'oeil stucco designs in shades of gray, black, and white, these papers imitated the European fashion of painting panoramic scenes directly onto wall panels that were surrounded by large areas of decorative stucco work. The paper itself was handmade in small sheets that were pasted together into long strips before the design was painted on.

The scenes depicted on the Lee House wallpaper were taken from popular eighteenth-century prints. The hallways have landscapes copied from engravings by the Italian artist Giovanni Paolo Pannini (c. 1691–1765). The Great Chamber, above the Great Room, features views of classical ruins, while the nearby Parlor Chamber, above the downstairs parlor, sports scenes of fishing villages and seaports, no doubt in reference to the source of Marblehead's (and Lee's) prosperity. The quality of these paintings is quite high. Wallpapers were a relatively new phenomenon in the 1760s and most had printed, rather than individually painted, designs.

The most elegant room in the Lee House is the Great Room on the first floor—the only room in the house fully paneled in wood, in this case native pine rather than the imported mahogany used in the partially paneled main hall. The paneling was originally painted a golden yellow, but in 1850 it was "grained" with skillfully applied paint to resemble stained wood, a popular fashion of that time. This was one of the Marblehead Bank's few decorative changes. The mantel in the Great Room is particularly fine. It is modeled after a drawing in Abraham Swan's *The British Architect-Builder's Treasury* (London, 1745). Copying architectural details from pattern books was a common practice in those days, even in houses as grand as Lee's.

The front façade of the house seems to have been similarly inspired, this time by a plate in Robert Morris's *Select Architecture* (London, 1755); the floor plan also resembles examples illustrated by Morris. Lee's brother Samuel, a well-known Marblehead builder-architect, designed and built his brother's grand dwelling using these English pattern books and the knowledge of "correct" building he gleaned while traveling in England.

The parlor, the smaller downstairs front room, was probably used as a less formal multipurpose room. The fireplace surround here is of typical Georgian design, with a

ABOVE *The sixteen-foot-wide main hall, with its broad mahogany stairway, lavish use of spiral balusters, and large expanses of hand-painted scenic wallpaper, was and is one of the grandest Georgian spaces in all of New England.*

OPPOSITE TOP LEFT *Unusual, recessed-curve handrail detailing.*

OPPOSITE BOTTOM LEFT *Detail of the Parlor Chamber showing the intricate intersection between the cornice molding and the top of a fluted pilaster.*

RIGHT *The stair treads are enhanced by carved Santo Domingan mahogany; the three balusters on each tread have slightly different spiral patterns. Beneath each tread is an inset panel and a carved floral "bracket."*

ABOVE LEFT *Jeremiah Lee by John Singleton Copley (1737–1815), 1769, life-size oil portrait. Collection of the Wadsworth Athenaeum, Hartford, Connecticut.*

ABOVE RIGHT *A large arched window lights the stairway landing; copies of Copley's portraits of Mr. and Mrs. Lee hang to each side.*

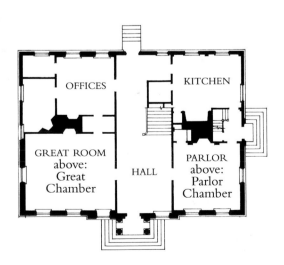

full-height pilaster on each side of the fireplace but without a mantel shelf. Such shelves over mantels were an innovation that was then just coming into fashion. One can be seen in the more stylish Great Room across the hall. The imported English Sadler and Greene tiles that surround the fireplace are rare survivors. The fireplace in the second-floor Parlor Chamber is quite similar, but here the tiles are of an even rarer polychrome design.

None of the original Lee furniture remained in the house during the bank's long occupancy, but the present furnishings, which are typical of the period of Lee's ownership, have been lovingly assembled by the Marblehead Historic Society, many with the assistance of long-time patron Louise Dupont Crowninshield. A few Lee items, including a fine set of chairs in the Great Room, have been obtained. Nineteenth-century copies of John Singleton Copley's full-length portraits of Jeremiah and Martha Lee hang on each side of the stair landing between the first and second floors, probably in the exact places for which they were intended. The originals are in the Wadsworth Atheneum in Hartford, Connecticut.

Two third-floor rooms are now furnished as original bedrooms, while much of the remaining third-floor space is occupied by the Marblehead Museum. The house's original kitchen was in a small exterior building, as was the usual practice at that time to reduce the risk of fire in the main dwellings. The interior kitchen was probably intended only for reheating food before serving it.

The Lee House, like the town of Marblehead itself, is a delightfully authentic survivor of another age. Gracious in size and concept, symbolic of the fortunes made at sea by early New Englanders, it has never been remodeled or "restored." It thus provides a unique link to our nation's distant Colonial heritage.

TOP LEFT *An upstairs bedroom opening onto the main hall has a crewel bed hanging and coverlet worked by a Westfield, Massachusetts, minister's wife in 1770–75.*

CENTER LEFT *The wallpaper in the upstairs Great Chamber features scenes of classical ruins, each surrounded by an elaborate painted "frame."*

ABOVE *The Parlor Chamber, across the hall, has scenes of fishermen and seaports—all overseen by Neptune. This detail shows the high quality of these rare original papers, all hand painted in gray, black, and white tempera.*

BOTTOM LEFT *The Great Room is completely paneled in pine. The design for the elaborate carved chimneypiece was taken from an English pattern book. Originally the paneling was painted a warm gold; in 1852 it received the faux wood graining seen today.*

Georgian Style

(1700–1780)

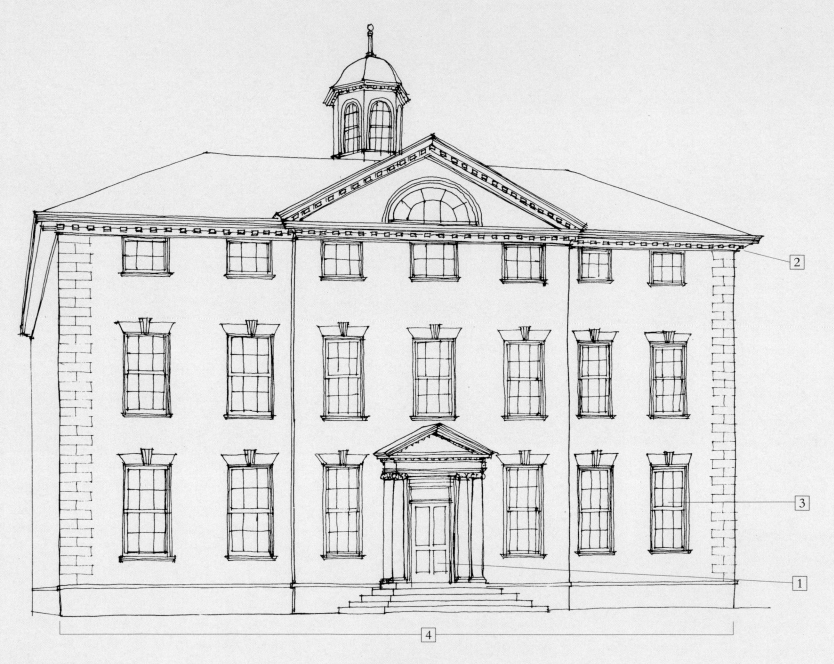

LEE HOUSE

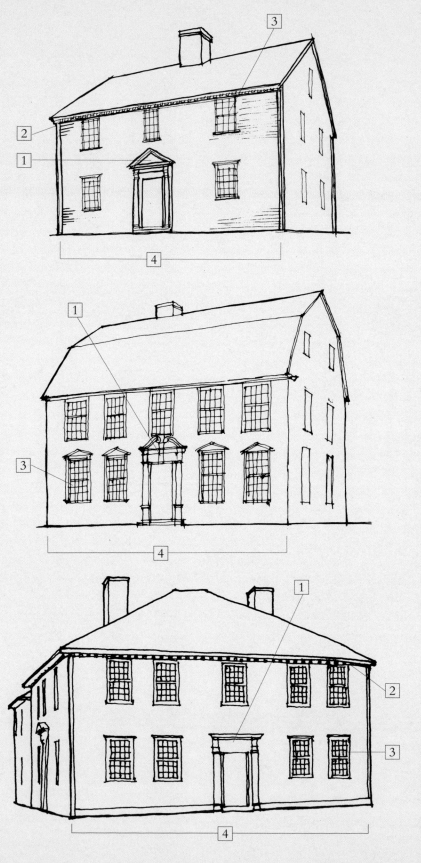

The artistic Renaissance that began in Italy in the 1400s and spread through France and Germany in the 1500s did not reach England until the 1600s. When it did, however, the medieval designs of English buildings began to be modified under its influence. Renaissance style took even longer to make its way across the Atlantic and take hold in England's thirteen colonies. But about 1700, balanced and symmetrical Renaissance-inspired buildings rapidly started replacing medieval designs in the colonies as well. This style is called Georgian after the several King Georges that ruled Britain through much of the eighteenth century. Georgian architecture dominated the colonies for most of that century until about 1780, when the closely related Federal style took its place.

In the 1700s, settlement in the thirteen colonies still clung closely to the Atlantic coast, and the most important towns were the seaports stretching from Portland, Maine, to Savannah, Georgia, that linked the colonies with distant Britain. Several of these Colonial towns—Boston, Philadelphia, and New York, for instance—were to grow into giant metropolises. In the process, however, they would lose most of their early architecture. Others were largely bypassed by later events and have survived as veritable museums of original Colonial buildings. Among these are Charleston, South Carolina; New Bern, North Carolina; Annapolis, Maryland; New Castle, Delaware; Newport, Rhode Island; and Marblehead, Massachusetts, site of Jeremiah Lee's splendid Georgian home.

IDENTIFYING FEATURES

1 PANELED DOOR WITH DECORATIVE CROWN

2 CORNICE EMPHASIZED WITH TOOTHLIKE DENTILS OR OTHER DECORATIVE MOLDING

3 WINDOWS WITH DOUBLE-HUNG SASHES, TYPICALLY WITH SIX TO TWELVE SMALL PANES PER SASH

4 WINDOWS IN SYMMETRICAL VERTICAL ROWS AROUND CENTRAL DOOR

*A striking pair of doors topped by an elliptical fanlight separate the reception room
beyond from the stair hall and the private rooms of the house.*

3
Russell House

Federal Style

*C*harleston, South Carolina, was the undisputed queen of southern cities in the years before the American Revolution. In 1663 several friends of King Charles II were made lord proprietors of Carolina and by 1670 the first settlers had arrived at Charles Town, as it was then called. By 1704 it was one of the few walled cities in North America, completely surrounded by fortifications built to protect it from incursions from nearby Florida, then a colony of Spain.

The town is located on a peninsula bounded by the Ashley and Cooper rivers before they merge with the sea. The rivers also served as barriers against attack, and within a dozen years the town was expanding beyond its original walls. With its fine natural harbor, Charleston soon became a principal New World trading center. Its first exports were furs attained through trade with the Indians, followed by locally grown indigo and rice, which were in turn supplanted by cotton. Small boats transported these products down inland rivers to Charleston, where they were repacked for shipment in oceangoing sailing vessels. By the outbreak of the American Revolution, Charleston's population of 12,000 made it the fourth-largest city in the American colonies, exceeded only by Philadelphia, New York, and Boston.

Charleston continued to grow and prosper for almost a century after America won its independence, right up until the Civil War, which began with shots fired on Federal troops at nearby Ford Sumter. The city and fort were soon a Confederate stronghold that fell under siege. Heavily damaged during the long conflict, Charleston then underwent a century-long period of austerity.

The city's economic decline did have one silver lining—it shielded a priceless legacy of early architecture from being replaced by newer construction. When prosperity returned in the 1940s, much of this splendid heritage was already protected by some of the nation's first historic-preservation ordinances. As a result, modern Charleston is a veritable museum of delightful historic houses and public buildings.

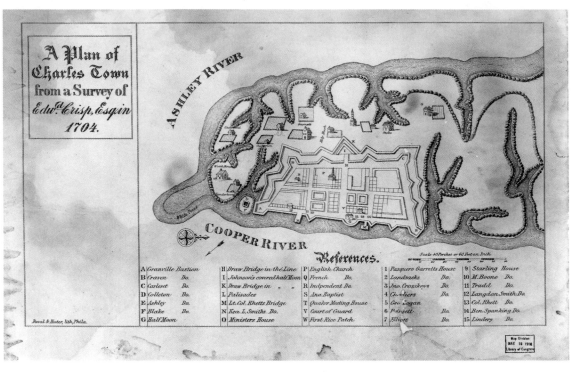

LEFT Nathaniel Russell *by Charles Fraser (1782–1860), c. 1818, watercolor on ivory, 6¼ × 5¼ in. Courtesy of the Historic Charleston Foundation.*

RIGHT *Plan of the original walled village of Charles Town, from a survey of 1704.*

In February 1765, during Charleston's golden days as the major port of the southern colonies, twenty-seven-year-old Nathaniel Russell (1738–1820), son of the chief justice of the colony of Rhode Island, moved to the city to become the local agent for several Providence merchants. South Carolina's bountiful crops of rice and indigo made Charleston a good place for the ambitious young man to seek his fortune. Upon his arrival, Russell placed an advertisement in the *South Carolina Gazette:* "Nathaniel Russell has just imported, in the sloop *Defiance,* from Rhode Island, a parcel of good Horses, Northward Rum, cheese, sperma-coated candles, onions and a few barrels of Apples, which he will sell cheap at his store in Colonel Beale's wharf." Thus began Russell's long and prosperous career as a Charleston merchant. During the American Revolution he sided with other merchants sympathetic to the British cause and in 1780 prudently sailed for England. It took special legislation to allow him to return to Charleston and regain title to his property in 1783.

In 1788 the fifty-year-old bachelor married for the first time. His bride, Sarah Hopton, was the daughter of another affluent local merchant. They soon had two daughters, Alicia and Sarah. For many years the family lived near Russell's wharfs and ships, as was common for merchants at that time. It was not until 1808 that he, his wife, and their now-teenaged daughters moved into a fashionable new dwelling he had built on Meeting Street.

The following years brought Russell great satisfaction. His house was hailed as a local landmark; he became known as "King of the Yankees" for his role in organizing and serving as president of a group of transplanted Northerners called the Charleston New England Society; and both his daughters married well, Alicia to a wealthy planter and Sarah to the Episcopal bishop of South Carolina.

Russell died in 1819 at the age of eighty-one, but his family continued to occupy the grand house until 1857, when it became the home of Robert F. W. Allston, then governor of South Carolina. Soon the privations of the Civil War reduced the women of

ABOVE *Early morning light accentuates the contrast between the "Charleston gray" (actually dull red) brick of the walls and the red rubbed brick used for the double belt courses, the second-story "blind" arches, and the first-floor window lintels.*

LEFT *The garden façade is dominated by a dramatic semi-octagon bay that lights the oval rooms within. The floor-length windows and exquisite iron balcony help make the garden feel like an extension of the house.*

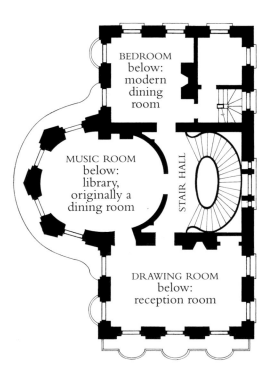

BEDROOM
below:
modern
dining
room

MUSIC ROOM
below:
library,
originally a
dining room

STAIR HALL

DRAWING ROOM
below:
reception room

Allston's family to running a school in their home. The Russell House was next turned into a convent school and then back into a private residence once again, before finally becoming the headquarters of the Historic Charleston Foundation in 1956. Since that time the foundation has maintained two floors of the house as a permanent museum.

Charleston was the mainland port closest to the sugar-rich islands of the British West Indies, with which it developed strong economic ties. Along with West Indies trade came architectural influences, including the use of porches, or verandas, to shade the south or west side of houses and to provide outdoor living space for hot evenings. This practice led to a penchant for positioning the narrow end of houses toward the street and for planting gardens along the houses' side. Although Russell rejected the typical Charleston side veranda for his house, he did opt for the lengthwise orientation and side garden. The tradition of having a private garden along the side of the house (usually the more breezy southerly side) led to what is called "northside manners" in Charleston, which meant not looking out your north-facing windows into your neighbor's garden. The narrowness of the houses also allowed them to be built quite close together, a particularly helpful feature given Charleston's location on a narrow peninsula.

Nothing is known about the designer of the Russell House. Russell himself may have sketched its plan with or without the help of a professional builder or architect. Whatever the source, the result was an unusually sophisticated façade in the then-fashionable Federal style. The house is built of local "Charleston gray" bricks, which, despite the name, are actually a dark, dull red; rubbed bricks of a brighter red are used for accenting the double "belt" courses between the stories, the rounded arches over the second-story windows, and the brick lintels over the first-floor windows. There are decorative stone lintels with keystones over the second- and third-story windows. The main entrance is somewhat unusual in its use of an elliptical fanlight without the usual side windows, or sidelights. Federal houses tend to have either a semicircular fanlight and no sidelights or a wide elliptical fanlight over both the door and two columns of sidelights. Above the doorway is a handsome wrought-iron balcony sporting the initials "N. R."; it serves a second-story room. A hint of the liveliness of the house's interior is seen in the three-story, semi-octagonal bay that projects outward on the garden side.

The house plan is remarkably true to the spirit of Robert Adam (1728–1792), originator of the Adam style, which was the British inspiration for American Federal designs. Adam was born in Scotland and learned his profession while working in his father's architectural firm there. He later set up his own firm in London, where he specialized in designing large country houses and their interiors.

At age twenty-six Adam left Scotland for Italy, where he spent three years gathering source materials that would serve him well for the rest of his career. He made plaster casts of moldings, prepared measured drawings of many antiquities, learned from fine craftsmen, and visited the excavations at Herculaneum, then just getting under way. Adam was particularly fascinated by these excavations, which included rare examples of well-preserved Roman houses. On his way home from Italy he and two draftsmen visited the remarkably preserved palace of the Roman emperor Diocletian at Split in what is now Croatia. The team spent a feverish five weeks there making measured drawings and gathering information for a book Adam was to publish in 1764. This book, *Ruins of the Palace of the Emperor Diocletian at Spalato in Dalmatia,* established his reputation as an expert on the newly discovered houses of ancient Rome.

After his return to Britain, Adam became concerned with what he called "movement" in house design. In the first volume of his *Works in Architecture* (1773) he states:

> Movement is meant to express the rise and fall, the advance and recess, with other diversity of form, in the different parts of a building, so as to add greatly to the picturesque of the composition. For the rising and falling, advancing and receding, with the convexity and concavity, and other forms of the great parts, have the same effect in architecture, that hill and dale, foreground and distance, swelling and sinking have in landscape.

In more concrete terms, by "diversity of form" Adam meant that he preferred adjoining rooms to have different shapes. The Russell House, with its rectangular, oval, and square rooms on each floor, is perhaps the finest American example of this principle. Another element of oval shape in the house—the elegant central stairway—further accentuates this unusual form.

The stairway itself is an engineering marvel. Built on the cantilever principle, it has no visible means of support and ascends from first to third floors without touching the

OPPOSITE TOP *A glimpse into the rear "room" of the Russell House garden, where a shaded pergola overlooks a bit of play-inviting lawn.*

OPPOSITE BOTTOM *Second-floor plan; this was the most formal floor of the house.*

Two curved mirrors mimic the four exterior windows of the elliptical music room. Among the few survivors of their type in the United States, the mirrors reflect and multiply daylight and candlelight. The entablatures and the cornice, made of a combination of wood and applied composition ornaments, typify the Federal style at its zenith.

The design of the graceful elliptical stairway is quite ingenious. Supported only by the second- and third-floor landings, it is entirely freestanding between stories and does not touch the walls. Each step is supported by, and cantilevered out from, the step below. Viewed from below (TOP), the subtle texture of the white plaster enclosure and the rhythm of the simple balusters dominate. Viewed from above (BOTTOM), the warm wood tones and the cantilevered stair treads prevail.

ABOVE *From the second-floor landing the stair hall's Palladian (lower) and elliptical (upper) windows can be seen. The 1786 George Romney portrait is of prominent Charlestonian Mary Rutledge Smith, shown with her twelfth child. After hanging for almost a century in England, the painting was returned to Charleston in 1975, purchased for the house by an anonymous donor.*

LEFT *The curving handrail is made of short sections of mahogany joined together. Its polished patina comes from nearly two centuries of constant use.*

adjacent walls. This ingenious construction allows two large windows to pierce the exterior wall, flooding the entire stairwell with light.

One of the stunning effects of the Russell House is that most of its rooms are similarly bathed in light. The rectangular front rooms on the second floor have windows on three sides. The oval middle rooms on both the first and second floors have four windows spaced around half of the oval. The overall light and airy feeling is an effect that Adam always attempted to achieve in his work. Combined with the delicate mantel and cornice decorations for which he was noted, this lightness gives Adam-inspired rooms an almost lacelike quality.

Visitors entering the Russell house find themselves in a large reception room; dramatic double doors, with windows in the top half and an elliptical fanlight above, connect this room with the stair hall beyond. The windows in these doors not only help bathe the stair hall with light but also offer a view that extends the entire three-room depth of the house.

The stair hall itself forms the core of the house—all of the nine main rooms open onto this central space, which is dominated by the spectacular oval stairway. The central stair rail makes a continuous sweep from first to third floor; it is made of hundreds of sections of Honduran mahogany carefully fitted together. Simple, slender, square-sided balusters allow the curve of the stairway and rail to dominate. Curved stairways were an Adam

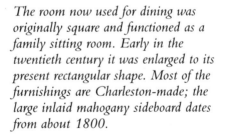

The room now used for dining was originally square and functioned as a family sitting room. Early in the twentieth century it was enlarged to its present rectangular shape. Most of the furnishings are Charleston-made; the large inlaid mahogany sideboard dates from about 1800.

speciality and this one, designed and constructed thousands of miles from the nearest buildings by Adam himself, is among the finest surviving examples of his decorative genius.

The first-floor oval room, now the library, was originally the dining room, while the square rear room, first used as an informal family sitting room, was expanded into a large rectangular dining room in the early twentieth century. It now features fine American furniture, most of it made in Charleston. The focal point is a rare table, circa 1800, set with Chinese Export porcelain.

Before the mid-1800s the main entertaining rooms of fine urban dwellings were often located on the second floor instead of the first, high enough to catch cooling summer breezes and to reduce dust and noise from the street. That the second floor was meant to be the Russell House's formal living area is underscored by the difference in detailing between the elliptical first-floor library below and the identically shaped music room above, which has much finer architectural decoration. Its cornice is quite deep and elaborately detailed, while that of the library is both shallower and simpler. The windows on the second floor are full length, while those below are a more normal window depth. In addition, the second-floor room has two identical false windows in the interior wall. Their mirrored-glass panes reflect and amplify the light. The window surrounds on the first floor are quite simple, while those on the second floor are flanked by "reeded" pilasters that support an ornate entablature above. A final contrast is in the mantels. Both have typical Adam

LEFT AND RIGHT *The second-floor drawing room, bathed in light from its seven full-length windows, has window surrounds and cornice details as delicate as, but different from, those in the music room. Classical scenes in bas-relief, inspired by Robert Adam's drawings of archaeological excavations in Italy, were favored enhancements for mantels and mirrors (see also the library mantel opposite).*

ornamentation—a centered rectangular panel with a bas-relief decoration applied to it—but the upstairs version is more intricate. Fine pilasters on each side of the fireplace in the music room support a wide decorative entablature, while downstairs these elements are much less elaborate.

• The square rear room on the second floor was originally a bedroom, as were all three of the third-floor rooms. This second-floor bedroom now features a handsome chandelier and a fine Hepplewhite bureau, another of the many fine Charleston-made pieces in the house.

Although Russell's original furnishings had been dispersed for almost a century when the Historic Charleston Foundation acquired the house, the foundation has made a great effort to fill it with objects appropriate to Russell's era and to his status as a wealthy merchant. Most of the furniture dates from 1770 to 1820, the years during which Russell would have been acquiring his belongings. Items from around the world are appropriately included in the collection since Russell's ships would have had access to quality goods from many countries.

The Charleston-made furniture in the house is particularly important because the city's cabinetmakers were renowned throughout the American colonies for their superb craftsmanship. The Charleston furniture industry began well before the American Revolution, and by 1810, when Russell was just settling into his new house, there were eighty-one furniture-making establishments in the city. The wood they used included local cedar, cypress, red bay, and poplar, as well as mahogany brought in from the West Indies. When the import tax on mahogany was removed in 1740, it became the favored wood for Charleston furniture. There were also many other artisans at work in Charleston: black-

smiths who executed delicate wrought-iron balconies and fences, silversmiths, plasterers, and others. The ease with which Russell could acquire items of such fine workmanship contrasts sharply with Jefferson's struggles only a few years earlier to obtain even construction bricks at remote and rural Monticello (see page 48).

The final Russell House room now on display is the pale green drawing room, which stretches across the front of the second floor. This elegantly sophisticated room would have been remarkable in London, yet it was built in a relatively small city in the young United States, far from the great houses of England where Robert Adam plied his trade. Its seven full-length windows open onto the second-story wrought-iron balcony. Light floods the room in a way not possible during the earlier Georgian era, because the technology for manufacturing large panes of glass had only recently been perfected. Adjoined with delicate, narrow glazing strips, these panes created the first picture-window effect in house design.

The windows are flanked by paired pilasters that support an elaborate entablature. These and the deep cornice moldings above are decorated with the Roman-inspired garlands and urns popularized by Adam. The room's soft greens were among Adam's favorite colors. It is now being discovered that many American homes of this era were painted in bright colors, almost shockingly bright to our modern eye, but original color renderings of Adam's commissions usually show nearly monochromatic color schemes of soft greens, blues, or ivories.

The Russell House superbly demonstrates those principles of space, light, and movement that made Adam's interiors, and the Adam-inspired American Federal style, so delightfully different from all that had come before.

LEFT *The second-story bedroom has several fine pieces of Charleston-made furniture, including this bed (c. 1800) and chest (c. 1770).*

RIGHT *The first-floor oval room has simpler detailing than the second-floor music room above it. Originally the dining room, it is now the library, presided over by Edward Savage's portrait of Nathaniel Russell (c. 1778).*

Federal Style

(1780–1820)

The American Georgian and Federal styles, both of which are based on British architectural trends, are conveniently separated in this country by the Revolutionary War and independence from Britain. Though derived from Georgian designs, the style that flourished in the newly independent United States is known as Federal, as if to underscore the end of two and a half centuries of British rule. The related architectural fashion in Britain is called the Adam style, after the influential architect brothers Robert and James Adam, who originated the style and were largely responsible for popularizing it.

The exteriors of many Federal houses are deceptively similar to those of the Georgian houses that preceded them. The principal differences are larger window panes, occasional bay windows, and an almost universal fanlight above the front doorway. Georgian and Federal interiors, however, are far less similar. The Federal style replaced Georgian wood-paneled walls with plaster ornamented by delicate raised swags and garlands; massive Georgian mantelpieces became smaller and more refined and also were embellished with delicate floral ornamentation. Still more striking is the Federal emphasis on unusual room shapes. In larger Federal houses ovals, half-octagons, and squares replace the rectangular rooms typical of Georgian dwellings, as does a new emphasis on larger windows and increased natural lighting of interiors.

By about 1820, when Federal designs began being replaced by newer fashions, the burgeoning new nation had already expanded westward into Ohio, Indiana, Kentucky, Tennessee, and Alabama. As a result, Federal houses were not confined to the coastal states as Georgian houses had been but were to be found over much of the eastern half of the country. Nevertheless, many of the largest and finest Federal houses were built in the prosperous port cities along the Atlantic coast, where much of the new nation's wealth was concentrated. It was in the affluent southern port of Charleston that merchant Nathaniel Russell built the grand house that is one of the high points of American Federal design.

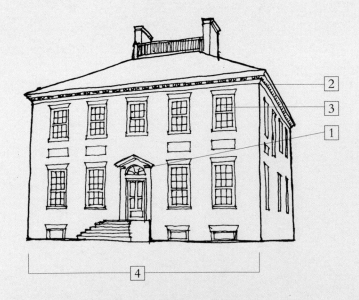

IDENTIFYING FEATURES

1 SEMICIRCULAR OR ELLIPTICAL
   FANLIGHT OVER PANELED DOOR

2 CORNICE EMPHASIZED WITH
   TOOTHLIKE DENTILS OR OTHER
   DECORATIVE MOLDINGS

3 WINDOWS WITH DOUBLE-HUNG
   (UPPER AND LOWER) SASHES,
   TYPICALLY WITH SIX PANES PER SASH

4 WINDOWS IN SYMMETRICAL VERTICAL
   ROWS AROUND CENTRAL DOOR

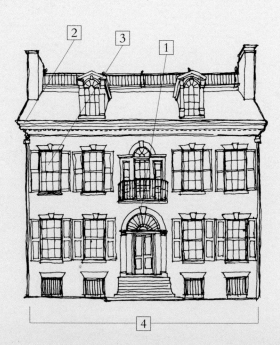

RUSSELL HOUSE

4

Monticello

Early Classical Revival Style

*N*o house in America more clearly echoes the thoughts, hopes, and ideals of one man than Monticello, designed and built by Thomas Jefferson, who planned and supervised every detail of its construction. Just as Jefferson was one of the most complex and multitalented leaders our country has produced, so, too, is his home—the work of his entire adult life—one of the nation's most fascinating houses.

Visitors to Monticello may not realize that during most of Jefferson's lifetime the house looked quite different from its appearance today. He began building the house in 1769, when he was only twenty-six, and did not finish it until 1823, when at the age of eighty he looked on as the columns of the west portico were finally raised into place. In the intervening fifty-four years Monticello was in a continuous state of flux as Jefferson's restless and searching intellect, and his passion for building, drove him to keep modifying and improving his grand plan for the house.

How, many have wondered, could it possibly have taken half a century to complete even as elaborate and personal a house as Monticello? In a recent book entitled *Jefferson and Monticello: The Biography of a Builder,* author Jack McLaughlin gives many fascinating insights into the difficulties Jefferson faced, and in some cases created for himself, in this lifelong building process.

Monticello means "little mountain," and Jefferson's initial decision to locate his home on a rural Virginia mountaintop was responsible for many of the complexities he had to solve. First there was the question of water supply, both for household use and for manufacturing the countless bricks used to build the house. Most rural houses are located near rivers, springs, or other sources of water, such as shallow wells. At Monticello even the deep well Jefferson eventually had dug proved to be erratic. During the ten years that his wife, Martha, lived in the house the well's flow was often insufficient for the household's needs, and for two of those years it was completely dry. In this period barrels of water had to be

PAGE 46 *Columns were so difficult to construct in remote western Virginia that the west portico of Monticello was supported by unfinished tree trunks until three years before Jefferson's death, when he finally had the Doric-style columns built of cut stone and shaped brick.*

hauled up to the mountaintop in wagons. Eventually a system of cisterns for collecting rainwater was constructed; this helped, but did not alleviate, the water-supply problem.

The dearth of water also impeded the manufacture of bricks. In the eighteenth century bricks could not simply be purchased and shipped to remote rural areas—they had to be made by hand on site. Suitable clay is first mixed with water and then molded into soft blocks that are hardened by a firing process, much like pottery. To produce the bricks for Monticello, either the scant supply of mountaintop water had to be used or they had to be made at a water source farther down the mountain and then carted up the steep road to the building site by horse and wagon. Both methods were tried, but neither was entirely satisfactory. The difficulty was compounded by a scarcity of experienced brick makers in that remote part of western Virginia.

Similar problems plagued every phase of the house's construction. Whether it was plaster for the walls, finished woodwork, windows, or hardware, all the building materials had to be either manufactured on the site or shipped by wagon over primitive roads. Finding competent workmen was equally difficult. Imagine trying to lure one of the relatively few skilled carpenters, brick makers, or plasterers of Colonial Virginia to an isolated mountaintop in the middle of nowhere.

To compound the difficulties even further, Jefferson was a tireless perfectionist; in the middle of the building process he completely changed the design of Monticello. The original design was based on the works of the Italian Renaissance architect Palladio, which Jefferson knew primarily from the architecture books he collected for his library. Palladian designs were then quite rare in this country, where much simpler, box-shaped Georgian houses were the prevailing fashion. The first Monticello featured a full-height, two-story Palladian porch on a central block that was flanked by lower, one-story wings. This design was nearing completion when, in 1784, Jefferson left the country to spend five years in Paris as America's minister to France. The architecture of that city gave him a wealth of new ideas for Monticello. He was particularly impressed with innovative French spatial plans and refined exterior designs.

Upon his return to America in 1789, Jefferson began planning his redesign of Monticello. He determined, for example, that the central block would be more pleasingly scaled if it appeared to be only a single story high. To achieve this effect he used a design he had seen in France in which the second-story windows appear, from the exterior, to be but the upper part of the first-floor windows. Monticello's original two-story porticoes were also redesigned to give a one-story appearance. A still more disruptive modification was Jefferson's decision to more than double the size of the house. These changes required demolishing part of the original house and rebuilding and expanding the rest.

Jefferson worked on the plans for the new design for the next five years. Most of that time he resided in Philadelphia, where he was serving as secretary of state under President George Washington. It was not until 1794, when he thought he had left government service for good, that he returned to his beloved mountaintop, first to renew his agricultural operations and then, in 1796, to begin the massive remodeling of Monticello.

To appreciate the enormity of Jefferson's task, one must remember that he returned to a house that had not been completed when he left for France. Much of the exterior woodwork had never been painted and was deteriorating from ten years of exposure. Once demolition began, walls came down and sections of roof were removed, sometimes not to be replaced for a year or more. Five years into the rebuilding the basic exterior was finished, but the interiors were still very rough—less than half the rooms were plastered and many of the floors were not fully laid down. At this point Jefferson was elected president of the United States.

His new responsibilities kept him away from Monticello for much of the next eight years. Luckily he found a skilled carpenter-builder, James Dinsmore, who met his exacting requirements and oversaw the remodeling in his absence. Dinsmore continued the rebuilding throughout Jefferson's presidency, but his efforts were often slowed or hindered by Jefferson's increasing financial problems. Scarce capital and labor frequently had to be redirected to other plantation projects that had the possibility of a direct financial return. The miracle is that Monticello's *interior* was at last completed in 1809, when Jefferson was sixty-six years old.

Through his most active years of raising a family, of public service, of entertaining dignitaries from the United States and abroad, Jefferson had lived in a house under construction, and so did his guests. A dedicated host, he entertained hundreds of visitors at Monticello, not at all deterred by its unfinished state. Some wrote ungraciously of their stay on the mountaintop. In 1802 Anna Thornton, wife of the well-known architect William Thornton, noted in her diary:

> We went thro' a large unfinished hall, loose plank forming the floor, lighted by one dull lanthern, into a large room with a small bow and separated by an arch. . . . The president has altered his plan so frequently, pulled down & rebuilt, that in many parts without side it looks like a house going to decay from the length of time that it has been erected. . . . Mr. J has been 27 years engaged in improving the place, but he has pulled down & built up again so often, that nothing is compleated, nor do I think it ever will be. . . . He is a very long time maturing his projects.

More understated were the comments of biographer Dumas Malone, "The house at Monticello was not for some time a convenient one."

Other guests were able to share Jefferson's vision despite the chaos. In 1796 the duc de La Rochefoucauld-Liancourt wrote:

> The apartments will be large and convenient; the decoration, both outside and inside, simple, yet regular and elegant. Monticello, according to its first plan, was infinitely superior to all other houses in America, in point of taste and convenience; but at that time Mr. Jefferson had studied taste and the

LEFT *The main entry door and two full-length windows, all topped with arched windows, flood the entrance hall/ Museum with light.*

RIGHT *Jefferson designed the Great Clock with cannonball weights that lower to indicate the day of the week. On Sunday an ingenious folding ladder was used to rewind the mechanism.*

fine arts in books only. His travels in Europe have supplied him with models; he has appropriated them to his design; and his new plan, the execution of which is already much advanced, will be accomplished before the end of the year, and then the house will certainly deserve to be ranked with the most pleasant mansions in France and England.

With Jefferson's great interest in architecture it is an irony that after the completion of Monticello's interior many exterior details remained unfinished for years. The steps were makeshift affairs, and crude tree trunks substituted for classical columns on the western portico. The last of the now famous porticoes was finally completed only three years before his death at age eighty-three. Despite its long gestation period, Monticello is very much as Jefferson planned it in his second design. It clearly reflects his concerns with elegant architecture, everyday practicality, and a place to pursue his many intellectual interests.

The main entry is through the east portico. Walking up the front steps, the visitor is immediately struck by three enormous glassed-in arches, the central one of which is the front door. Inside, light from these openings floods the entrance hall, which also served as Jefferson's Museum; it was filled with archaeological artifacts, natural history specimens, and marble busts. Jefferson felt that science and history were essential disciplines; how better to enjoy them himself, and to share his enthusiasm with visitors, than by displaying important objects from his own collection?

In the entrance hall visitors see the first of many practical gadgets and innovations Jefferson installed through Monticello. A clock over the door, built to Jefferson's specifications, is connected to a scale on the far right wall that indicates the day of the week. When the clock is wound, cast-iron weights travel up the wall to the Sunday mark at the top. As the clock moves through the week the weights pass the other day marks. By Friday they have disappeared through a hole cut in the floor. Jefferson's design was too long for the room, so the weights spend Saturday in the basement before being rewound on Sunday morning. In other rooms mechanical dumbwaiters bring up food from basement service rooms, and double doors have hidden interconnections to open them in unison.

Jefferson's spatial innovations include his liberal use of octagonally shaped rooms, which admit far more light than do the usual squares or rectangles. Beds are placed in alcoves to save floor space. Jefferson's own alcove bed is placed *between* two rooms—his

ABOVE *Jefferson's alcove bed is nestled between his bedroom and his cabinet (private study). In theory this arrangement allowed him to retire from either room, but in practice one side of the alcove was covered first with glass and later with paper panels to prevent drafts. The space above the alcove, marked by three elliptical openings, was a closet for out-of-season clothing and linens.*

PAGE 52 *Jefferson's cabinet is one of the semi-octagonal rooms at Monticello. It housed his collection of scientific instruments, one of the first in the nation.*

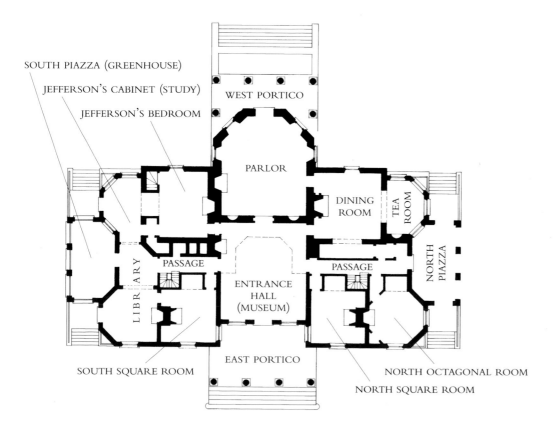

SOUTH PIAZZA (GREENHOUSE)

JEFFERSON'S CABINET (STUDY)

JEFFERSON'S BEDROOM

WEST PORTICO

PARLOR

DINING ROOM

TEA ROOM

LIBRARY

PASSAGE

PASSAGE

NORTH PIAZZA

ENTRANCE HALL (MUSEUM)

SOUTH SQUARE ROOM

EAST PORTICO

NORTH OCTAGONAL ROOM

NORTH SQUARE ROOM

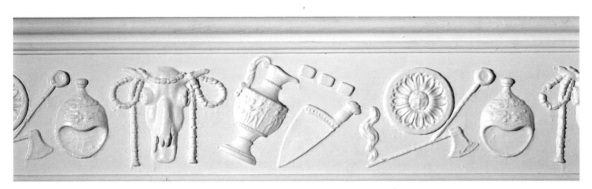

Monticello's many entablatures were constructed of basic wooden moldings embellished with cast composition ornaments, such as the rosettes in the tea room's Doric entablature (TOP LEFT). The decorative ornaments in the frieze of the parlor's entablature (BOTTOM LEFT) are all symbolic of ancient sacred sacrificial rites. The ox skull was a particular Jefferson favorite and is found in many entablatures and mantelpieces at Monticello.

BELOW The elegant dining room mantelpiece, with its blue-and-white jasperware plaques and marble shelf, was also very practical. The panel doors on each side hide dumbwaiters for delivering bottles from the wine cellar below.

dressing room and his study—a theoretically ideal arrangement that in practice proved quite drafty. Glass and later paper-covered panels were added to the alcove for warmth.

Jefferson toiled long and hard over the decoration of the principal interior rooms. The difficulty of finding skilled craftsmen forced him to abandon pilasters and devote his energy instead to the design and installation of the entablatures. Historically, each order of classical column—Doric, Ionic, Corinthian, and so forth—supported a corresponding type of entablature. For the entrance hall Jefferson chose an Ionic entablature; Doric was used in the dining room, and the parlor features Corinthian. Other variations are used in the other rooms, but all are quite close to the proportions prescribed by Palladio.

Fortunately for Jefferson, the entablatures did not have to be made entirely of wood. James Dinsmore would carve a representative section out of wood, make a mold of it, and then cast the requisite number of copies in "composition," a mixture of linseed oil, powdered chalk, and glue. Jefferson found another skilled craftsman in Washington, D.C., to carve and cast the delicate frieze ornaments. Dinsmore then mounted the various elements onto the cornice boards around the top of each room. When painted, the composition parts of the entablature were indistinguishable from the wooden ones.

One of Jefferson's favorite decorative motifs for both entablatures and mantelpieces was the ox skull, sometimes with floral swags suspended from the horns. The ox was the most sacred of ancient Roman sacrifices, and the skull motif ornamented the temples of Vesta in many Roman cities, signifying "the hearth and home as the center and source of Roman life and power." Jefferson felt much the same about Monticello—it was his source of peace and strength—and he also believed that the individual family was the source of America's power.

The parlor has a striking cherry and beechwood parquet floor designed by Jefferson. He brought many of the house's furnishings from Paris, including the large rectangular mirror on the left, one of a pair installed in this room in 1809; they cover two brick niches left over from the house's original design.

The great dome of Monticello was patterned after Rome's temple of Vesta, goddess of the hearth. No longer furnished, the room is not accessible to the public.

The semi-octagonal tea room is bathed with light entering from four different angles. Called by Jefferson his "most honourable suite," it holds likenesses of his friends and heroes.

In addition to the famous gadgetry, Jefferson also designed some of the furnishings for Monticello. For example, he devised an ingenious variation on bookcases. Instead of shelves he used boxes that he stacked one on top of another with the open end facing out. The effect was the same as shelves, but the boxes could easily be moved about and rearranged. Anyone who has built inflexible, fixed bookshelves only to move to another home and leave them behind, or who has had to pack books in boxes only to spend days putting them back on shelves, can't help but be impressed by this strikingly simple idea.

Jefferson was also intensely interested in landscaping and garden design. Wishing to preserve the pristine beauty of Monticello's mountaintop views, he sought a way to avoid cluttering the grounds with the many outbuildings a working plantation required. His solution was to build two dependency wings, which began beneath the main part of the house and extended outward along the sides of the mountaintop. This plan retained unimpeded vistas in all directions from the house. To keep working gardens out of view he had them cut into terraces below the crest of the hill.

In the last years of Jefferson's life, Monticello, finally complete, was already falling into disrepair because of his accelerating financial problems. Shortly before his death, Jefferson even attempted to sell off parcels of land, including his beloved Monticello, in a lottery. This desperate move failed to raise sufficient funds, however, and after his death most of Monticello's furnishings and equipment were sold at auction to pay off his debts. No one wanted to buy the house itself because its location made it impractical and expensive

ABOVE *Jefferson enclosed the piazza outside his library to make a small greenhouse.*

RIGHT *This terrace was cut into the mountain's sunny southern slope for the plantation's vegetable gardens. The brick pavilion is a modern reconstruction.*

to maintain. In 1831 it was finally sold for $5,000 to a druggist as a silkworm farm. When this venture failed it was sold for $2,700 to Lt. Uriah P. Levy, a naval officer who admired Jefferson and appreciated the house's unique historical value. Levy and his descendants owned and preserved Monticello for almost a century until 1923, when it was purchased and restored as a permanent museum by the Thomas Jefferson Memorial Foundation.

The importance of Monticello today is not only that it affords a glimpse of the way America's third president lived, but also that it reflects the extraordinary dreams Jefferson spent much of his life fulfilling. The man who could see a remote Virginia mountaintop, imagine a Monticello, and work toward perfecting this vision for half a century is the same man who could look at a small, undeveloped country and conceive of a great nation in which all men were created equal, who could observe the vast wilderness of the Louisiana Territory and envision a nation stretching from ocean to ocean.

The house and west lawn are reflected in an ornamental fish pond added in 1808. The Roundabout Walk surrounding the lawn was designed by Jefferson, who often varied the flowers in the beds that flank it.

Early Classical Revival Style

(1770–1830)

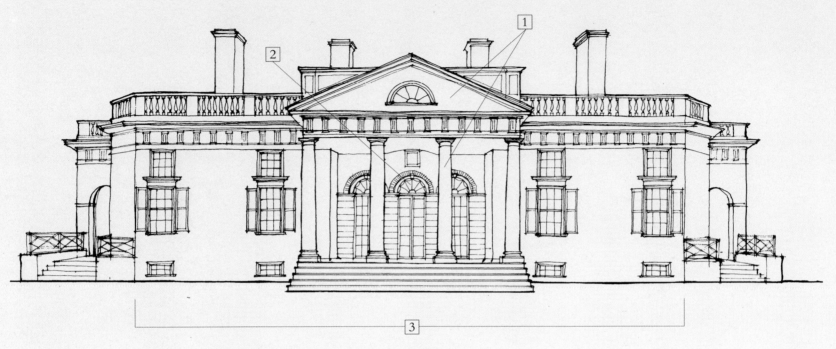

MONTICELLO

The Early Classical Revival style owed its popularity to the restless intellect and persuasive influence of Thomas Jefferson, so much so that it is sometimes called the Jeffersonian Classical style of American architecture. In his youth Jefferson became bored with the simple and sedate Georgian buildings that dominated Colonial Virginia. A man of vast curiosity and a voracious reader, he was particularly impressed by one of the great works of the Italian Renaissance, Andrea Palladio's *Four Books of Architecture,* first published in 1570. The primary focus of these volumes are the subtypes, or orders, of Greek and Roman design as expressed in the details of porch columns and the decorated roofs that the columns support. Palladio gives

exact mathematical rules and "correct" ratios for each part of the classical orders and for their applications to buildings of differing size, shape, and function. The underlying theme is that careful use of the classical orders, particularly as perfected in ancient Rome, is the key to producing buildings of timeless beauty.

Jefferson firmly believed in Palladio's thesis and was strongly influenced by it in designing Monticello. An articulate lobbyist for his ideals, Jefferson also spread his architectural convictions to his friends and even occasionally sketched plans for their houses. As his political influence grew, he helped insure that many buildings constructed in the nation's new capital, Washington, D.C., were designed

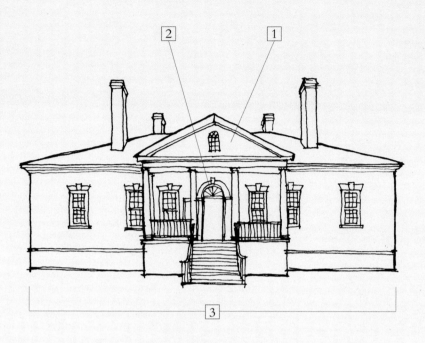

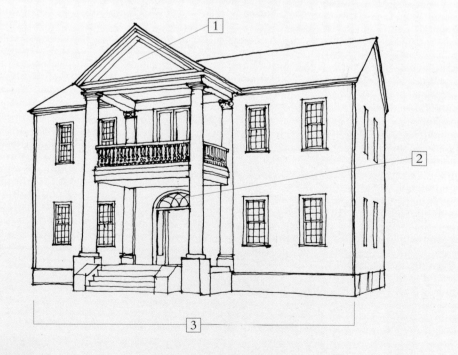

IDENTIFYING FEATURES

1 FAÇADE DOMINATED BY ENTRY PORCH WITH FOUR COLUMNS

2 SEMICIRCULAR OR ELLIPTICAL FANLIGHT OVER PANELED DOOR

3 WINDOWS IN SYMMETRICAL VERTICAL ROWS AROUND CENTRAL DOOR

according to Palladio's principles. Jefferson himself developed into an accomplished architect and personally designed the fine Palladian buildings of the University of Virginia in his native Charlottesville.

Jefferson's Roman house designs never achieved the wide popularity of the contemporaneous Federal style, which was far less difficult to construct, yet Jeffersonian columns graced the façades of many fine dwellings in Virginia and the Old South. His pioneering ideas also paved the way for a much more widespread classical style based on the Greek precursors of Roman designs. The Greek Revival style dominated American building from 1830 to 1850 (see pages 86–97).

5

Parlange

NEW ROADS, LOUISIANA

French Colonial Style

Today we easily forget that for more than three hundred years following Columbus's historic voyage most of our country's vast lands were controlled by Spain and France rather than England, whose thirteen small colonies closely hugged the Atlantic Coast. What is now the southwestern United States was then the northernmost outpost of Spanish dominion, which stretched southward through Mexico and the West Indies into South America (see Spanish Governor's Palace, pages 72–83). France, in turn, claimed an enormous triangle of land in central North America that included the entire drainage area of the Mississippi River, the "Mother of Waters," and its many tributaries. From the 1500s until its purchase by President Thomas Jefferson in 1803, all of this vast but sparsely settled region, which makes up about half of the present United States, was called Louisiana in honor of France's King Louis XIV.

Except for scattered fur trappers and Indian traders, French settlers in the New World were concentrated in eastern Canada and in the flat, fertile lands bordering the lower reaches of the Mississippi. Here, in what is now the state of Louisiana, large plantations produced crops for export to the mother country—first valuable indigo, from which a much sought-after deep blue dye for cloth was made, then sugar, and eventually cotton. These products, along with furs from upriver, were marketed and exported through the busy port city of New Orleans, where cargoes arrived by flat-bottomed river boats and left for Europe in ocean-going sailing vessels.

For this reason, most of the extant French Colonial buildings are found in modern Louisiana, both in New Orleans, where the majority of early French houses were small cottages, and upriver, where wealthy planters built large plantation houses. Of the several dozen French Colonial plantation houses that survive, none is more authentically preserved or historically fascinating than Parlange, built about 1800 a hundred miles upriver from New Orleans by an aristocratic Frenchman named Claude Vincent, marquis de Ternant (1757–1818).

An 1842 watercolor of a rural-style dwelling in suburban New Orleans, probably built about 1810.

PAGE 60 *A centuries-old live oak draped with Spanish moss graces this rear view of Parlange.*

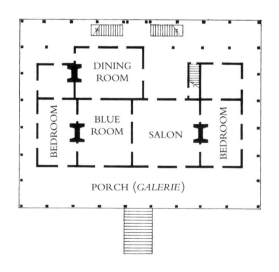

Few documented facts appear in the published references to Ternant. He is buried near Parlange and his gravestone records that he was born in Damviller-sur-Meuse, a small village in the Lorraine district of northeastern France. Buried near him are his wife and several of their descendants. Ternant's name is carved on the tombstone simply as Claude Vincent Ternant, which might have cast doubt on the veracity of his noble birth if his son and namesake, who died in 1842, had not left a remarkable estate. Painstakingly inventoried, this included not only his father's land, slaves, farm equipment, and large house, but also an unusual quantity of extraordinarily valuable personal property—fine furniture, linens, laces, silks, china, crystal, jewels, even rare wines. Equally revealing was a cache of gold and silver coins valued at $300,000, the equivalent of about ten million dollars today.

The enormous wealth and refined taste of Ternant's son, who died only twenty-four years after his father, suggests that the elder Ternant was indeed a wealthy French aristocrat who, unlike so many of his peers, managed to escape the French Revolution's bloodstained aftermath with both his life and fortune intact. All noble titles were abolished by the revolutionary government, and even thirty years later in a distant but antiroyal land, his heirs may have been reluctant to call attention to their ancestor's aristocratic origins on his gravestone.

Ternant's New World plantation house, though large and comfortable, adhered to the unpretentious building practices of other local planters. As originally built, Parlange consisted of a linear series of four interconnecting main rooms. The two larger central rooms probably served as parlor and dining room; the smaller end rooms, with breeze-creating doorways on three sides, as bedrooms. After the younger Ternant's death in 1842 his wealthy widow, Virginie Trahon Ternant, expanded the house rearward, adding a large new dining room and two smaller bedrooms. The foundation story, rear *galerie,* and roof of the extension closely followed the original style so that the house, which has had no major modifications since, remains a unified architectural whole.

Virginie Ternant, or the marquise de Ternant, as she styled herself, was a colorful figure who dominated Parlange's nineteenth-century history. She was the younger Ternant's second wife; they were married in 1835, shortly after the death of his first wife, about whom little is known. Virginie bore Ternant four children, three of whom died tragically while still young. One son drowned at age five. Another, lavishly indulged by his mother's wealth, died a "gambler and wastrel" when he was twenty-five. A daughter, forced by her mother to marry a titled aristocrat whom she didn't love, committed suicide on her wedding night.

As the widowed marquise, Virginie was fond of travel and the kind of urbane social life not possible on a remote Louisiana plantation. She apparently spent much of her time in New Orleans and Paris. In both cities she is reported to have entertained lavishly and maintained her own box at the opera. In Paris she met her second husband, French army colonel Charles Parlange. Their son, also named Charles, inherited the plantation at her death; it has borne his name ever since. The younger Charles became a distinguished Louisiana attorney, jurist, and the state's lieutenant governor in 1892. Today

The long, straight entry road to Parlange, flanked by a pair of pigeonniers, *used to be framed with ancient live oaks until most were destroyed by Hurricane Andrew in 1992. Young live oaks are now being planted for future generations.*

the house and lands are owned by his grandson Walter Charles Parlange II, who still manages it as a working farm.

Set in a grove of ancient, moss-draped live oaks, from the roadway Parlange resembles a typical, storybook southern plantation. On closer examination, however, the house's more subtle Gallic charms are revealed. Unlike the porches of most large southern plantation houses, with their massive classical columns, Parlange's two levels of exterior porches are supported in the French style—by graceful two-part columns that appear to taper upward from ground to roof. Surrounding the house's brick-walled raised basement is a series of thick but slightly tapered columns made of specially shaped triangular bricks that relate to the wall behind. On this flood-protecting foundation level sits the main house, which has walls of heavy timber framing instead of brick. As if to echo this change in material, each ground-level brick column supports a carefully turned and tapered wooden column on the level above. Squared and massive at their base, these columns became delicate and tapered "colonets" above the balustrade, thus minimizing obstruction of the door and window openings behind.

A closer look at the doors and windows reveals a still more fundamental difference between French and English architectural traditions. English houses tend to be directed inward. Typically, a single entry door opens onto halls and stairways that lead to still other doors opening onto the principal rooms. By contrast, French houses tend to look outward.

OVERLEAF *Parlange's steeply pitched hipped roof covers both the house and the porch in one straight sweep. The porch, or* galerie, *as it is called by the family, encircles the entire house and is used as a passageway among rooms because Parlange, like most French Colonial houses, lacks interior hallways.*

ABOVE *One of the five French doors along the front façade. All are enhanced by transom lights with decorative mullions in a fanlight shape.*

TOP RIGHT *The roof framing of one of the octagonal* pigeonniers *features heavy timber construction with pegged joints. The shelves, which once supported hundreds of pigeon nests, are today filled with books.*

BOTTOM RIGHT *The raised basement, which protects the main floor above during floods, contains wine cellars and provision rooms; it is constructed of brick handmade on the plantation. The columns are built of bricks shaped like pie wedges, each with a slightly smaller diameter than the one below.*

Every room usually has one or two doorways that lead directly outside or, as at Parlange, onto a wraparound external porch, or *galerie,* that serves as a passageway among rooms. In this type of house the distinction between door and window becomes blurred because the many paired French doors are glazed with panes of glass to admit light. The front façade of Parlange's main floor, for example, has no "windows" at all but five doorways that lead into the four principal rooms.

Parlange's doorways were carefully handcrafted of local cypress, one of the most durable and decay-resistant woods known, and feature delicate glazing strips and surround moldings as well as solid external shutters for storm protection. Above each doorway is a small transom window—the house's only Anglo touch. These windows are glazed in the fanlight pattern, which was almost universal on the Federal-style houses that dominated the English-speaking United States at that time.

Originally, all of Parlange's eighteen main-floor openings were probably French doorways with fan transoms above. Over the years, however, some of those along the side and back walls have been converted to Anglo-style windows by filling in the lower part of the doorway and adding two sliding sashes to the upper part.

Because of the external circulation facilitated by these many external doorways, French houses typically lack internal hallways. Instead, adjacent rooms open directly onto

LEFT *The upper story is built of local materials—a heavy wooden frame of cypress filled with a mixture of mud, moss, and deer hair. The upstairs porch, or galerie, makes a shaded outdoor living room overlooking False River, a lake that was once a bend in the Mississippi.*

CENTER *Compound columns, made of brick on the basement level and of delicately carved wood on pedestal bases on the living level, were typical of rural French Colonial dwellings.*

RIGHT *This pigeonnier, once a source of squab for the table, has been converted into a charming guest house by the Parlanges' son Brandon, a civil engineer who has been very active in the house's preservation.*

LEFT *The mantelpiece of the Blue Room features a rare clock from Orleans, France, and a photo of "Miss Lucy," the present mistress of Parlange.*

RIGHT *The melodeon in the salon holds a vintage copy of "La Marseillaise" and a photograph of the B-17 piloted by Walter Charles Parlange II during World War II.*

OPPOSITE TOP LEFT *An armoire made at Parlange holds several generations of toys.*

OPPOSITE TOP RIGHT *Portraits of Marie Virginie de Ternant and Marius de Ternant hang in corners of the salon to give the room the illusion of being circular, a nineteenth-century French fashion.*

OPPOSITE BOTTOM LEFT *A portrait of Mrs. William Lindsay Brandon, Lucy Parlange's great-great-grandmother, hangs above the dining room mantel.*

OPPOSITE BOTTOM RIGHT *A portrait of Virginie de Ternant Parlange by Claude-Marie Dubufe dominates the salon.*

each other, and internal circulation thus passes directly through the rooms, rather than through adjacent passageways. When the internal doors to a room are closed for privacy, one uses the external doors to reach the rooms beyond. Such is the pattern at Parlange.

Among the most charmingly French details at Parlange is the matching pair of early brick pigeon houses (*pigeonniers*) that grace the entryway. Squab has long been a favorite French delicacy, and most French manor houses have one or more such structures. The houses are designed so that the semidomesticated pigeons can range freely and fend for themselves, thus requiring little or no feeding. The birds enter the house through small openings near the top and build nests on platforms along the walls. A small ground-level door permits entry to gather the succulent young birds from movable ladders. Called dovecotes in England, where they are less common than in France, these structures can provide an almost effortless supply of springtime dinner fare. At Parlange, however, they have recently been adapted to a higher calling—one has been turned into an office; the other, into a delightful guest room.

Walter Parlange and his charming wife, Lucy, have lovingly maintained and preserved their historic dwelling and generously open it to all interested visitors (although its out-of-the-way location and unadvertised status keep it from being deluged by tourists). Its rooms are now filled with a delightful collection of mostly French family antiques, some dating from the original Ternants and from Virginie's nineteenth-century visits to Paris. With the help of their engineer son, the Parlanges recently completed a costly and painstaking structural restoration to insure that their extraordinary family house, occupied for more than two centuries, will also be enjoyed by future generations.

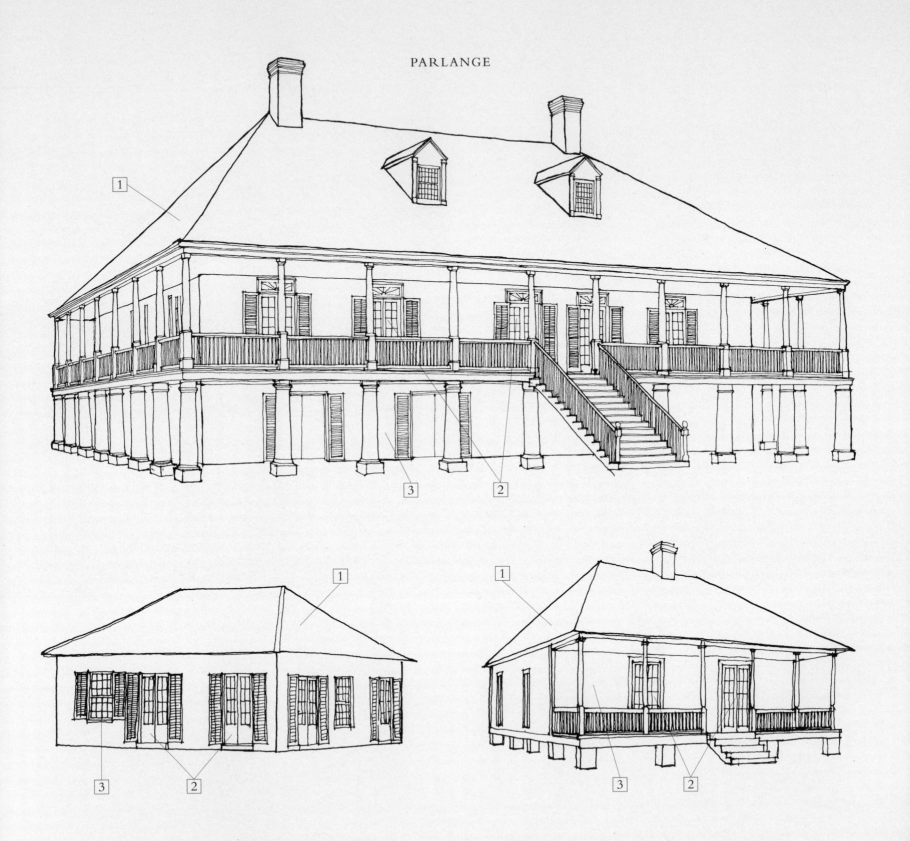

French Colonial Style

(1700–1830)

Original French Colonial buildings are among the rarest of our country's architectural styles. Most surviving examples are located in Louisiana along the Mississippi River. Some are small urban dwellings in the original French Quarter of New Orleans. Others are the grander homes of wealthy planters built on riverside farms that extended for 120 miles upriver from New Orleans.

These plantation houses are picturesque, timber-framed structures featuring the tall and steeply pitched hipped roofs characteristic of rural French manor houses. The French prototype, however, had to be adapted to sub-tropical Louisiana in two important ways. First, the main living area of the house, made of heavy interlocked timbers as in France, was built on a very tall brick foundation to protect it from the Mississippi's periodic floods. This foundation allowed for a series of service rooms—wine cellars, work areas, storage rooms, and so forth—at ground level beneath the house. Second, unlike their French predecessors or French urban houses in the New World, these Louisiana plantation houses were usually surrounded by wide external porches, or galeries. These porches provided refreshingly cool yet sheltered outdoor living areas during the hot and rainy Louisiana summers. Similarly galeried houses were also common in the more tropical West Indian colonies of both France and England, and may have originated there. In keeping with French tradition, exterior openings on the raised main floors were either tall, narrow casement windows or narrow, double French doors, which give each room direct access to the porch. Parlange is the outstanding survivor of this rare and picturesque style of early-American house design.

IDENTIFYING FEATURES

1   STEEPLY PITCHED ROOF, USUALLY HIPPED (FOUR-SIDED)

2   TALL, NARROW DOOR AND WINDOW OPENINGS WITH VERTICALLY PAIRED DOORS AND SASHES

3   STUCCO-COVERED WALLS

6
Spanish Governor's Palace

SAN ANTONIO, TEXAS

Spanish Colonial Style

Until the early nineteenth century the southwestern quarter of what is now the United States, as well as most of present-day Florida, were Spanish colonies. This enormous region was but the northernmost fringe of Spain's Colonial empire, which stretched southward through Mexico and the West Indies and included much of South America. By the time the first small and ill-prepared band of permanent English settlers reached Virginia in 1607, this vast empire had been thriving for more than a century.

Florida and our desert Southwest offered the early Spanish explorers no riches comparable to those of Peru or Mexico. Instead, these regions, sparsely settled by missionaries and military men, served to buffer the Spaniards' northern frontier from French or English expansion.

Today only a handful of important buildings erected in this region during the three centuries of Spanish and Mexican rule survive. Chief among these are handsome mission chapels established by Franciscan and Dominican friars in parts of California, Arizona, New Mexico, and Texas. Spanish Colonial houses throughout the region were less grand —most were modest structures of adobe or stone. The relatively few extant examples date principally from the mid-nineteenth century, when Anglo settlement had already begun to modify the traditional Hispanic building practices of the region.

Perhaps the most important of our country's very few surviving eighteenth-century Spanish Colonial houses is a structure in the heart of modern San Antonio, Texas, that is known today as the Spanish Governor's Palace. This dwelling has been closely intertwined with San Antonio's colorful history for more than 250 years.

By the time the San Antonio region was first settled in 1718, the Spaniards had already established missionary villages populated by priests, Indian convert-workers, and soldiers in western Louisiana and eastern Texas—on the very borders of French territory. The San Antonio region became an important stopover on the long road connecting these

73

The Spanish Governor's Palace just before restoration.

PAGE 72 *Detail of the carved-walnut entry door.*

remote outposts with the nearest sizable town, which was Saltillo, in the mountains of northern Mexico. The San Antonio area was favored with an abundance of the desert's most precious commodity—water. A series of cool, rushing springs, fed by rainfall in the low hills to the north, issued from sinkholes in the ground to form clear, swiftly flowing rivers. Soon the Spaniards abandoned the Louisiana border missions and between 1718 and 1731 established five new mission-villages within a dozen miles of modern San Antonio. Amazingly, all of the original chapel buildings of these missions survive in varying states of preservation. Most familiar is the chapel of the mission of San Antonio de Valero, better known by its later name, the Alamo.

As was the usual Spanish Colonial practice, a military garrison protected the first San Antonio mission. In 1722 the governor of the northeastern Spanish provinces decided to strengthen this military presence and ordered a new fort, or presidio, to be established near the mission. It included a large central parade ground, or military plaza, partially surrounded by barracks and storehouses. Somewhat later, but probably before 1749, a large, formal residence for the local military commander—then the highest Spanish official in the region—was built near the northwest corner of the plaza. This structure, restored in 1930 as it might have looked in the 1700s, is the Spanish Governor's Palace. The former parade ground is now the site of the city hall.

The title Governor's Palace is something of a misnomer. For its place and time the house was certainly palatial, and even by modern standards it is a large and comfortable dwelling. But there is scant evidence that any of the regional governors who resided in San Antonio beginning in the 1730s displaced the local military commander from the presidio house. Indeed, in the late Colonial era the center of local government, and most likely the governor's dwelling, was located two blocks away on the east side of the military plaza facing San Fernando Cathedral. In any event, as the dwelling of a high Spanish official the presidio house must have been one of the few imposing residences in the town during the Colonial era.

By the 1780s the house and several smaller adjacent structures had become privately owned. The first recorded owner was, not surprisingly, a former local military commander, Captain Luis Menchaca. In 1804 his heirs sold the house to a wealthy local businessman named Ignacio Perez, whose descendants owned the property until it was bought by the City of San Antonio for restoration in 1929. Perez was interim governor of Texas during the turbulent period of Mexican revolt (1814–17), and his daughter married Antonio Cordero, governor from 1805 to 1807. This could account for the name Governor's Palace.

In the mid-nineteenth century the old military plaza became San Antonio's principal open market area and the once grand house was put to more humble uses. At first it was converted into a school, and then it was occupied by a long series of shops and bars that served the nearby marketplace.

Restoration of such long-neglected Colonial buildings verged on a national obsession in the first decades of the twentieth century. Not only were numerous early English Colonial landmarks rebuilt (for example, the Iron Works House, pages 10–19), but so were many Spanish Colonial missions and related structures in Florida and the Southwest. All of this restoration work is praiseworthy, for it preserved countless architectural treasures that might otherwise have been lost forever. The only regret is that most preservation architects of the period were not yet aware of the importance of, and techniques for, conducting precise historical and architectural research. Thus they seldom documented which architectural elements were truly original to the structure, which were later modifications, and which were added during the "restoration."

The Governor's Palace, restored more than half a century ago, is a case in point. That the massive rubblework exterior walls and their early door and window openings were left intact is clear from photographs of the street façade taken just before restoration (following Spanish custom, the walls are now covered with a uniform layer of protective stucco). Early published descriptions of the restoration mention renovations that were made to match the "hand-hewn timbers," "wooden lintels," "wrought-iron lanterns and wall brackets," "flagstone floor," and "kiln-made tiles," so apparently some of the house's earlier fabric had withstood its many years of neglect. The handsome carved-walnut front doors are faithful reproductions of those seen in an early etching. Other details of the room arrangements, fireplaces, interior finishes, and patio may be less historically precise but are at least typical of Spanish building practice of the period.

The street façades of Spanish Colonial houses were rather severe. Massive wooden doors provided direct access to different rooms; wrought-iron window grilles allowed ventilation while keeping out unwelcome visitors.

One of the most remarkable surviving original details of the house is a large and elaborately carved keystone over the main entrance. It bears the coat of arms of Spain's King Philip V (reigned 1700–46), which features a double-headed eagle and the inscription "1749—Se acabo [finished]." Historians surmise that part of the house may be older than that date (as the word finished implies) or younger, if the keystone was installed when only one or a few rooms were completed. Spanish Colonial houses were commonly expanded with gradual room-by-room additions.

Inside, the house seems much larger than its simple and unimposing rectangular façade suggests. The interior is divided into a 3 × 3 grid of long, narrow rooms whose walls are only slightly thinner than the outer walls. The main entrance opens onto the northern (right-hand) row, where the front and back rooms have been further subdivided—the front into an entry hall with a small chapel to the right, the rear into a stair hall and storage loft with the simple kitchen to its right. Between these is a long dining room with doorways leading into each of the four smaller surrounding rooms. The wider, central row of rooms comprises a large ballroom at the front, behind which is an equally large reception room or living room. To the rear of this room is a walled

The main entry door (BOTTOM) is topped by an early keystone (TOP) carved with the coat of arms of Spain's King Philip V. The door itself is of hand-carved walnut and is patterned after an early etching of the original.

RIGHT The octagonal garden fountain emits but a trickle of water, as is typical of such fountains in arid locales.

ABOVE *In Spanish Colonial houses rooms opened directly onto one another. Here aligned doorways permit a view of the entire length of the house, from the chapel through the entry hall and the ballroom into the governor's office at the far end. Note the different floors and door surrounds in each room.*

LEFT *This view of the steep stairway leading to the food-storage loft shows the handmade character of the thick interior and exterior walls.*

The walled terrace served as an outdoor living room.

The house's handsome pebble-paved patio was part of the 1930 reconstruction. It is uncertain whether any of it, except perhaps the location of the well, was based on archaeological findings. The architect is said to have noted that the current terrace area to the left of the patio showed evidence of having been a series of rooms connected by a porch-corridor.

Today the Governor's Palace is a much-venerated jewel among San Antonio's surviving treasures from the Spanish Colonial era. It provides a glimpse of the exotic lifestyle of a high government official serving on Spain's New World frontiers more than two centuries ago.

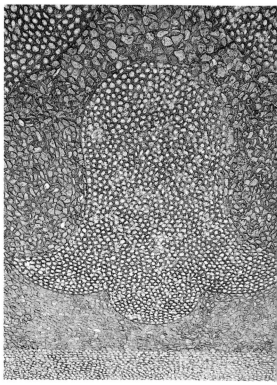

ABOVE *A detail of the pebble mosaic that paves the garden.*

LEFT *View from the walled terrace into the garden, with its banana trees and octagonal fountain.*

Spanish Colonial Style

(1600–1850)

Today's southwestern United States was once the northern fringe of a vast Spanish empire that extended through Mexico, Central America, northern South America, and most of the West Indies. Having neither the gold and silver wealth of Mexico and Peru nor the valuable sugar crops of the Caribbean Islands, our Spanish Southwest was only sparsely populated with forts and missionary settlements that provided a frontier buffer against the southward expansion of the adjacent French and English territories.

Spanish Colonial houses in the region are of two principal types. In the arid lands of Texas, New Mexico, and Arizona flat-roofed dwellings predominate. These have massive walls of stone or adobe brick in which heavy timbers are embedded to support a thick roof of earth or mortar. The Spanish Governor's Palace belongs to this type, which was first brought to Spain from North Africa by the Moors. In slightly different form it was developed independently by several groups of Native Americans long before the Spaniards arrived.

The second type of Spanish Colonial house is found along the California coast. It, too, has stone or adobe brick walls but is topped by a traditional pitched roof made of timber frames covered with semicylindrical clay tiles. This type is also deeply rooted in Spanish architectural tradition.

The southwestern United States became a part of independent Mexico in 1821 and was ceded to, or annexed by, the United States in the 1840s. During the subsequent Anglo immigrations traditional Hispanic buildings were modified by the addition of multipaned windows, decorative window crowns, paneled doors, and fired-brick wall copings. But after the expansion of the western railroads in the 1880s, traditional thick-walled Hispanic buildings of stone or adobe brick were rapidly replaced by wooden-framed Anglo dwellings throughout most of the region.

SPANISH GOVERNOR'S PALACE

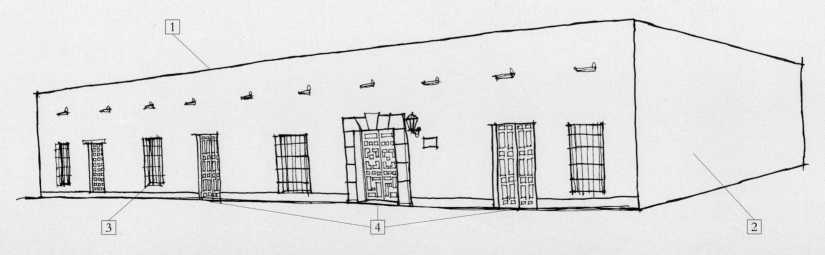

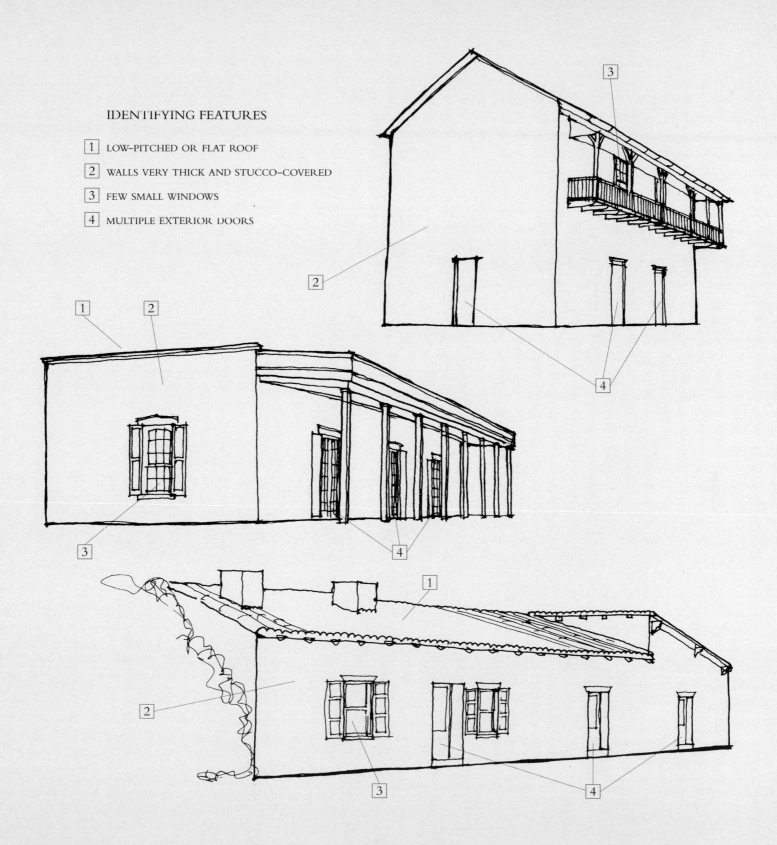

IDENTIFYING FEATURES

1   LOW-PITCHED OR FLAT ROOF

2   WALLS VERY THICK AND STUCCO-COVERED

3   FEW SMALL WINDOWS

4   MULTIPLE EXTERIOR DOORS

Romantic Houses

(1820–1880)

For several decades after independence the United States still looked to Britain in matters of style and taste. Most American houses from 1780 until about 1820 were built in the Federal style, which was directly borrowed from the British Adam style. It took a second conflict with the former motherland—the devastating War of 1812, in which, among other outrages, British troops burned the new capital city of Washington—to create a nationwide distaste for borrowed English culture.

Following Thomas Jefferson's lead of looking to the ancient world for architectural inspiration, Americans now turned not to Rome, as Jefferson had, but to the still earlier architecture of ancient Greece, the "mother of democracies." Thus arose the Greek Revival style (pages 96–97), which dominated American building from about 1830 until 1850. So all-pervasive was this new fashion that it was referred to simply as the "national style" of architecture.

The Greek Revival style was to be the last in the long tradition of building the majority of new houses in a single, currently fashionable style. In the 1840s the first pattern books appeared featuring plans and drawings for new houses in several styles. Instead of the prevailing Greek Revival fashion, these books emphasized new designs based on either medieval or Renaissance building precedents. The medieval designs drew on shapes and details loosely borrowed from the castles, cathedrals, and manor houses of the Middle Ages. This fashion came to be known as the Gothic Revival style (pages 110–11). The Renaissance designs took the shape of picturesque Italian farmhouses embellished with Americanized door, window, and cornice-line decorations borrowed from formal Renaissance town houses. This fashion is now known as the Italianate style (pages 122–23).

Along with a decreasing number of Greek Revival holdovers, both Gothic Revival and Italianate houses were common in the 1840s and 1850s. Of the two new fashions, the Italianate was less expensive to construct because of its simpler shapes and roof forms. For this reason it always outnumbered its Gothic competitor and became the dominant style for American houses constructed in the 1860s and 1870s.

The shift toward several competing architectural fashions was facilitated by America's rapid industrialization in the mid-nineteenth century. Transportation in particular was revolutionized as railroads replaced wagons and riverboats as the principal means of moving goods and people long distances. Our first commercial railroads were built in the early 1830s; less than thirty years later the eastern United States was honeycombed by a 30,000-mile rail network. The expansion of the railroad enabled fast and economical distribution not only of high-value manufactured items, such as building hardware or house pattern books, but also of relatively inexpensive factory-milled doors, windows, and decorative detailing. No longer dependent on highly skilled local craftsmen to produce such items, home builders could now choose from a wide selection of ready-made architectural components in various fashionable styles.

A. J. Davis (1803–1892), "Knoll," east elevation (detail),
watercolor and ink on paper, 14¼ × 10¼ in.

7
Melrose

Greek Revival Style

The town of Natchez is perched on high bluffs overlooking the mighty Mississippi River. The bluffs, a rarity along the lower Mississippi, gave the town ready access to river transportation and rich riverside farmland while offering protection from the rampaging floods and yellow-fever epidemics that plagued most of the land bordering the river.

The area that now comprises most of Mississippi and Alabama, as well as the panhandle of Florida, was a political pawn during the Colonial era. Sandwiched between French Louisiana, the Spanish part of Florida, and British Georgia, it was claimed by all three countries and passed back and forth among them as a victory trophy in the aftermath of their various conflicts. Founded as a French fort in 1716, the small town of Natchez was passed to the British in 1763, to Spain in 1779, and, finally, to the newly independent United States in 1798. Throughout this period Natchez remained a sleepy frontier village.

The town's fortunes changed in 1803 when President Thomas Jefferson purchased the vast Louisiana territory from France. Now free from French control of river shipping, Natchez began to boom as the principal Mississippi port along the five-hundred-mile stretch between Memphis and New Orleans. Banks were chartered, import-export offices were opened, and land speculators, politicians, and lawyers flourished. By 1817 Mississippi was a full-fledged state with Natchez as its capital.

The Natchez region's principal economic resource was the fertile farmland along the Mississippi, which proved to be ideal for growing a new variety of cotton first imported from Mexico in 1806. Called Petit Gulf, its yield was very high because it did not tend to rot in the humid, coastal-plain climate as had earlier varieties. This new type of cotton became the white gold of Natchez and the deep South. By 1830 the southern states were producing 731,000 bales of cotton; by 1850 the number had grown to 2.5 million, and by 1859 had reached 5.3 million. During this period Natchez matured into a cosmopolitan

John T. McMurran, c. 1860.

city where prosperous cotton planters built town houses and enjoyed an urbane social life when not occupied with administering their rural land holdings.

In the mid-1820s an ambitious young lawyer from Ohio named John T. McMurran (1801–1866) moved to Natchez. In 1827 he formed a law partnership with John A. Quitman (1798–1858), a friend from Ohio who had been living in Natchez since 1821. Quitman later became a major general in the Mexican War and governor of Mississippi.

His friendship with Quitman also advanced McMurran's social life; in 1831 he married Mary Louise Turner, a first cousin of Quitman's wife and the daughter of a prominent judge who, like many Natchez professional men during that era, had become wealthy as a cotton planter. As a wedding gift Judge Turner gave the young couple Holly Hedges, a local landmark cottage built in 1796. Soon McMurran would enter the small circle of professional-men-turned-cotton-growers who ruled Natchez society. In 1840 Holly Hedges was damaged in a tornado that destroyed part of the city and the McMurrans, now the parents of two young children, set out to build a larger home that would be "among the most splendid" in all of Natchez. With the help of a talented Maryland architect-builder named Jacob Byers, they succeeded.

Melrose, as the McMurrans called their new home, is an elegantly understated design in the then-fashionable Greek Revival style favored by wealthy Natchez planters. The couple spared no expense in building their dream house. It was constructed of carefully fired local bricks made and laid under the supervision of a skilled Philadelphia mason who moved to Natchez for the project. All of the house's architectural details—porch support columns, windows, doors, cornice moldings, stairways, and floors—were hand carved from cypress, heart of pine, and other fine woods. The furnishings were equally lavish— top-of-the-line pieces from the most renowned cabinetmakers and craftsmen of New York, Philadelphia, and New Orleans.

To complete all this work took four years, and it was 1845 before the McMurrans and their two children, twelve-year-old John, Jr., and his ten-year-old sister, Mary Eliza, finally occupied Melrose. For the next fifteen years the house was a centerpiece of fashionable Natchez society. An inkling of that life-style, and of the interrelated families that dominated Natchez, is given in a journal kept by the young bride of John, Jr., when she first arrived from her native Maryland in 1856: ". . . the long lines of white-washed cabins of the slaves, all so new and strange. The first arrival of moonlight at Natchez, the servants awaiting and the ride out and John's pointing out in the dim starlight the different places: Monmouth (Gen. Quitman's), Linden (Mrs. Connor's), Sedge Hill (Aunt Fanny's), Woodlands (Grandma Turner's), and last in a quiet corner, beautiful Melrose. The first impression the following day of that quiet elegant household, the most perfect arrangement that I ever saw. . . . All seemed like fairy land."

The Civil War brought an end to this and many other fairy lands. Melrose and most other Natchez buildings escaped destruction in the war, but the house's occupants were less fortunate. In 1864 the McMurrans' daughter, Mary Eliza, and her own young daughter both died in quick succession. Mary Eliza's son, John, died a year later—only two

PAGE 86 *The front façade of Melrose is dominated by a full-height classical entry porch with four Doric-style columns supporting a triangular pediment.*

days after his father finally returned from the war. Also in 1864 John McMurran, Sr., suffered a severe facial wound when fired upon by a Union sentry.

Whether because of financial necessity or the unhappy memories Melrose now held, the McMurrans sold the estate in 1865 to their neighbor Elizabeth Davis, the wife of Natchez attorney George Malin Davis. Included in the sale were all of the house's lavish furnishings, the first of several such fortunate transfers. In fact, many of the original furnishings installed by the McMurrans in the 1840s and 1850s are still miraculously in place today, providing a uniquely accurate view of an elegant antebellum home.

After the death of George Davis in 1883, all of his large estate, including Melrose, which the family rarely used, passed to his six-year-old grandson, George Malin Davis Kelly, of New York City. Virtually unoccupied since 1865, Melrose was to remain so until the end of the century. During this long period it was cared for by two remarkable women, former slaves of the Davis family, Jane Johnson and Alice Sims. It fell to them to ward off repeated attempts to break into the house and steal its valuable furnishings. They both lived at Melrose until their deaths at age 103 and 96, respectively, long after new occupants arrived in 1901.

Mary Louise McMurran, 1880s.

That year George Malin Davis Kelly, now twenty-four, married Ethel Moore, a fellow New Yorker. Shortly after their marriage, he and his bride set out for Natchez to inspect the numerous properties he had inherited. In an interview many years later, Mrs. Kelly explained what a surprise this had been to her, as she had had no idea that her husband owned vast lands and several fine houses in Natchez. Her reactions to the charming town and to Melrose must have been similar to those of the McMurrans' daughter-in-law almost half a century earlier, for the Kellys chose to live at Melrose during their frequent visits to Natchez.

In refurbishing the long-dormant dwelling, the Kellys made two propitious decisions. First, they decided to preserve the house as it was rather than to remodel or update it. They even left the kitchen in its original location—a rear outbuilding. Second, they decided to leave all of the early furnishings intact, including the 1850s curtains!

By 1910 the Kellys had made Melrose their permanent residence; George Kelly died there in 1946. His wife continued to live in the house until her death at age ninety-seven in 1975. In her later years she was greatly assisted by Fred Page, who had come to Melrose as a teenager and became the Kellys' longtime butler. He continues to work at the house as an interpreter with the National Park Service. Mrs. Kelly's daughter and heir, Mrs. Dexter Ferry, adhered to Melrose tradition when she sold it, again with many of the original McMurran and Davis family furnishings, to Mr. and Mrs. John S. Callon in 1976.

Mr. Callon is a seventh-generation citizen of Natchez. When he and his wife set out to "refurbish" Melrose, they carefully added new heating, air-conditioning, electricity, and plumbing, but they, too, left the kitchen in the outbuilding, kept most of the early furnishings, including the curtains, in place, and dedicated themselves to documenting and protecting their house. Among their remarkable discoveries were the extremely rare floor cloths in the foyer and back hall, which had been buried under generations of dust and wax.

LEFT *View of the parlor and drawing room from the library. Opening the two pairs of pocket doors creates a spacious three-room salon for entertaining. Note the differing door surrounds and the handsome ceiling rosette.*

RIGHT *The original painted floor cloths in the entry foyer and the back hall beyond are now extremely rare. The windows (lights) around both the interior and rear doors are typical of Greek Revival entryways.*

OPPOSITE TOP LEFT *Two of a set of three folding-top tables, attributed to Charles White of Philadelphia, are surrounded by the house's original set of Gothic Revival dining room chairs, c. 1845–1860. The pier table to the left is also an original piece.*

OPPOSITE TOP RIGHT *The original mahogany punkah (overhead fan) still hangs in place over the dining room table. Carved in Natchez with the honeysuckle-leaf motif typical of Greek Revival, it was operated by a servant who pulled on long cords attached to it.*

OPPOSITE BOTTOM LEFT *A seating arrangement in the back hall with two of the original parlor chairs, an American Empire sofa, and a portrait attributed to Thomas Sully.*

OPPOSITE BOTTOM RIGHT *A detail of the painted floor cloth in the back hall. Still intact after almost 150 years, it was woven and meticulously hand painted in England.*

These floor cloths are probably of English origin, for by the early nineteenth century several English companies had developed machinery that could weave heavy canvas cloth in widths of up to twenty-seven feet and lengths of seventy feet or more, thereby avoiding any seams. The cloth was then stretched on a giant frame, covered with sizing, smoothed, and painted with several layers of oil paint. Finally, a decorative pattern was stenciled or hand painted on the surface. A critical part of the process was the aging of the finished cloth, as it could take several years for the oil paint to harden sufficiently for use underfoot. Floor cloths were not inexpensive, and they were priced by the quality of the canvas base, the number of coats of paint, the complexity of the decorative pattern, and the length of time they had been aged.

Judging by their complex patterns and long survival, the Melrose floor cloths were of very high quality. The one in the entry foyer is of a geometric design, imitating an inlaid marble floor, an appropriate pattern for a formal entry area. The back hall pattern, copied from a Brussels carpet design, was appropriate for this more informal room. The elaborate pattern also made it easier to repair any chipped paint unobtrusively. In the popular household-management books of the day, floor cloths were recommended for high-traffic areas such as halls and kitchens. Melrose's use of them was therefore typical of the period.

Melrose has very fine interior architectural detailing. Particularly noteworthy are the elaborate surrounds of the foyer doors leading into the dining room and drawing room and the ceiling rosettes from which the chandeliers are hung. The drawing room, parlor, and library are connected by columned pocket doors that open to form a dramatic three-room "salon." Many of the details resemble those in Asher Benjamin's illustrated books of architectural details, which were popular at the time.

One enters Melrose through the foyer with its original floor cloth. To the left is the dining room, in which an enormous original mahogany punkah hangs over the table. When operated by a servant this fanlike device provided constant air movement. The air flow both cooled the diners and prevented flies from landing on the food.

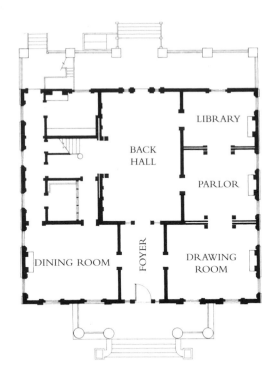

To the right of the foyer is the drawing room, which is still decorated with its original curtains and Rococo Revival furniture. The adjoining parlor contains furniture brought by the elder Davises from their nearby home Choctaw, as well as several original pieces, including a piano from Knabe Graeble and Company of Baltimore. The rear room of the three-room salon suite is the library. The back hall at the center rear of the house functions as a large, informal living space. The section of the ground floor behind the dining room contains assorted service and storage rooms as well as pantries. Upstairs are bedrooms with many fine early furnishings.

From the colonnaded rear porch behind the back hall one can see the early paired outbuildings that served the house. To the left is the colonnaded kitchen house with servants' rooms above. The matching building to the right is the dairy house, again with servants' rooms above. These form a U-shaped courtyard that is surrounded by columns on three sides and extended by two additional pairs of smaller outbuildings. First come a pair of cisterns, each with an octagonal lattice-work surround, followed by a matching privy and smokehouse. Other nearby buildings include a carriage house, a stable, and two slave cabins.

Melrose's outbuildings remain remarkably intact. The dairy still has its troughs. The nine-hole privy has both men's and women's compartments, with seating for children as well as grown-ups. The cistern pumps date back to 1842, and the slave bell system, which has a bell of a different tone for each room of the main house, still functions.

Many acres at Melrose are carefully landscaped, and the grounds cast a spell upon visitors. Entering through the main gate, one passes a large reflecting pond planted with giant cypress trees. The original entrance road winds through what knowledgeable early

A highly unusual tête-a-tête sofa and a marble-top Rococo Revival sofa table, both original Melrose pieces, adorn the parlor.

The furnishings in the front bedroom include a dressing table brought from nearby Auburn plantation and the four-poster bed in which George Malin Davis died. The French gilt mantel clock may have been the only clock at Melrose prior to 1865.

The drawing room's high-quality, remarkably well-preserved original furnishings, including the 1845 Philadelphia chandelier, the suite of matching Rococo Revival furniture, the overmantel mirror, and the draperies, valances, and tiebacks, make it one of the most important drawing rooms in the South.

The door to the upstairs front porch (TOP) and the main entry door beneath it (BOTTOM) have almost identical elaborations. The pattern of the surrounding lights is the same. Both doors are inset, allowing a pair of fluted Doric-style columns (which, in traditional Doric fashion, lack bases) to join a pair of simple unfluted outer pilasters in supporting the wide entablature. The upstairs porch railing incorporates the same honeysuckle-leaf motif found on the dining room punkah.

The rear of Melrose has a commanding full-façade porch, supported by simplified square "columns." The pair of matching outbuildings to each side also have full-façade porches. The kitchen house is to the right and the dairy to the left; both had servants' rooms on the second floor.

visitors identified as an "English landscape park," a large lawn with huge trees and shrubs planted in naturalist groupings. Beyond the house are two magnificent live oak trees, dripping with Spanish moss, their extensive root system plunging in and out of the surrounding earth. Beyond this magical pair is a more formal garden area, while an orchard lies to the rear. Many species of birds make their homes in the huge ancient shrubs and bring the grounds alive with their constant darting about.

Today Melrose has a new and permanent owner, the U.S. National Park Service. The house was the first major acquisition for the Natchez National Historical Park, which was founded in October 1988. The park's purpose is to "preserve and interpret the history of Natchez, Mississippi, as a significant city in the history of the American South." The park will also contain the site of the original 1716 French settlement, Fort Rosalie, and the circa 1841 house complex of William Johnson, a free African-American who was a prosperous businessman and property owner in antebellum Natchez. In addition, it will include a preservation district of privately owned residences—one of the best assemblages of distinguished antebellum structures in the South.

And so Melrose will continue to be, as it was to begin with, part of a town of quiet distinction, a town bypassed by most of the vicissitudes of the twentieth century. The beneficiary is the modern visitor, who can experience something of the gentle pace and subtle charm of a long bygone era.

MELROSE

IDENTIFYING FEATURES

1. NARROW LINE OF TRANSOM AND SIDELIGHTS AROUND DOOR

2. ENTRY OR FULL-WIDTH PORCH SUPPORTED BY COLUMNS

3. CORNICE LINE EMPHASIZED WITH WIDE BAND OF TRIM

4. GABLED OR HIPPED ROOF OF LOW PITCH

Greek Revival Style

(1825–1860)

The Greek Revival style marked the young United States' first break with the architectural fashions of England. After their victory in the debilitating War of 1812, Americans seemed to have lost all remaining nostalgia for the culture of their homeland. Following Thomas Jefferson's lead, they developed instead a passion for the "pure" architecture of ancient Greece and Rome. Whereas Jefferson preferred Roman precedents, the Greek Revival movement that dominated American building for several decades harkened back to ancient Greece, which not only had been the inspiration for the Roman designs but was also the "mother of all democracies." So popular did this new fashion become that by the 1830s it was known as the National style of American architecture.

Only the grandest Greek Revival houses, featuring façades dominated by massive, full-height columns, actually resemble Greek temples. More commonly the classical columns support only a smaller entry porch or are reduced to flattened pilasters applied to the façade for decorative effect. All of these variations, however, share two characteristic features: 1) a very wide band of cornice-line trim just beneath the roof, and 2) front doors surrounded by a narrow band of rectangular panes of glass.

The popularity of the Greek Revival style coincided with the nation's first period of large-scale westward expansion, and it moved with Americans as they crossed the Appalachians into Tennessee, Kentucky, and what is now the Midwest and followed the cotton boom into the "New South" states of Alabama and Mississippi. Melrose is among the most splendid of the surviving southern examples. By the middle decades of the nineteenth century the Greek Revival style was losing favor to the Gothic Revival and Italianate styles, which were popularized by the first pattern books of house plans and drawings.

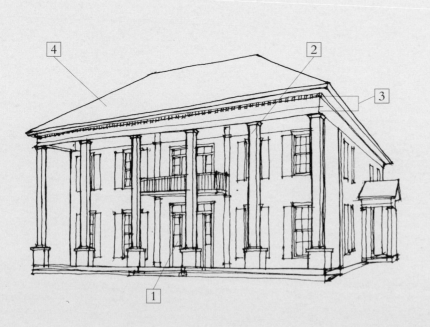

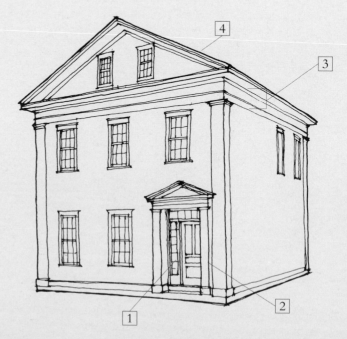

8

Lyndhurst

Gothic Revival Style

Lyndhurst, sited atop a rolling hill overlooking the Hudson River just north of New York City, is the sort of country house that inspired rhapsodic prose from nineteenth-century romantic writers. James Fenimore Cooper, who lived nearby, considered the Hudson to be America's equivalent of Germany's fabled Rhine. After a trip through the Rhine Valley he went even further:

> To me it is quite apparent that the Rhine has [no scenery] of so great excellence [as the Hudson]. [The Rhine] wants the variety, the noble beauty, and the broad grandeur of the American stream. . . . In modern abodes, in villas, and even in seats, those of princes alone excepted, the banks of the Hudson have scarcely an equal in any region.
>
> There are finer and nobler edifices . . . in other favored spots, certainly, but I know no stream that has so many that please and attract the eye.

Thanks to writers such as Cooper and his neighbor Washington Irving, as well as to the landscape painters of the Hudson River school, the Hudson Valley became the prototypical setting for romantic American houses—and Lyndhurst is among the finest. Its castellated turrets, picturesque chimneys, verandas, bay windows, nooks, and crannies all call to mind the age of chivalrous knights and damsels in distress, perhaps even one imprisoned in its tall tower.

Few houses in America so clearly define both the beginning and the end of an architectural fashion as does Lyndhurst. This is because the house, as we see it today, was built in two stages—the first was finished in 1838 just as the Gothic Revival movement was becoming popular, and the second in 1865 as its popularity was beginning to wane (note that Château-sur-Mer, pages 126–137, similarly brackets the somewhat later Second Empire style). The architect for both building phases was Alexander Jackson Davis

Portrait of Alexander Jackson Davis, c. 1850.

(1803–1892), the acknowledged master of residential Gothic Revival design. Lyndhurst is his masterpiece.

As first built—without the tall tower—Lyndhurst was less dramatic in appearance and even in name. It was then known simply as Knoll because of its location atop a small hill. A very early "villa in the pointed style," as Davis's writings described such houses, it was designed for General William Paulding (1770–1854), a commander in the War of 1812 who had served twice as mayor of New York City. Fortunately, some of the main rooms of this first design are still intact, including the present entry hall, reception room, and drawing room.

In 1864 the house was purchased by George Merritt (1807–1873), an affluent New York merchant and inventor who wanted a larger home to suit his social ambitions—he almost doubled the size of the original house and changed its name to Lyndhurst. Luckily, he did not seek out some newly fashionable architect who might well have changed the entire spirit of the house, but instead rehired Davis to build an addition compatible with the original design. Davis had always maintained that one of the advantages of Gothic-style houses was the ease with which they could be expanded, an opinion that Merritt gave him a unique opportunity to demonstrate. And he did so with spectacular success.

Davis had begun his career as an architectural illustrator; his forte was making exquisite watercolor renditions of proposed buildings. This work gave him a strong background in design and the ability to present his ideas beautifully to clients. The prominent New York architect Ithiel Town appreciated Davis's talents and invited him to become a partner, which he did from 1829 to 1835 and again from 1842 to 1843. Town owned a renowned architectural library and from these illustrated volumes Davis learned much about architectural history. Taking advantage of this knowledge, in 1838 Davis prepared a short book of his own called *Rural Residences.* This was our country's first house pattern book, and it illustrated views and plans of entire houses, not just individual architectural details. The book was not widely circulated, but from 1839 to 1850 Davis collaborated with writer and landscape architect Andrew Jackson Downing (1815–1852) on a series of much more popular pattern books. The house designs and illustrations Davis prepared for these books greatly influenced American architectural fashion during the mid-nineteenth century.

In its original form Lyndhurst was a much simpler central-gable house, quite similar to those that Davis and Downing featured in their pattern books. It was distinguished, however, by unusual parapeted walls and ornate stone detailing. For his expansion of Lyndhurst, Davis incorporated the dramatic and now-familiar towers as major elements of the design. He also transformed an upstairs library into an art gallery, converted the downstairs dining room into a new library, and added a service wing and a magnificent new dining room on the north side of the house. A glance at the floor plan (see page 101) shows the basic changes, and a comparison of Davis's original east elevation (see page 84) with today's Lyndhurst (see page 98) gives an idea of the overall scope of this work.

PAGE 98 *The front façade of Lyndhurst.*

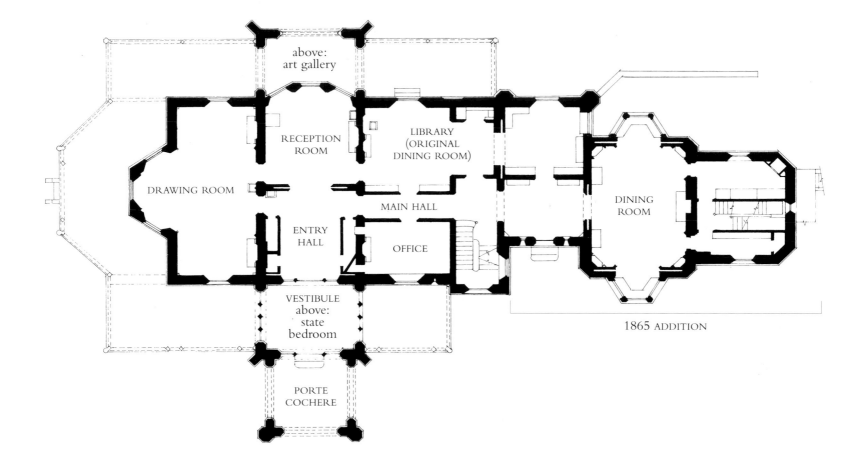

above:
art gallery

RECEPTION
ROOM

LIBRARY
(ORIGINAL
DINING ROOM)

DRAWING ROOM

MAIN HALL

DINING
ROOM

ENTRY
HALL

OFFICE

VESTIBULE
above:
state
bedroom

1865 ADDITION

PORTE
COCHERE

In addition to his grand remodeling of the house, Merritt, an avid horticulturist, undertook a large-scale renovation of Lyndhurst's landscaping. The grounds today consist of sixty-seven acres of rolling hills that surround the house and descend to the Hudson. Drives and paths curve gently through green lawns accented by magnificent century-old specimen trees. Native American beeches, dogwoods, maples, chestnuts, and oaks are supplemented by more exotic imported varieties, such as European weeping beeches, Japanese split-leaf maples, Oriental gingkos, Norway spruces, and European beeches. There also were formal geometric gardens, but these were placed out of view of the main house to preserve its naturalistic setting. The many outbuildings added by Merritt and later owners were also carefully sited so as not to interfere with the romantic landscape views from the house.

The most dramatic of the outbuildings Merritt added was a large greenhouse located halfway between the entry gates and the main house along the northern property boundary. It burned down in 1880, shortly after financier Jay Gould (1836–1892) purchased the property, but Gould, who also was interested in horticulture, quickly had it rebuilt on the old foundation. The new greenhouse is thought to be the first in the country to employ metal framing to hold the glass. It remained in use until 1961 and still stands today, although without glass and in somewhat deteriorated condition. Long-range plans call for its complete restoration.

Merritt was able to enjoy his newly expanded and landscaped showplace for only seven years. He died in 1873 but left as a lasting monument his transformation of a relatively simple "villa in the pointed style" into a magnificent Gothic castle. Merritt must have been precisely the kind of patron that Downing had described in his *Architecture of Country Houses* (1850):

> And, lastly, there are the men of imagination—men whose aspirations never leave them at rest—men whose ambition and energy will give them no peace within the mere bounds of rationality. These are the men for picturesque villas—country houses with high roofs, steep gables, unsymmetrical and capricious forms. It is for such that the architect may safely introduce the tower and the campanile—any and every feature that indicates originality, boldness, energy, and variety of character. To find a really original man living in an original and characteristic house, is as satisfactory as to find an eagle's nest built on the top of a mountain crag.

Lyndhurst's third owner, Jay Gould, was even more of a mountaintop eagle—a true American original. A builder of the railroads that helped open up the Southwest, he

LEFT *The formal rose garden, with its domed gazebo, is separated from Lyndhurst's mostly naturalistic grounds by hemlocks, poplars, and a low barberry hedge.*

RIGHT *Jay Gould, an avid horticulturist, commissioned this greenhouse to replace one that burned in 1880. Built by Lord and Burnham, it is probably the first in the country to use metal framing to create broad, open spans. Although it is in a deteriorated state today, a plan has been prepared for its eventual restoration.*

bought, sold, and consolidated lines throughout the country and in the process became one of the nation's most successful financial speculators. He made large profits through complex stock manipulations and single-handedly caused an infamous "Black Friday" in 1869 through speculation in gold. Indeed, his inventive financial schemes led to many of today's stock market regulations.

In the first years after he purchased Lyndhurst in 1880, Gould was at the height of his power. With controlling interest in the Missouri Pacific Railroad, the Texas and Pacific Railroad, the Wabash Railroad, and the Manhattan Elevated Railroad, as well as large holdings in the Union Pacific Railroad and the Western Union Telegraph Company, he was perhaps the wealthiest man in America from 1881 to 1884.

Gould was never popular with the press. He did not like to talk to reporters, and his complex transactions invariably received bad reviews, much worse than those of his charismatic contemporaries, such as "Commodore" Vanderbilt and Jim Fisk, who were busy doing exactly the same things. Gould was particularly disliked in Manhattan, so rural Lyndhurst provided him and his family with a refuge from harassing reporters and outraged citizens. For additional privacy he commissioned a spectacular steam-powered yacht. Launched in 1883, it permitted Gould to commute to his New York office via the Hudson River rather than aboard crowded trains.

Gould's greatest personal pleasure at Lyndhurst was the huge greenhouse, where he raised exotic plants, including 250 varieties of palm trees from around the world. It also contained a rose room, an azalea room with 2,000 plants, and a fernery with 600 different varieties. Rare orchids were a particular favorite and his collection numbered almost 8,000 plants representing about 150 varieties.

Gould died in 1892, leaving a substantial fortune to his children. Lyndhurst was purchased from the estate by Helen, his oldest daughter, who occupied the house until her death in 1938. She became a much respected philanthropist and willingly opened Lyndhurst to groups of young people and civic projects of various kinds. She kept the main house virtually unchanged but over the years added numerous outbuildings, including a bowling alley, indoor swimming pool, laundry, and kennel.

After Helen's death her younger sister Anna, the duchess of Talleyrand-Périgord, returned from France and purchased Lyndhurst from Helen's husband and heir. Anna also carefully maintained the estate until her death in 1961; she left it to the National Trust for Historic Preservation as a museum and permanent monument to her father. Lyndhurst's remarkable state of preservation, with interiors virtually unmodified and with many original furnishings designed by Davis, is due to the careful stewardship of the Gould family for almost a century.

A visit to Lyndhurst today begins with the handsome entry gates and a long approach drive through grassy lawns dotted with handsome specimen trees to a parking area tucked out of sight behind what was originally a large stable complex. A stroll up the hill to the main house takes in the parklike setting and the fine westerly view across the Hudson Valley.

The marble-clad tower, part of Davis's 1865 addition, is crowned by stair-step battlements. All the windows have drip moldings to deflect rain water as it runs down the wall. The moldings' ninety-degree turn at either end further deflects the flow.

Built of light gray marble quarried at nearby Ossining, Lyndhurst's exterior is exquisitely detailed. Davis had a thorough knowledge of Gothic design gleaned from his study of books illustrating Gothic details and façades. Lyndhurst's design, however, represents his own personal synthesis of these sources, using proportions and scaling he felt to be the most pleasing. The delicate window tracery, the hooded windows with "drip" molds at each side, the beautiful roof parapet with its many varieties of crenellation, the multiple chimneys, and the handsome pinnacles all contribute to the picturesque effect that he sought.

One of Davis's boldest devices was the projection of both the library and state bedroom out over the veranda that wrapped around the house. Altered on one side of the house by the entry façade of the Merritt addition, this configuration is still clearly visible on the riverfront side, where the art gallery (originally the library) overhangs the veranda below. When the first version of the house was built in the 1830s, most American houses were simple symmetrical boxes, perhaps with colonnaded porches. Davis's interweaving of porch with house was at that time a most daring architectural innovation.

Inside the house, the walls of the main hall, which runs the length of the house, are painted to resemble the marble exterior. In the hall, as elsewhere in the house, the ceiling is perhaps the most dramatic feature. At a time when ceilings were usually flat and rarely decorated, Davis introduced an entire repertoire of elaborate ceiling detailing, mostly inspired by the vaulted ceilings of Gothic churches. Every main room on the ground floor

ABOVE *Detail of window ornamented with stone tracery; strips of lead hold the panes of clear and colored glass.*

LEFT *The glass in the art gallery's large, Gothic-style window was replaced in the late nineteenth century and is attributed to Louis Comfort Tiffany. The stained glass depicts an "Emblem of the Arts" holding an artist's palette, an architect's drafting tools, and a sculptor's mallet and chisel.*

RIGHT *Gothic chairs designed by Davis for Lyndhurst are aligned in front of the two-story window that dominates the west end of the art gallery and overlooks the Hudson River.*

OPPOSITE *Originally the library, this room was converted into an art gallery when Lyndhurst was expanded in 1865. Its ceiling has fine exposed timber vaulting. The magnificent window, intricately patterned wood floor, and faux ashlar walls complete what was one of the most ambitious domestic spaces in the country when it was built in 1838.*

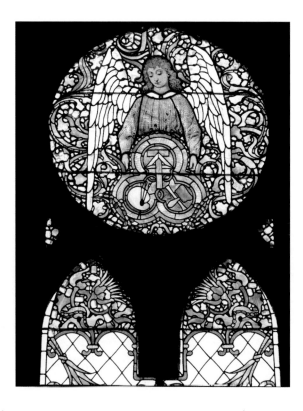

ABOVE *A portrait of Jay Gould hangs on a faux-marble painted wall in the entry hall above two of Davis's Gothic-style wheel-back chairs.*

RIGHT *All three of these bedrooms have Gothic-inspired windows. The window in the south bedroom (*TOP*) has an ogee-shaped frame. Elaborate tracery embellishes the window in the state bedroom (*CENTER*), which juts out over the original porte cochere (now the enclosed vestibule). This room also features a remarkable Gothic Revival bed. The Eastlake-inspired furniture in the east bedroom (*BOTTOM*) was added by the Goulds.*

ABOVE *The quatrefoils ornamenting the ceiling squares in the office are trompe l'oeil, as is the cornice detail, which resembles a series of Gothic corbels (supporting wall projections). Here they appear to support the ceiling.*

LEFT *The office is home to a Wooten patent desk with a fold-and-lock design and numerous compartments. It belonged to Jay Gould.*

has a different pattern of vaulting, giving each a distinctly different feel. The reception room has simple, parallel, almost flat vaulting enhanced by painted panels between the ribs. The vaulting in the entry hall, drawing room, and original dining room (now the library) is livelier and more complex.

The original upstairs library (now the art gallery) features elaborate exposed-wood trusses and a very high ceiling that rises up to the roofline. A large Gothic-style window overlooks the Hudson at one end, while the other end boasts a carved wooden screen similar to those found in Gothic cathedrals. The great window has varied stained-glass designs at the top and clear leaded glass below. The combination of great window, screen, and vaulted ceiling creates an amazingly inventive interior space for an American dwelling built in 1838.

The most opulent room in Davis's 1865 expansion of the house was the Gothic dining room. It has a deep red color scheme accented by pointed arches, huge bay windows, wood-grained ceilings, and matching table and chairs that were designed by Davis himself. These furnishings join other Gothic Revival pieces that Davis designed for the original house.

Davis and other designers of the day faced a special problem in creating appropriately "Gothic" furniture for such houses. Most medieval domestic-scale furniture that survives or can be seen in contemporary paintings was relatively massive and crude; it did not provide a sophisticated precedent for nineteenth-century designers, who wanted elegant furniture in their Gothic Revival houses. They solved the problem by melding Gothic *architectural* details with basic furniture shapes of much more recent design.

The first designers to create such furniture were English. At the precocious age of fifteen the talented revivalist Augustus Welby Pugin (1812–1852) was designing "Gothic" furnishings for King George IV's redecoration of Windsor Castle. Between 1844 and 1852, Pugin designed many such Gothic Revival pieces for the new Houses of Parliament in London. Pugin's lead was followed by others, including Davis. It is not entirely clear whether all of Lyndhurst's fine Gothic Revival furniture was designed by Davis, but much of it undoubtedly was. Other furnishings in the house are of later vintage—Merritt added Renaissance Revival Victorian furniture in the drawing room; the Goulds, the wonderful bedroom suite of Eastlake inspiration in the east bedroom. The National Trust has restored most of these furnishings and is proceeding with the lengthy and expensive task of revitalizing Lyndhurst, the nation's premier example of Gothic Revival design.

ABOVE *A corbel in the form of a cherub holding a fleur-de-lis supports the base of a ceiling vault.*

OPPOSITE *The dining room, added in the 1865 remodeling, is the most opulent room at Lyndhurst. The multi-unit column, typical of the Gothic Revival style, is a dominant feature. Those flanking the fireplace are of marble, the rest are of wood painted to resemble marble. Another typically Gothic-style feature that figures prominently is the narrow pointed arch embellished with five small scallops. It can be seen in the tracery in all six sections of the bay window and at the cornice line between the beams of the ceiling. Even the tops of the Davis-designed chairs have a similar rhythm.*

Gothic Revival Style
(1840–1880)

Proponents of the Gothic Revival style idealized the architecture of the Middle Ages, seeing it as particularly appropriate for romantic country houses. These houses loosely incorporated architectural details from medieval castles or Gothic churches to evoke images of a remote and heroic past. This new medievalism was a central theme of the Romantic movement that swept through the artistic world of England and much of western Europe in the late eighteenth and early nineteenth centuries.

The new romanticism was introduced into American architecture by Alexander Jackson Davis, and Lyndhurst was to become his masterpiece. Davis and other devotees of the Gothic Revival style advocated picturesque irregularities and "asymmetrical" massing, features that contrasted sharply with the formal and balanced designs of the preceding era. Davis wrote: "The English collegiate [Gothic] style is for many reasons to be preferred. It admits of greater variety of plans and outline . . . while its bay windows, oriels, turrets, and chimney shafts give a picture effect."

In fact, many American Gothic Revival houses were built without any picturesque irregularity or asymmetry. Instead they are simple, symmetrical boxes whose principal medieval reference is a steep central gable pierced by a decorative window of Gothic pointed-arch shape. This was because most American houses of the era were built with heavy frames of interlocking timbers rather than with stone masonry as were the medieval houses that inspired them. Heavy timber framing is relatively simple to fashion into rectangular, boxlike structures with planar walls but is very difficult to adapt to the angular projections, nooks, and crannies of the stone originals.

The pioneering house pattern books by Davis's collaborator, Andrew Jackson Downing, and those by the many Romantic-era architect-writers who followed him,

showed about equal numbers of Gothic Revival and "Italianate" examples, the latter loosely based on quaint Mediterranean farmhouses and villas. In this country, Italianate designs were to become far more numerous than their Gothic rivals, which were more complex and more expensive to construct. Nevertheless, scattered Gothic Revival houses became memorable additions to the mid-nineteenth-century American landscape. Of these, none was more picturesque than Lyndhurst.

IDENTIFYING FEATURES

1. WALL SURFACE EXTENDING INTO GABLE WITHOUT BREAK

2. STEEPLY PITCHED ROOF, USUALLY WITH STEEP CROSS GABLES

3. WINDOWS EXTENDING INTO GABLES, OFTEN WITH GOTHIC (POINTED-TOP) SHAPES

4. ONE-STORY ENTRY OR FULL-WIDTH PORCH, COMMONLY WITH FLATTENED GOTHIC ARCHES

5. GABLES WITH DECORATED VERGE BOARDS

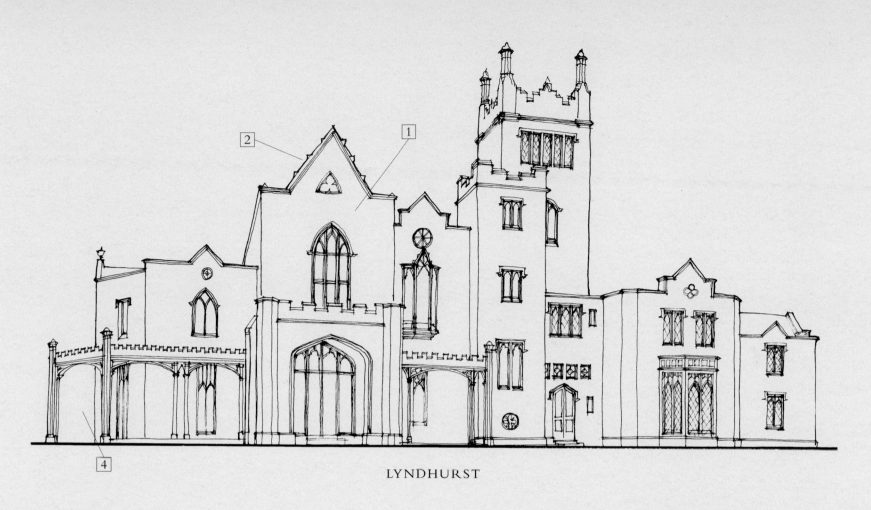

LYNDHURST

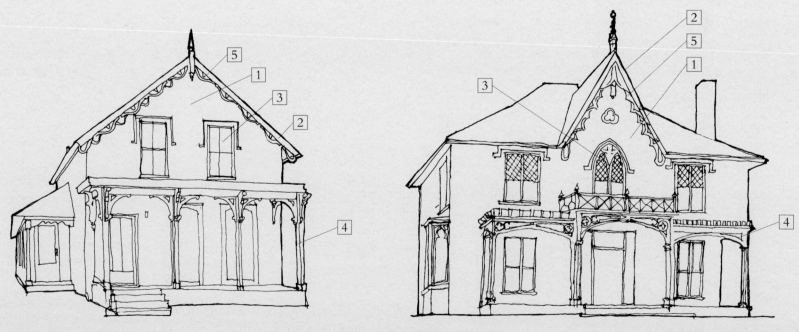

9
Morse-Libby House

PORTLAND, MAINE

Italianate Style

*I*f ever a city should have been named Phoenix, after the mythical Egyptian bird that rose from its own ashes, it is Portland, Maine. First settled by English colonists in 1628 on a small, hilly peninsula adjacent to a fine natural harbor, the town was twice burned by Indians during the lengthy French and Indian War—in 1676 and again in 1690. During the early eighteenth century a lively shipping trade brought renewed prosperity, but in 1775, when the gutsy town refused to surrender its weapons to the British in a skirmish preliminary to the American Revolution, the British set fire to the town and destroyed 414 of its 500 homes.

For the third time Portland rebuilt and by the mid-nineteenth century boasted the largest fleet of merchant ships on the eastern seaboard. The port had a varied economy based on fishing, light manufacturing, the export of timber and grain, and the lucrative West Indies trade, which entailed bringing wood and other necessities to the Indies in return for molasses, which was processed by the city's seven distilleries into rum, a principal export commodity. Then, on July 4, 1866, tragedy struck for the fourth time. A devastating fire destroyed 1,800 homes and narrowly missed the fashionable Italianate mansion completed seven years before for Ruggles Sylvester Morse (1816–1893), a prosperous New Orleans hotel man who spent the summers in his native Maine. The house's tall square observation tower, or campanile, as it would be called in Italy, must have witnessed a terrifying sight as the city burned around it on that fateful night. Soon, however, it overlooked a more positive scene as workmen set about rebuilding once again, a process completed in the remarkably short time of two years.

Morse and his wife, Olive, both of whom had grown up in Maine, began building their grand summer home in 1858. Morse had left the state in the 1830s to work, first at Boston's famed Tremont House Hotel and then in New York's equally renowned Astor House. After learning about the management of "palace" hotels, as these luxury establishments were then called, Morse moved on to New Orleans, where he worked, perhaps as a

Nineteenth-century engraving of the Morse-Libby House.

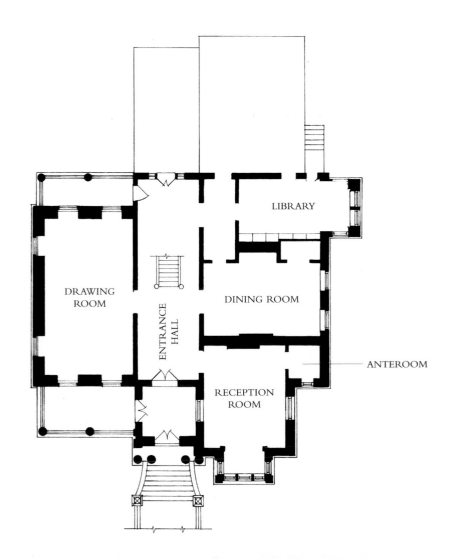

Round arches and paired doors are typical of Italianate doorways. Here the doors and the keystone of the arch are elegantly detailed.

PAGE 112 *A four-story tower and seven different window patterns ornament the façade.*

manager, at the fashionable St. Charles. He must have been both a very competent and a very frugal executive, for he soon became the owner of three of that bustling city's most important hotels. By the time his house in Portland was begun, Morse was a man of wealth and taste, the latter acquired during years of serving the needs of wealthy and demanding clients.

As a hotel man, Morse was accustomed to making grand statements in decor and to pampering his customers with the latest technological improvements. Nothing less would do for his home in Maine. To design the house, Morse chose one of the foremost architects of the day, Henry Austin (1804–1891) of New Haven, Connecticut, who had learned his trade under Ithiel Town of the influential New York firm of Town and Davis (see Lyndhurst, page 100). In 1842 Austin had designed the acclaimed Yale College Library in the newly fashionable Gothic Revival style. He had also designed several fine houses in the new Italianate style and thus was proficient in both of the trendsetting Romantic styles of the day.

In choosing the Italianate fashion for his house, Morse followed the advice of Andrew Jackson Downing (1815–1852), the writer who popularized these Romantic

LIBRARY

DRAWING ROOM

ENTRANCE HALL

DINING ROOM

ANTEROOM

RECEPTION ROOM

styles through his influential books *Cottage Residences* (1842) and *The Architecture of Country Houses* (1850). According to Downing:

> There is a strong and growing partiality among us for the Italian style. . . . Its broad roofs, ample verandahs and arcades, are especially agreeable in our summers of dazzling sunshine, and though not so truly Northern as other modes that permit a high roof . . . it [is] . . . remarkable for expressing the elegant culture and variety of accomplishment of the retired citizen or man of the world. . . . It is also very significant of the multiform tastes, habits, and wants of modern civilization. . . . The Italian style is one that expresses not wholly the spirit of country life nor of town life, but something between both, and which is a mingling of both.

Downing's hint about the style's lack of adaptability to northern climes was ignored by architect Austin, probably because of Morse's desire to be perceived as a tasteful man of the world, one who was in touch with the most modern fashion trends.

The house was built of dark brownstone, then a favorite building material in New York City. This gives its exterior a feeling of dignity, formality, and unity. The somber stonework of the façades is enlivened however, by an informal, asymmetrical plan typical of many Italianate dwellings and by a rich variety of decorative elements.

The exterior design of the two earlier American housing fashions with roots in the Italian Renaissance, the Georgian and Federal styles, were more symmetrical and formal. All windows were identical or nearly so, with perhaps one carefully centered window of different design for accent. In the Morse-Libby House a whole repertoire of window design elements is introduced; there are seven different patterns on the front façade alone. The variations are in the window shape itself—rectangular, round-arched, circular, single, and triple—and in the crowns above the windows—triangular pediments, arched pediments, flat entablatures, or no crown at all. According to Downing, "the great variety of forms in the windows introduced . . . [in the Italianate style is] a variety which denotes different uses in different apartments." Indeed, the different window types on the Morse-Libby front façade do belong to rooms with differing uses.

On entering the house one is greeted by a dramatic three-story entry hall. The spacious hall and stairway, the grand gaslit chandelier, and the large paired statues are almost commercial in scale and feeling, a reminder of Morse's hotel background. He apparently felt comfortable welcoming guests into this large, exuberant, even slightly ostentatious space. Although the hall is distinctly urban in feel, the informal "country" theme of the asymmetrical exterior is picked up in the wall paintings—bucolic scenes of Italian peasant girls!

A small reception room lies immediately to the right of the entry hall. After presenting a calling card to the servant who answered the door, a visitor would have been escorted to this room to await further recognition. The art of "visiting" was a highly developed and ritualized process during the Victorian era. One paid calls, left cards,

This pair of arched windows has segmental arched pediments. Rows of modillions are found beneath the main and porch roofs.

Triangular pediments crown a single window, a triple window, and the front-facing gable of the roof. Quoins ornament the corners of the house.

The large entrance hall is dominated by a central staircase. Deep brackets support the upstairs balconies. The original eighteen-foot-tall gas chandelier hangs from the gallery ceiling three stories above.

and returned calls. The process is easiest to understand when compared to modern telephone etiquette—one places calls, leaves messages, and receives return calls. Visiting served the same purpose as a local telephone call, while letters were the equivalent of long-distance calls.

A guest escorted into the reception room was on "hold" while the servant (secretary) checked to see if the intended callee was "out" or otherwise occupied (in a meeting or on the other line). If the callee was not available, a further refinement of the visiting ritual involved turning down different corners of one's calling card to signify different messages, such as "condolence" or "felicitation" or that a daughter was included in the visit. Visiting was of particular importance to ladies, who, according to an etiquette book of the day, "were advised to keep an account of visits made and visits owed, a balance book of social obligations."

At the same time that the Morses' visitors were showing their sophistication by offering a proper calling card, their hosts were subtly using the reception room decor to express their interest in the arts. Writing, music, architecture, and painting are symbolized in delicate paintings on the coved ceiling. A small side room featuring a face of Bacchus encircled by grape leaves suggests that wines or liquor may have been kept there for special occasions—an early version of today's home bars.

The reception room's chandelier, wall-to-wall carpeting, and intricately painted walls and ceiling are all original. Portraits of Mr. and Mrs. Morse flank the fireplace and an elegant ottoman, a circular sofa popular in the mid-nineteenth century, occupies the center of the room.

One of the extraordinary aspects of the Morse-Libby House is the integrated design of its interiors. Each room's walls, ceilings, floor coverings, furnishings, and window treatments were carefully coordinated. This total approach to interior design was introduced to nineteenth-century Americans in public spaces—hotel lobbies and sitting rooms, railroad parlor cars, and the saloons of luxury steamboats. This is particularly well illustrated by the Morse-Libby drawing room.

Drawing rooms were intended for receiving and entertaining visitors. Romance is the theme of this room's decor in the Morse-Libby House. Wall paintings feature cherubs, or "children of Venus," and garlands of roses. These motifs appear again in the corners of the room, over the mirrors, and in smaller paintings at the tops of the wall panels. They are also carved into the furniture, woven into the design of the rug, and even incorporated into the chandelier. It is believed that the person responsible for this meticulously coordinated design was Gustave Herter, who later headed a distinguished furniture and interior design firm in New York City.

The general style of the drawing room furnishings is French Rococo, a favorite mid-Victorian fashion that was considered particularly appropriate for the formal living areas of Italianate houses. Occupying the center of the room is a large table that might seem more appropriate for a dining room. In mid-Victorian times, however, such center tables were reported in a contemporary magazine account to be "an institution, as orthodox as the hymn book. [They are] practically universal; in expensive as well as in humble houses [they are] still the object point and the *pièce de résistance* of the room." Today we can only speculate about the reason for this custom. Perhaps it was because the center of the drawing room had the greatest amount of light and the family could gather around the table in

the evenings to read, or because it was the most prominent spot to display one's important possessions. Whatever the reason, tables in this position are seen in most photographs of mid-Victorian drawing rooms and parlors, as the best room was called in smaller Victorian houses that had neither a formal reception room nor a drawing room.

During the Victorian era rooms often had highly specialized functions, such as receiving, dining, entertaining, reading, and smoking. And for each type of room there were design schemes that were thought to be particularly appropriate. The Morse-Libby House, for example, has a smoking room decorated in a Turkish theme. It is one of the earliest such rooms in the country; Turkish motifs later became common for smoking rooms, perhaps because Turkish tobacco was then the best available. The Morse-Libby library, in contrast, is decorated in Gothic Revival style, which, according to Downing, invoked the "quiet domestic feeling" needed in such rooms.

Both smoking rooms and libraries were considered male retreats during the Victorian era. The Morse-Libby House has a third such retreat, a large billiard room on the third floor. After dinner, while the men smoked, played billiards, or sipped brandy in the library, the women would "withdraw" to another room, probably the drawing room (the name is derived from *withdraw*) or, if the guests were intimate friends, the upstairs parlor, an informal room that usually served as a private family retreat—a place to read, sew, talk, or play games.

According to Downing, dining rooms should be "rich and warm . . . [and] the furniture should be substantial," as opposed to drawing rooms or parlors, which should be "lighter, more cheerful and gay . . . and the furniture . . . delicate in design." In the Morse-Libby House the decor of the dining room is indeed in striking contrast to that of the drawing room. The walls of the dining room are covered in dark wood paneling with molded plaster carvings of fruits, vegetables, game, fish, and even a Maine lobster—a handsome setting for a multicourse Victorian dinner. The natural wood tones of the walls carry over to the ceiling, which is painted to simulate wood graining. Both walls and ceiling are enhanced with decorative plaster that is also grained to look like carved wood.

Morse's background as a hotelier is particularly evident in the second-floor master suite, a series of interconnected living spaces for him and his wife. Undoubtedly inspired by the guest suites found in grand hotels, it consists of a large bedroom, a dressing room, and separate rooms for bath and toilet. Such suites were rare in American houses at that time; they began to appear in very large American houses in the late nineteenth century but did not become common in smaller houses until the 1960s.

Another luxury of the Morse-Libby House was complete indoor plumbing—sinks, toilets, and bathtub—still a rarity in the mid-1800s. Americans were first introduced to the pleasures of indoor plumbing in luxury hotels, some of which boasted bathtubs and washbasins with hot and cold running water and a built-in drain, and flush toilets, which alleviated trips to an outside "necessary" or the use of chamber pots. The built-in double washbasin in the Morse-Libby guest room is an example of this up-to-date plumbing technology, as is the full bathroom that serves the master suite.

The theme of the drawing room is romance; many painted cherubs decorate the ceiling and walls.

A cherub is carved into the arm support of this drawing room chair.

*The rich wood tones of the dining room are an eye-fooling combination of real
wood and carefully grained faux-wood finishes.*

It is only through several lucky strokes of fate that this magnificent house, now a public museum, was preserved for our enjoyment. Morse died in 1893 and a year later his widow sold the house to Joseph Ralph Libby, a leading Portland merchant and department store owner. Libby appreciated the quality of the house and its contents and left it intact even though changing fashions in interior design during his family's long occupancy eventually made the decor seem old-fashioned.

Hard economic times kept the house vacant from the late 1920s until 1940, when it was scheduled to be demolished. Wishing to save the historic structure, local preservationists Dr. William Holmes and his sister Clara stepped in and acquired the house. They were influential in forming the Victoria Society, which has preserved the house and operated it as a museum ever since.

The preservation of the Morse-Libby House has not been an easy task, for slow deterioration of its elaborate interior and exterior detailing has required complex and expensive conservation procedures. The exterior problems stem in part from the unsuitability of the Italianate style to northern climates, as Downing had observed. In winter, ice tends to accumulate in the house's broad gutters and on sections of its low-pitched and flat roofs. Then, as the ice melts on warm days, water seeps into the stone walls, keeping them damp. When nighttime temperatures drop below freezing, a freeze-and-thaw cycle develops that causes the soft brownstone to flake away in layers. This flaking is intensified by the way the stone was originally laid; its natural layered structure was placed vertically rather than horizontally as it was found in the quarry. This problem has required an inventory of every stone and its condition. The progress of deterioration is then closely monitored and, when necessary, the stone is either replaced, restored, or resolidified.

Restoration of the heavily deteriorated front porch followed advice given by Downing himself: "Should economy oblige us to construct the balcony and terrace of wood, they should be made in a bold manner, and thoroughly painted and sanded, to imitate the material of the house." The porch was recently reconstructed of wood and, finished to look like stone, it closely matches the original masonry.

Similar care is being given to the problems that plague the interior. Some of the decorative paint finishes in need of repair are water-based, and the technology is not yet available to clean and restore them. These areas will not be touched until there is a safe preservation technique on the market. Other paint finishes are oil-based, and for these careful reapplication of flaking pieces can be undertaken. The elaborate dining room ceiling has been fully restored in this manner. The society's approach has been to survey each conservation problem and then search for the best modern technology to solve it. This could serve as a model for anyone entrusted with the care of irreplaceable historic buildings.

The Morse-Libby House is of importance today as a document of high-style Italianate design, as a rare and unmodified example of the integrated interior design fashions of the mid-nineteenth century, as a symbol of that era's enthusiasm for propriety, gaiety, and forward-thinking technology, and, finally, as a lesson in the patient and thoughtful preservation of an irreplaceable landmark.

This dressing room is part of the master bathroom suite. Such suites were the very latest domestic innovation when the house was designed in 1858.

Italianate Style
(1840–1885)

Like its contemporary, the Gothic Revival style, the Italianate style was an outgrowth of the wave of artistic romanticism that swept western Europe at the turn of the nineteenth century. Romantic-era architects focused on two very different models for the "ideal" country house. The medieval churches, castles, and manor houses of France and England were the source of Gothic Revival architecture, while the picturesque villas of rural Italy were the inspiration for the Italianate style.

The style first spread to the United States from England, where it had gotten a boost when Queen Victoria chose it for a new summer palace—Osborne House on the Isle of Wight, begun in 1845. In spite of this royal endorsement, however, Italianate fashions were greatly overshadowed in Victorian England by Gothic designs, which seemed to suit the English temperament and countryside better than a fashion based on sun-drenched Mediterranean farmhouses.

When these two Romantic fashions crossed the Atlantic, however, the reverse proved to be true. Although

MORSE-LIBBY HOUSE

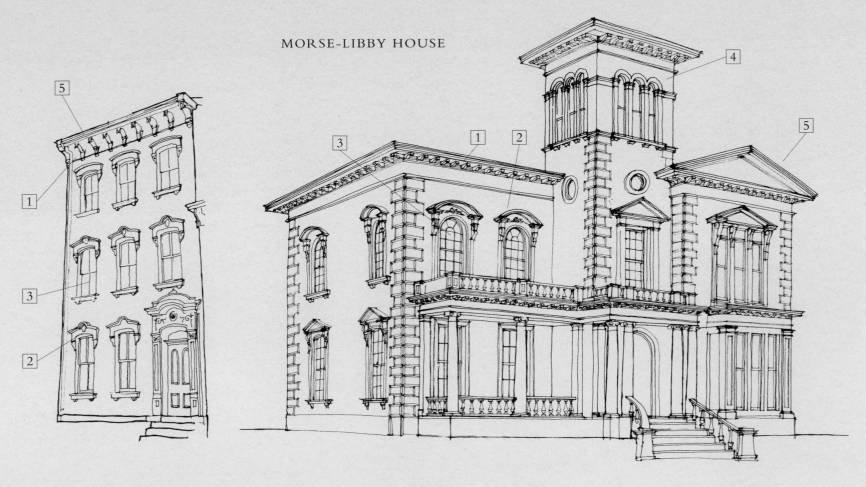

both styles were advocated for American country houses in the influential Downing-Davis pattern books of the 1840s, Americans, having neither Gothic nor Italian originals close at hand, preferred the simpler Mediterranean-based designs, and the Italianate style became the dominant fashion in American domestic architecture for a quarter of a century—from about 1855 to 1880.

Architect Henry Austin learned his trade as a junior colleague of Alexander Jackson Davis, whose 1838 pattern book had introduced both Gothic Revival and Italianate models to Americans (see Lyndhurst, page 100). Austin's Morse-Libby House is the finest surviving Italianate design by the first generation of American Romantic-era architects. In it he skillfully combined the opposite extremes of Italian domestic design: the formal elements of a Renaissance town house—classical columns, pedimented window crowns, and corner quoins—with the asymmetrical shape and picturesque tower of a simple Italian farmhouse.

IDENTIFYING FEATURES

1 WIDELY OVERHANGING EAVES WITH DECORATIVE BRACKETS BELOW

2 ELABORATED WINDOW CROWNS

3 TALL, NARROW WINDOWS, SOMETIMES ARCHED ABOVE

4 SOMETIMES HAVE SQUARE CUPOLA OR TOWER

5 LOW-PITCHED ROOF

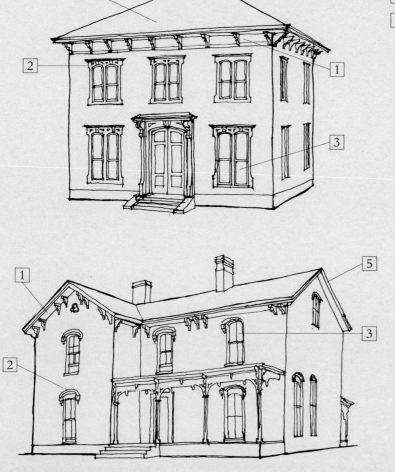

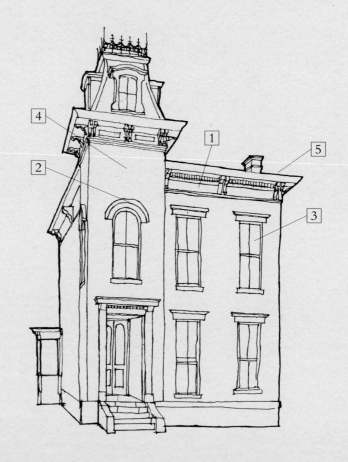

Architect's sketch of the Mark Twain House, 1873.

Victorian Houses

(1860–1900)

The last four decades of the nineteenth century brought still other architectural styles into competition with the Greek-Gothic-Italianate triumvirate of the preceding Romantic era. Both the Gothic Revival and Italianate styles persisted, with declining popularity, into the 1880s, but they were being overshadowed by newer fashions imported from Europe. From France came the mansard-roofed Second Empire style (pages 136–37), named for its popularity during the mid-century rebuilding of Paris under the aegis of Emperor Napoleon III. In this country it so dominated reconstruction-era building that it was sometimes called the General Grant style. In the 1870s the rustic Stick style (pages 150–51), a then-popular fashion for French and German country houses, was introduced into this country by the Paris-trained New York architect Richard Morris Hunt. This style ushered in a new propensity for houses based on medieval prototypes, a taste that was to endure for the rest of the century. By far the most popular of these was the Queen Anne style (pages 164–65), loosely copied from the contemporaneous Old English style in Britain. Queen Anne designs were to dominate American house construction from about 1880 to 1900.

These late Victorian decades also saw the introduction of our first two home-grown architectural fashions, both of them inspired by Boston architect Henry Hobson Richardson, one of the towering figures of American design. While studying in France, Richardson had become intrigued by the beauty and simplicity of early medieval churches in the round-arched Romanesque style. He modified and adapted these early designs into a new American fashion that has come to be known as the Richardsonian Romanesque style (pages 188–89).

Richardson's style featured massive stone walls and was most popular for large public buildings, although it was also used for some large and expensive dwellings, particularly in the 1890s. He and his followers also adapted the style to less complex, wooden-walled houses. Characterized by a uniform wall covering of dark shingles, this fashion has come to be known as the Shingle style (pages 176–77). With their highly stylized exteriors and open-flow interior planning these two styles paved the way for the first "modern" house designs that were to dominate the first two decades of the next century.

A technological innovation of the Victorian era facilitated the building of wood-framed houses based on medieval prototypes. Known as the "balloon-frame" system, it allowed heavy frames of massive timbers with complex hand-hewn joints to be replaced by much lighter frames of 2 × 4– or 2 × 6–inch lumber joined together with simple wire nails. By the 1870s the balloon-frame system had become the standard technique for house construction and remains so today. Not only was it less expensive than heavy timber framing, but it also simplified the construction of complex and irregular shapes—bays, nooks, crannies, peaks, and gables—all favorite features of the picturesque late Victorian styles.

10
Château-sur-Mer
NEWPORT, RHODE ISLAND
Second Empire Style

Through several remarkable turns of fate, the small city of Newport, Rhode Island, is today home to the nation's premier collection of grand and imposing historical houses. Located on an island in sheltered Narragansett Bay, Newport's fine deep-water harbor made it one of the principal seaports of Colonial America. In 1770 it had ten thousand inhabitants and was the fifth-largest city in the American colonies—exceeded in size only by Philadelphia, New York, Boston, and Charleston, South Carolina. Newport's fortunes were soon to decline, however. Partially destroyed by a long British occupation during the American Revolution, the town's fate was sealed after the war when nearby Providence, farther inland and not handicapped by being located on an island, began to replace it as the region's main seaport.

By 1840 Newport had become a sleepy seaside village whose quaint old buildings and cooling breezes made it a favorite summer getaway for artists and intellectuals. As is the case with so many picturesque artist colonies, the town's charms were quickly discovered by more affluent visitors. Beginning as a trickle in the 1840s and 1850s, the influx of the rich steadily increased to a flood. Between 1880 and 1914 many of the nation's wealthiest families built palatial "cottages" on the island. During those decades the town was the undisputed summer capital of Gilded Age society, complete with lavish costume balls, countless dinner and garden parties, and grand yachting events.

For the first thirty years of the town's rise to fashion, from about 1850 to 1880, the grandest of all Newport houses was a massive gray structure built of rough-hewn granite known as Château-sur-Mer (Castle-by-the-Sea). Like Lyndhurst (see pages 98–111), this remarkable house has the unusual distinction of representing both the beginning and end of an architectural era. When completed in 1852 it was among the first and most imposing American examples of the latest French building fashion—the mansard-roofed Second Empire style that became popular in mid-century France during the reign of Emperor Napoleon III. Twenty years later, just as American enthusiasm for Second Empire

Before Hunt's remodeling, Château-sur-Mer had a prominent front entry and its mansard roofline had a different profile.

PAGE 126 *Architect Richard Morris Hunt designed this carved-oak mantel for the billiard room in the style advocated by English designer Charles Eastlake. The tiles above the fireplace were made by English craftsman Walter Crane. The room's beamed ceiling can be seen reflected in the mantel's mirror.*

designs was beginning to wane, Château-sur-Mer was remodeled in the same style to become one of the country's grandest late Second Empire houses. This remodeling marked a crucial turning point in the hitherto unspectacular career of a forty-year-old French-trained American named Richard Morris Hunt (1827–1895), who was soon to rise to fame as the dean of American architects (see Biltmore, pages 232–45).

Avant-garde as it was when built, the original house apparently did not boost the first architect's career. He was a Newport designer-builder named Seth Bradford (1801–1878), about whom very little is known. One suspects that Bradford's up-to-the-minute design was strongly influenced by his worldly client William Shepard Wetmore (1801–1862), a retired New York merchant who had amassed a large fortune in the lucrative but dangerously unpredictable Pacific trade.

Wetmore's career had begun in Providence, where his uncles owned a prosperous shipping company. At age nineteen he was given the important job of "supercargo" (cargo sales and purchase agent) aboard one of their vessels, which was headed around the world via England, Africa, China, and South America. William was quick to realize that the greatest opportunity for an ambitious and adventuresome young man lay not in such time-consuming shipboard journeys but in on-site management of American shipping interests in some foreign port. So he and two financial partners formed an import-export firm in remote Valparaiso, Chile, which then had no American agent. When this venture prospered he sold his interest and founded a similar partnership in Canton, China, at the time a major and highly competitive source for the riches of the Orient. Here he succeeded once again and about 1840 sold his holdings for a substantial fortune. The forty-year-old Wetmore planned to retire to New York, but the lure of international trade proved irresistible, and he formed yet a third and still more successful foreign trading company, this one based in New York. Finally, as he approached fifty, he decided to retire for good. Drawn back to his native New England, he chose fashionable Newport for his final home. In 1851 he acquired fifteen acres of what was then rural pastureland on Bellevue Avenue and commissioned Bradford to build him the town's most imposing dwelling.

In spite of its ultrafashionable exterior, the original plan of Château-sur-Mer was a conventional center-hall arrangement with four main rooms on each of the three floors. In 1854, only two years after the house was completed, Wetmore redecorated the largest first-floor room, originally the drawing room, to create Newport's first ballroom, an amenity that was to become a standard, and increasingly lavish, feature of the Gilded Age town. To insure that the room was properly elegant for formal balls, Wetmore commissioned one of New York's most knowledgeable designers, the French-born cabinetmaker Léon Marcotte, to do the decor. Designed in Louis XV Revival style, Marcotte's ballroom was an elegant novelty in Newport at the time, but today seems downright modest in comparison to many of the ballrooms that were subsequently built.

Unlike many grand Newport houses, which were designed as costly stage sets on which to play out the dramas of the brief summer social season, Wetmore's house was his

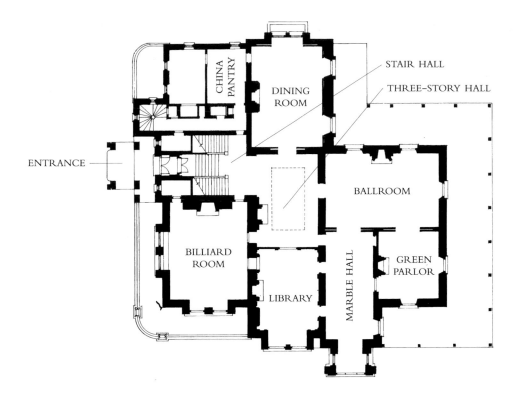

CHINA PANTRY

DINING ROOM

STAIR HALL

THREE–STORY HALL

ENTRANCE

BALLROOM

BILLIARD ROOM

GREEN PARLOR

LIBRARY

MARBLE HALL

principal residence. He had lived in the dwelling for only ten years when he died at age sixty-one in 1862. The house passed to his only surviving son, George Peabody Wetmore (1846–1921), then a sixteen-year-old student preparing to enter Yale. Suitably appreciative of his father's legacy, George also retained the house as his main residence throughout his long and active life, which included two terms as governor of Rhode Island (1885–87) and three as United States senator from the state (1895–1913).

In 1869, after completing his studies at Yale and then at Columbia Law School, George married Edith Malvina Ketletas. He soon decided to spend some of his inherited fortune to insure that Château-sur-Mer would maintain its status as Newport's grandest residence. To remodel and expand the house he chose New York architect Richard Morris Hunt. Hunt hailed from a distinguished New England family, and his wife and her parents had long summered in Newport.

Many of the forty-year-old Hunt's previous commissions had been stylish and innovative Newport summer houses for his family and friends. It was during this period that he introduced the new Stick style, then popular in French and German resort towns, into this country (see Mark Twain House, pages 138–51). In spite of these fashionable designs, Hunt had not yet received an assignment as grand as that handed to him by George Wetmore. In addition to much larger and more dramatic public rooms, Wetmore wanted greatly expanded service areas, nurseries for his growing family, and more bedroom suites. Carried out in several phases over more than a decade, these renovations completely transformed

One of a pair of arched niches that ornament the rugged brownstone of the entry gate.

the house's interior arrangement and decoration. They had somewhat less effect on the house's exterior appearance, particularly as viewed from Bellevue Avenue.

Faced with the exterior's fortresslike granite walls, Hunt wisely decided to retain much of Bradford's original façade and gain space by adding a single large wing, built of the same granite, to the building's inconspicuous northeast (left rear) corner. He did, however, replace Bradford's American-style curved mansard roof with a steeper and more fashionable French-style version, which is most evident in the tall, straight-sided roof of the projecting tower. A roof of the original type can still be seen on a surviving gatehouse designed by Bradford.

To better serve his redesigned interior, Hunt moved the house's principal entrance to the north (left) façade of the new wing, where it is announced by a large porte cochere of sculpted granite. The new wing houses a large dining room and two new stairways—a principal grand stairway just beyond the entrance and a spiral service stairway located in the small, pointed-roof tower that projects from the wing. The rest of the space in the new wing was devoted to service areas and to second-floor nurseries over the dining room.

Hunt also cleverly modified the functions of several of the existing first-floor rooms. The former kitchen, now moved to the basement, became a billiard room; the original dining room became the library; and the former study was transformed into a three-story, skylighted entry hall circled by balconies on the second and third levels. Not surprisingly, the interior decoration of the entire house was modernized with 1870s fashions during these extensive architectural changes. Only the grandest feature of the original house, the ballroom, was spared and remains essentially unmodified today.

Château-sur-Mer's principal downstairs rooms reflect two extremes of 1870s decor. Hunt himself was responsible for the design of the new grand stairway, one of the most dramatic features of the house, as well as the adjacent three-story entry hall and the nearby billiard room. These are finished in handsome golden oak, complete with turned spindles and stylized carvings, as advocated by the Englishman Charles Eastlake in his influential book, *Hints on Household Taste,* first published in the United States in 1872.

The decor of the new dining room and library had a very different inspiration. George and Edith Wetmore spent much of the 1870s living in England and traveling on the Continent, where they were introduced to the work of the gifted Italian wood-carver and decorator Luigi Frullini (1839–1897), whom they commissioned, probably over Hunt's objections, to create elaborate carved paneling and tooled-leather wall coverings for both the library and dining room. These were fashioned in a sort of Neo–Italian Renaissance style and were not installed until 1876, four years after Hunt completed his work on the house. Frullini's traditional carvings in dark walnut are in striking contrast to Hunt's more trendy and modern detailing in light oak.

The only first-floor room that has been significantly altered since the 1870s is a small parlor adjacent to both the ballroom and the original entry hall (Bradford's Bellevue Avenue entrance was seldom used after Hunt's new entrance was added, and in 1914 it was

finally replaced by a window; the early entry hall now serves merely to connect the library, ballroom, and parlor). In 1897 the parlor was redecorated in a subdued Louis XV style by a distant Wetmore cousin, Ogden Codman, Jr., who, with coauthor Edith Wharton, had in that same year published *The Decoration of Houses,* a book that was to have a profound influence on American interior design for the next half-century. Codman's parlor in Château-sur-Mer is one of the important early examples of his design philosophy, which emphasized light-walled and uncluttered rooms with furnishings and detailing borrowed from a variety of eighteenth-century French (or occasionally English) sources.

Upstairs, Château-sur-Mer's five bedrooms show more stylistic unity than do the downstairs rooms. The Wetmores' long stay in England brought them into contact with the current rage for "Aesthetic" interiors, which featured subtly colored and patterned wallpapers designed by William Morris, a principal advocate of simplified, "modern" design. The Wetmores used a variety of Morris-inspired furniture and wallpaper to decorate the five bedrooms. George Wetmore's bedroom, which was left

Château-sur-Mer sits in the midst of expansive, parklike grounds.

Richard Morris Hunt designed the grand staircase; its underside is painted to simulate an arbor with foliage and trellis work. The wall cloth is painted to resemble tapestry, and the stained glass window, dated 1876, was made by William McPherson of Boston.

Italian designer Luigi Frullini's intricate carving on a fall-front desk in the library depicts a man seated at a library table.

LEFT *This is one of the oldest complete bathrooms in Newport. Looking much as it did in the 1850s, it is an excellent example of the earliest period of interior plumbing, when fixtures were installed to look as if they were built-in furniture.*

RIGHT *George Wetmore's bedroom survives unmodified and is a superb example of the British Arts and Crafts movement. The ceiling was stenciled to complement the original William Morris wallpapers.*

untouched by his children after his death, survives intact. The other bedrooms were variously redecorated in later years but have recently been restored to their 1870s English Aesthetic appearance.

After George Wetmore's death in 1921, Château-sur-Mer passed to his two spinster daughters, the elder of whom, Edith Wetmore, was to become the last family owner. She died at age ninety-eight in 1968, and her heirs sold most of the furnishings at auction and then offered the house for sale. It was purchased by the Preservation Society of Newport County, which had been founded in 1945 to save Hunter House, Newport's grandest surviving eighteenth-century dwelling. These and several other of Newport's finest mansions have been saved from destruction and are now public museums operated by the society and other benefactors. Many of Château-sur-Mer's original furnishings bought at the estate auction were donated back to the house by friends of the Preservation Society; other original pieces have since been acquired through gifts or purchase.

Because of these efforts visitors today can see Château-sur-Mer much as it looked after Hunt's extensive remodeling more than a century ago. It serves as a grand monument to the early years of fashionable Newport society, to a remarkable Rhode Island family, and to one of the most gifted American architects of the last century.

Frullini covered the dining room walls with stamped, silvered, and painted leather. A carved sideboard sports a majolica inset depicting a boar hunt.

Decorated in 1854 by Leon Marcotte, this was one of the earliest ballrooms in Newport. The furnishings are upholstered in reproduction fabric that closely resembles the original; the walls are painted in seven subtle shades of gray highlighted with gold leaf.

Second Empire Style
(1855–1885)

When introduced into this country in the 1850s, Second Empire buildings, with their distinctive mansard (doubly sloped) roofs, were viewed as very avant-garde and "modern" because they were based on the latest Parisian architectural fashion. To our eyes, however, Second Empire designs, which in fact drew on earlier architectural precedents, tend to look quaintly old-fashioned. The mansard roof, for example, was first used in the seventeenth century by French architect François Mansart, from whom the name derives. This and other historical architectural features were simplified and recombined into a new building style that flourished in the massive rebuilding of Paris undertaken in the mid-nineteenth century by Emperor Napoleon III, whose reign is known as the Second Empire. Grand expositions (the Victorian term for what we now call world's fairs) were held in Paris in 1855 and 1867 and helped to spread the new style to other countries where it became especially popular for large public buildings.

In the United States the Second Empire style was widely used for both houses and larger buildings during the 1860s and 1870s. Architect Seth Bradford's original Château-sur-Mer, completed in 1852, is a particularly early example, probably inspired by owner William Wetmore's frequent trips to Europe.

Richard Morris Hunt had firsthand knowledge of the style because, while studying architecture at the Ecole des Beaux Arts in Paris from 1846 to 1855, he was given the unusual honor of assisting in the design of a new extension to the historic Louvre palace. This building was to become the prototype for many Second Empire designs. Several of Hunt's early commissions after returning to New York to establish his own practice in 1855 were Second Empire designs. His 1872 roof alterations and new wing for Château-sur-Mer are the best surviving demonstrations of his familiarity with the French originals.

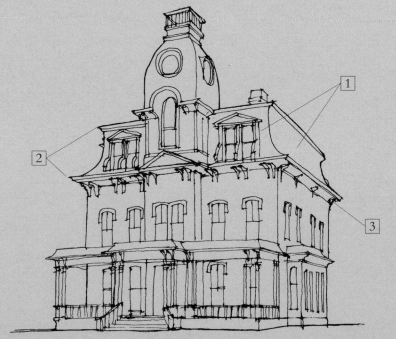

CHATEAU-SUR-MER

IDENTIFYING FEATURES

1 MANSARD ROOF WITH DORMER WINDOWS ON STEEP LOWER SLOPE

2 MOLDED CORNICES BOUND LOWER ROOF SLOPE

3 EAVES USUALLY WITH DECORATIVE BRACKETS BELOW

11
Mark Twain House

HARTFORD, CONNECTICUT

Stick Style

There is no doubt that author Samuel Clemens (1835–1910), better known by his pen name, Mark Twain, loved this extraordinary house, as did his wife, Olivia Langdon Clemens (1845–1904). Sam and Livy, as they were known to friends, left volumes of correspondence about the house, its construction and furnishing. One critic provided a whimsical view of the dwelling in 1874, the year that Sam and his young family first moved in:

> This is the house that Mark built.
> These are the bricks of various hue
> And shape and position, straight and askew,
> Which makes up the house presented to view,
> The curious house that Mark built.

The Clemens family had chosen a unique setting for their new home—the small, intellectual community of Nook Farm on the outskirts of Hartford, Connecticut. Sam had first seen Hartford in 1868 and had been impressed by its fine houses and lush landscapes, "Everywhere the eye turns it is blessed with a vision of refreshing green." The Nook Farm neighborhood was particularly appealing to the Clemenses. Begun in 1853 by John Hooker and his brother-in-law Francis Gillette, it consisted of about 140 acres settled by relatives of the two men along with some of their intellectual friends. This amazing group ultimately included Hooker's sister-in-law Harriet Beecher Stowe (author of *Uncle Tom's Cabin*); his nephew, the actor and playwright William Gillette; women's suffrage leader Isabella Beecher Hooker; writer Charles Dudley Warner; and other talented writers, artists, and musicians. It was a neighborhood where literature, progressive ideas, and political causes were openly discussed, and it welcomed the already famous Samuel Clemens and his family.

The Clemenses purchased two Nook Farm lots in early 1873 and hired the

Samuel Clemens was a patron of sculptor Karl Gerhardt, paying to send him to the Ecole des Beaux Arts in Paris. Gerhardt executed this 1884 bust of the author from life; it sits in front of Louis Comfort Tiffany's silver-stenciled wall in the entry hall.

PAGE 138 *An inviting one-story porch, or* ombra, *as Clemens preferred to call it, surrounds the entry façade.*

fashionable New York architect Edward Tuckerman Potter (1831–1904) to plan the house. Potter had recently designed a house for George Warner and his wife, Elizabeth Gillette Warner, the Clemenses' good friends and Nook Farm neighbors. He had also just completed three Hartford-area churches, including one sponsored by Mrs. Elizabeth J. Colt, a local social leader and widow of the firearms manufacturer Samuel Colt. These commissions gave Potter impeccable credentials in the Hartford area.

Potter must have worked very quickly because when Sam and Livy set sail for Europe two months later, in May 1873, they had already seen a color rendering of the house and had left behind workmen to begin readying the site. By the time the Clemenses returned from Europe at the end of 1873, the structure of the house was complete and they moved in the following September.

The house caused much comment in Hartford. Like Mark Twain himself it was unusually flamboyant, carrying to an extreme a dominant architectural dictate of the day, "Avoid plain walls at all cost." Multicolored and otherwise elaborated exterior walls of brick, stone, or slate are common in several American architectural styles that became fashionable after 1860, but are found mainly on large public buildings. A similar effect was achieved for houses by decorating the walls with "stickwork"—wooden boards applied in patterns to wooden siding and variously painted to create striking designs.

In his monumental Stick-style design for the Twain House, Potter took the unusual step of having walls of solid brick masonry instead of wood. As the critic's poem so charmingly points out, the architect made use of several clever devices to enliven these high-style brick walls. To avoid the expense of laying multicolored bricks, which were also difficult to obtain because they had to be specially glazed and carefully fired, Potter created wall patterns simply by painting plain red bricks black and vermilion. In addition, as the poem suggests, he laid the bricks themselves in unusual patterns—many are set diagonally, for example, creating interesting shadows and textures. He also used slate of different hues to form patterns in the roof.

Finally, Potter wrapped a one-story *ombra* around the southeast side of the house. Nothing so simple as a porch, veranda, or gallery would do for the Twain House. It had to be an *ombra,* a word whose Latin root conjures up the image of dark, quiet shade beckoning on a hot afternoon. On this porch, as we shall call it, Potter liberally applied the wooden motifs that are typical of Stick-style designs, including squared porch supports with beveled edges and trusslike triangular braces at the top. Sometimes, as in the porte cochere, such braces even appear at the *bottom* of supporting columns. The porch's balcony railing and hanging frieze also have this characteristic "trussed" appearance.

No two of the house's numerous gables have identical stickwork decoration; even the small dormers sport variations of trusslike design, as do the triangular braces that support the roof eaves. The frieze beneath the roof of the porte cochere also bears the upside-down-picket-fence pattern that is so typical of Stick-style design. To add still further texture and interest to the exterior walls, Potter applied decorative wood and brick panels to the outside of the service staircase and on part of the south end of the house.

ABOVE *This detail shows how bricks laid at various angles combine with painted bricks to produce an unusually lively wall surface.*

LEFT *Applied wooden "stickwork" and painted brick enliven the exterior wall of the servants' stairway, part of an 1881 addition.*

Like its owner, this house was most definitely *not* shy and retiring. It had a commanding presence that some loved and others loathed, a presence that might go in or out of fashion but could never be ignored. Having spent a small fortune on the basic house and its exterior detailing, Sam and Livy could not at first afford elaborate interior decoration. Instead they encouraged Potter "to let up on the fancy touches til we know how things [will] turn out." As a result, much of the interior remained quite simple while they waited to see how successful Sam's latest writings would be.

One room that Potter may have been allowed to finish was the third-floor billiard room. Here the architect's well-known love of symbolism is seen in the crossed pool cues and drinking and smoking motifs etched into decorative panels of translucent marble. Either Potter or a later designer extended these masculine themes to the ceiling, on which similar motifs were stenciled. Restoration of the house in the 1960s turned up sketches for equally imaginative wall decoration for other rooms, but these were never executed.

With the instant success of *Tom Sawyer* and a long-running play based on one of his novels, by 1878 Sam's finances had improved and he and Livy set off for Europe to gather furnishings for the house and material for his book *A Tramp Abroad*. When they returned in 1879 Livy hired a decorator to complete many of the second-floor rooms while the furnishings were still packed up. The delightful wall decoration of the upstairs nursery was done at this time. It features a Walter Crane–designed English wallpaper based on "Ye Frog He Would A-Wooing Go" and fireplace tiles showing scenes from Cock Robin's funeral. Another child's room, the school room, the master bedroom, and the second guest room were also finished that year.

It would be another two years before final decoration of the ground-floor rooms was undertaken. Several structural changes were made first—principally an addition to the kitchen wing and the expansion of the entry area. The walls of a small reception room next to the entry area were removed to create a larger, lighter entry hall, one similar to the "living halls" that were then becoming fashionable in large Victorian houses (see Glenmont, page 155).

As this construction work was nearing completion, the Clemenses made the fortunate decision of hiring the brilliant Louis Comfort Tiffany (1848–1933) to oversee the finishes of the enlarged entry hall and other downstairs rooms. Son of the founder of the famous New York jewelry firm, in 1895 Tiffany was to found the renowned Tiffany Glass Company (later Tiffany Studios), which utilized new techniques that he had perfected for making art glass. But in 1881 he was still primarily an interior designer with a special interest in the powerful effect of color. Working under him on the Twain house were several noted artists and craftsmen: Lockwood deForest, Candace Thurber Wheeler, and Samuel Colman. A $5,000 contract Tiffany submitted to Sam in 1881 outlined the scope of work to be undertaken:

ABOVE *This translucent marble panel in the billiard room—a male domain in the nineteenth century—is etched with symbols of drinking and smoking.*

OPPOSITE *The porte cochere is a fine example of the exposed roof structure and triangular bracing typical of the Stick style.*

RIGHT *This statue of David and Goliath by Marius-Jean-Antonin Merci won first prize in an 1870 competition in Rome. It stands in the drawing room beside a clever bipart door that can fold neatly against the wall or be braced into one solid door. The walnut door's silver stenciling and the silver-stenciled, salmon-colored walls are restorations of Louis Comfort Tiffany's original decoration.*

BELOW *Tiffany's original decor of silver stenciling on wood paneling below and red paint with black-stenciled borders above have been restored in the inviting front hall.*

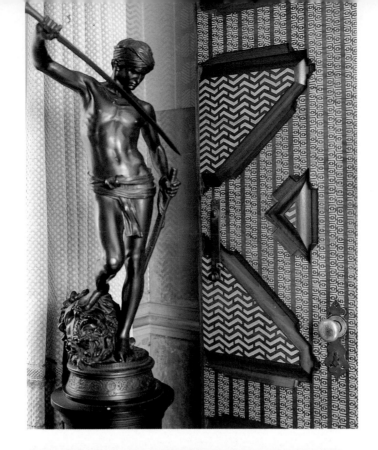

TIFFANY CONTRACT

First Floor Hall
　Walls painted and stenciled
　Ceilings painted & stenciled
　　in metals
　Wood work decorated, or not,
　　at our option
　Marble floor stained if
　　practicable

Halls above First Floor
　Walls and ceiling plainly
　　painted

Parlor
　Doors stenciled
　Wood work painted
　Walls and ceiling papered or
　　stenciled at our option

Dining Room
　Walls papered
　Ceiling painted or papered at
　　our option

Library
　Walls covered with metal leaf
　　& stenciled
　Ceiling covered with metal leaf
　　and paint
　Colored glass transom to be
　　furnished for upper part of
　　centre window in bay

Bed Room
　Wall and ceiling papered

The work will commence forth-
with and be completed as soon
as possible.

Under the terms of this vague contract, which left much to Tiffany's discretion, work was indeed begun. The result is one of the most spectacular surviving interiors from the Aesthetic period of American design. The ingenious use of color for which Tiffany is renowned is evident in the base colors chosen for the walls—handsome rich red for the entry hall, a subtle salmon pink in the drawing room, and clear turquoise for the library. Stenciled over these colors, and over the dark woodwork in the entry hall, were geometric patterns incorporating motifs that resembled American Indian and African symbols as well as decorative elements from India, where Lockwood deForest maintained a workshop. Silver, black, and gold were the colors used for these stenciled designs.

As was typical of Victorian-era decor, the Twain dining room was given a rather masculine treatment (see also Morse-Libby House, page 119). The walls were covered in

ABOVE LEFT *The Eastlake-style mahogany bed and dresser in the downstairs guest bedroom were purchased at the Household Art Company, a custom furniture store on Tremont Street in Boston. The furniture is so at home in the house that it was long thought to have been designed by the architect, Edward Tuckerman Potter.*

ABOVE RIGHT *A re-creation of Clemens's oldest daughter Susy's bedroom. The wallpaper is a roller stencil pattern, the only roller stencil work in the house.*

LEFT *A fragment of Walter Crane's 1877 "Nursery Rhymes Design" wallpaper was found behind the nursery mantel; it was carefully reproduced and rehung.*

Japanese leather embossed with a lily pattern and glazed in oxblood red, gold, and bronze. The wood dado was stenciled and a new Tiffany-designed mantel with a fireplace surround of square glass tiles set in brass was added. Subtle gilt stenciling helped to lighten the dark woodwork in the room and to integrate it with the other public rooms. The architectural changes and much of the interior decoration were completed by 1882.

The next ten years spent in this wonderful dwelling were the happiest of Sam and Livy's life. Their three daughters grew up here. Livy visited with her stimulating neighbors and entertained a constant stream of the era's most important people. Sam retired to his study/billiard room almost daily and turned out many of his most important works: *Tom Sawyer* (1876); *The Prince and the Pauper* (1881); *The Adventures of Huckleberry Finn* (1885);

ABOVE *The library walls are painted blue and stenciled with bronze paint, as specified in the Tiffany contract.*

RIGHT *The Clemenses purchased the library mantel in Scotland in 1873 and carefully removed it when they sold the house in 1903. In 1958, during the house's restoration, it was discovered disassembled in a barn and reinstalled in the house.*

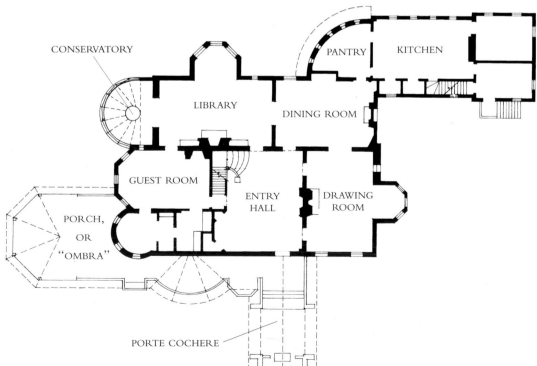

The unusual placement of a window above the fireplace in the dining room was made possible by diverting the chimney flue to the right.

CONSERVATORY

KITCHEN

PANTRY

LIBRARY

DINING ROOM

GUEST ROOM

ENTRY HALL

DRAWING ROOM

PORCH, OR "OMBRA"

PORTE COCHERE

Architect Edward Tuckerman Potter, c. 1875.

and *A Connecticut Yankee in King Arthur's Court* (1889). Life seemed idyllic, yet it was during this period that the seeds of the tragedies that would ultimately engulf and impoverish the family were being sown.

In 1880 Sam invested in the development of the new Paige typesetting machine and also set up the Charles L. Webster Company to publish his own and others' books. By 1887 he was struggling to keep the faltering publishing company afloat. And by 1891 he had invested almost $200,000—an enormous sum in those days—in the typesetting enterprise, whose inventors made constant demands for more cash to perfect their design. That same year Sam finally realized he could no longer keep the expensive house operating; it was closed and the family moved for a time to Europe, where the cost of living was lower.

For Livy, whose own separate funds had been used to build the house, and who had poured so much energy into its creation, parting with it was particularly hard. As described by A. B. Paine in *Mark Twain: A Biography:* "The day came for departure and the carriage was at the door. Mrs. Clemens did not come immediately. She was looking into the rooms, bidding a kind of silent good-by to the home she had made and all its memories. Following the others she entered the carriage, and Patrick McAleer drove them together for the last time. They were going on a long journey. They did not guess how long, or that the place would never be home to them again."

Despite the lower cost of living in Europe, the Clemenses' financial situation did not improve. In 1894 they were hit by a double blow. In April the Charles L. Webster Company closed its doors, leaving debts of $200,000. Then in October it was decided that the typesetting machine would never succeed, thus destroying Sam's hopes of recouping his large investment. The couple faced financial ruin. They decided to rent their house to their friends John Calvin Day and Alice Hooker Day. Sam visited the house when the Days were moving in during the spring of 1895. In a letter to Livy he expressed his love for the house and his anguish at their self-imposed exile:

> Livy darling, when I arrived in town I did not want to go near the house, & I didn't want to go anywhere or see anybody. I said to myself, "If I may be spared it I will never live in Hartford again."
>
> But as soon as I entered this front door I was siezed [*sic*] with a furious desire to have us all in this house again & right away, & never go outside the grounds any more forever—certainly never again to Europe.
>
> How ugly, tasteless, repulsive, are all the domestic interiors I have ever seen in Europe compared with the perfect taste of this ground floor, with its delicious dream of harmonious color, & its all-pervading spirit of peace & serenity & deep contentment. You did it all, & it speaks of you & praises you eloquently & unceasingly. It is the loveliest home that ever was.

Despite their yearnings for the Nook Farm house, Sam and Livy embarked on a round-the-world lecture tour that greatly helped reduce their debts; by 1899 all their creditors had been paid in full. In the intervening years, however, another tragedy struck. Their twenty-four-year-old daughter Olivia Susan Clemens (1872–1896) contracted spinal meningitis while visiting friends in Hartford. She died in her familiar childhood home, and shortly thereafter Sam wrote a letter that referred to the house in the past tense:

> Ah, well, Susy died at *home*. She had that privilege. Her dying eyes rested upon no thing that was strange to them, but only upon things which they had known & loved always & which had made her young years glad. . . . If she had died in another house—well, I think I could not have borne that. To us our house was not unsentient matter—it has a heart & a soul & eyes to see us . . . & approvals & solicitudes & deep sympathies; it was of us, & we were in its confidence.

The Clemens family on their porch, c. 1885.

In 1900 Sam and Livy returned from Europe to live in New York. Their debts were paid, their lives were starting over. Sam visited Hartford for a friend's funeral and wrote, "I realized that if we even enter the house again to live our hearts will break." An era had ended, and the house was put up for sale. Three years later the by now unfashionable dwelling was bought for only $28,000, a fraction of its original cost. Livy, who was ill at the time and had not visited the house for twelve years, planned the disposition of its contents from memory; much was finally sold at auction. The new owners lived in the house until 1917; over the next ten years it was used as a school, then sold to real estate speculators, and ultimately converted into apartments. During this period various unsuccessful attempts were made to raise enough money to acquire the historic property. Finally, in 1929 the house was purchased by the Mark Twain Memorial and Library Commission, whose trustees borrowed some of the purchase money. By 1930 the apartments had been removed from the first floor and the building was being used as a branch of the Hartford Public Library. During the Depression and World War II the mortgage was paid off and the building was maintained, although little could be done to restore it. In 1955, however, the trustees adopted a series of long-term goals that included restoring "the house as it was in Mark Twain's day," and a well-researched and careful restoration was soon begun. It took nineteen years to complete this enormous task. Many of these years were spent conducting research and oral interviews and raising funds for the project. Most of the actual restoration work was done between 1969 and 1974.

Today efforts continue to obtain original Clemens furnishings, to insure that the home is well maintained, and to keep up with the restoration process. This is a challenge that the commission, which preserved the grand house through many lean years and then meticulously restored it, is sure to meet. It is most fitting that this curious, flamboyant house, so treasured by Sam and Livy, now stands as a permanent memorial to the happy years when Mark Twain wrote the timeless stories that have captured the hearts of his countrymen for generations.

Stick Style
(1860–1885)

The Stick style, whose appropriate name was suggested in the 1950s by architectural historian Vincent Scully, is a relatively rare American architectural fashion. Loosely based on medieval precedents and popular only during the period from about 1860 to 1880, it bridges the gap between two more widespread fashions based on medieval themes—the Gothic Revival style that preceded it (see Lyndhurst, pages 98–111) and the Queen Anne style that followed (see Glenmont, pages 152–65).

Much of the credit for popularizing the Stick style in this country goes to architect Richard Morris Hunt, the French-trained American who somewhat later also introduced the dramatic Châteauesque style (see Château-sur-Mer, pages 126–37, and Biltmore, pages 246–57). While studying at the prestigious Ecole des Beaux Arts in the 1850s, Hunt became familiar with rustic Picturesque-style houses built of wood that were then all the rage as second homes in the fashionable seaside and mountain resorts of

MARK TWAIN HOUSE

France and Germany. Among Hunt's earliest commissions after returning to the United States were summer houses for wealthy friends in Newport, Rhode Island, where his family spent the summers. Drawing on his knowledge of current European fashion, Hunt produced a half-dozen delightfully original Picturesque-style designs for Newport clients between 1861 and 1872. Widely admired and illustrated in architectural magazines of the day, they became the harbingers of a new housing fashion, examples of which can be found scattered throughout the country.

New Yorker Edward T. Potter was among the many American architects who were fascinated by Hunt's adaptations of European Picturesque houses. Best known for his High Victorian Gothic churches, in the Mark Twain house Potter created what is arguably our nation's most spectacular remaining example of Stick-style design.

IDENTIFYING FEATURES

1 DECORATIVE TRUSSES IN GABLES

2 DIAGONAL OR CURVING PORCH-SUPPORT BRACES

3 GABLED ROOF, USUALLY STEEPLY PITCHED WITH CROSS GABLES

4 OVERHANGING EAVES, USUALLY WITH EXPOSED RAFTER ENDS

5 HORIZONTAL AND VERTICAL BANDS (LESS COMMONLY DIAGONAL) RAISED FROM WALL SURFACES FOR EMPHASIS

Note: All identifying features rarely present in any single house

WEST COAST VERSION

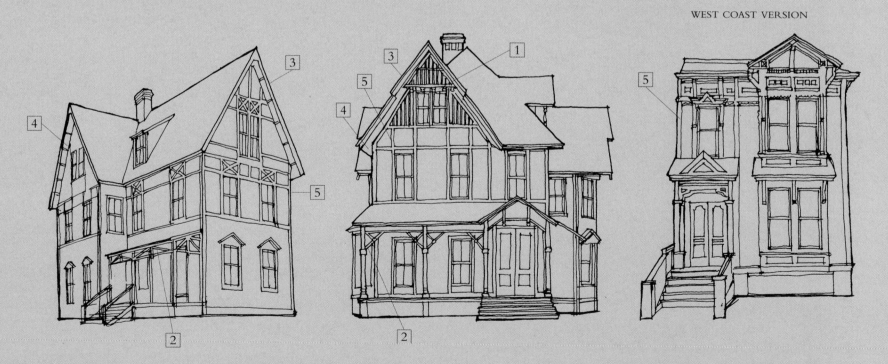

12
Glenmont

WEST ORANGE, NEW JERSEY

Queen Anne Style

*G*lenmont was the home of Thomas Alva Edison (1847–1931), who, as every schoolchild knows, revolutionized American life by inventing the first practical electric lighting, the phonograph, and motion pictures.

Early in his career Edison had lived, worked, and earned a modest fortune in the town of Menlo Park, New Jersey. His first wife died there in 1884, leaving him with three young children. Soon afterward the bereft widower was introduced by friends to the attractive young Mina Miller (1865–1947), daughter of another prosperous inventor, Lewis Miller of Akron, Ohio. The two fell in love and were married in 1886.

At that time Edison had already decided to expand his research laboratories and had found a much larger site in nearby West Orange. Before their marriage he offered Mina a choice of homes—either a large country house in West Orange or a fine town house across the Hudson River in New York City. She wisely chose the country, perhaps because, as the daughter of a successful inventor, she had some insight into the all-consuming dedication of such creators and sensed that she should live close to her husband's laboratories if she hoped to see much of him.

Edison's proposed country house was a large, stylish frame dwelling called Glenmont that was then up for sale. It was located on fourteen wooded acres in Llewellyn Park, an exclusive section of West Orange that was only a few blocks from Edison's new laboratories. The house had been completed in 1880 for Henry C. Pedder, an executive of the New York department store Arnold Constable & Company. Financial reverses were forcing Pedder to sell the almost-new house and all of its lavish furnishings, fixtures, and decorative objects. The idea of acquiring a fully furnished and decorated household greatly appealed to the twenty-year-old Mina. Soon she was not only the stepmother of three young children but also the mistress of a grand Queen Anne mansion.

With its wooded hills and winding roadways Llewellyn Park was one of the earliest planned suburbs in the country and the first to feature the romantic landscape planning advocated by the influential Andrew Jackson Downing (see Lyndhurst, page 100).

The introduction of rapid rail transportation in the late nineteenth century made such suburbs possible. People now had an alternative to living in the city near their place of work. And the lure of a home in a peaceful country setting instead of in a dirty, congested city proved irresistible. "Streetcar suburbs" began sprouting up all over the country.

Llewellyn Park was the creation of Llewellyn S. Haskell (1815–1872), a prosperous New York pharmaceutical importer. An ardent admirer of natural landscapes, Haskell had been an early supporter of the move to create Central Park. The origin of his idea to develop Llewellyn Park is not entirely clear. He was a friend of both landscape designer Downing and his equally distinguished associate, architect Alexander Jackson Davis, designer of Lyndhurst. Indeed, Davis was later to build his own home, Wildmont, in Llewellyn Park. These two friends may have influenced Haskell's visionary plan. Whatever the inspiration was, between 1853 and 1857 he purchased 350 acres for his new development and set aside 50 of them as shared parkland to be "used and enjoyed, as a place of resort and recreation." All home owners were assessed for the costs of the common land and it was controlled by an elected board. Such community-owned open spaces eventually became a common planning practice, but it was an extremely farsighted idea in the 1850s.

Glenmont's architect was New Yorker Henry Hudson Holly (1843–1892), author of two influential house pattern books, the second of which helped to make the Queen Anne style the most popular housing fashion in late-nineteenth-century America. Published in 1878, this book bears the cumbersome Victorian title *Modern Dwellings in Town and Country: Adapted to American Wants and Climate with a Treatise on Furniture and Decoration.* The first chapter discusses the virtues of the Queen Anne style, treating such details as sites, building materials, roofing, chimneys, plumbing, heating, and lighting. The book includes renderings and floor plans for twenty-three Queen Anne designs and ends with many chapters on appropriate furniture and interior decoration. Two years after the publication of *Modern Dwellings* Holly began building Glenmont for Henry Pedder. Not surprisingly, the house, including furnishings and interior detailing, closely reflects the ideas expressed in the book.

One of the characteristic features of the Queen Anne style is an emphasis on multiple decorative patterns for wall surfaces, both exterior and interior. The entry hall of Glenmont is an excellent example. Its wall surface is divided into three sections: a dark wood dado at the bottom, a field covered with lighter-colored, patterned wall covering above, and a decorative frieze at the top. Holly's rationale for this tripartite division was based on his conviction that people and furniture looked best when seen against a dark background, that pictures looked best when hung against a lighter background, and that the cornice and ceiling, being set apart, might have any number of brilliant hues as accents. The three-part wall thus showed everything to best advantage. Holly's inspiration for this scheme came from nature itself:

This gradation of color from deep to gay is borrowed from the Great Architect; for, in nature, how often do we see the same system carried out;

as, for instance, in a mountain capped by brilliant clouds at sunset! Or, take the tree, for example: the roots and trunk are dark and substantial, giving evidence of strength and durability; the branches are covered with leafy verdure, not pronounced in color; the blossoms, with their ever-varying and brilliant hues, are confined to the summit; while the sky (corresponding to the ceiling of a room) is blue—the color of all others which gives an appearance of distance.

When the Edisons purchased Glenmont from Pedder it was completely furnished and decorated in the precise manner described by Holly in *Modern Dwellings*. Several of its rooms remain to this day exactly as Holly designed them, while others were redecorated by Mina Edison.

One of the rooms that has remained virtually unchanged is the entry hall. It is an example of what was known in late-nineteenth-century parlance as a "living stair hall." Whereas earlier houses usually had narrow entry halls with enough room for only a table or two around the stairway, the Victorians decided that this was a cold and unfriendly introduction to a house. The solution was to substitute a larger, roomlike living hall with a cozy fireplace and comfortable places to sit—a room where guests could be welcomed with warmth and hospitality.

The front stairway landing features an original stained-glass window and a painting by New Jersey artist A. A. Anderson, which, ironically, was purchased at an 1889 exposition in Paris.

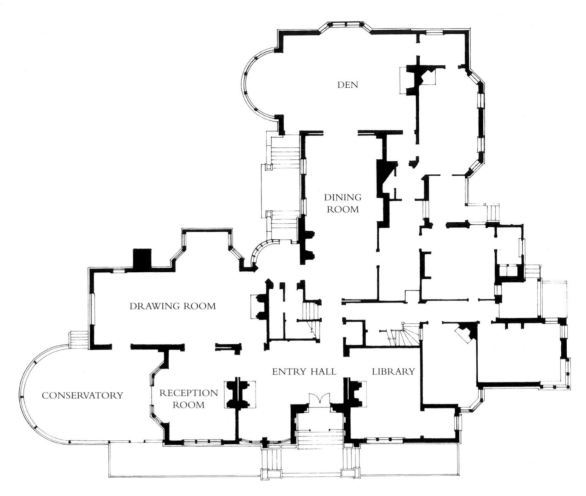

DEN

DINING ROOM

DRAWING ROOM

ENTRY HALL   LIBRARY

CONSERVATORY   RECEPTION ROOM

The wall covering chosen for the field of Glenmont's living hall was Lincrusta-Walton, a Victorian innovation that was particularly recommended for high-traffic areas. Unlike simple wallpaper, it was a composite material made of wood pulp and linseed oil into which various patterns could be embossed before the linseed oil dried and gave it a hard finish. Conceived in 1877 by Englishman Frederick Walton, the inventor of linoleum, it was exceptionally sturdy when glued into place. It was then painted or glazed to blend with the room's decor. In this case a green glue sizing was applied first, then a coat of silver-colored paint, and finally a coat of orange shellac, resulting in its "bronze" appearance.

The principal stairway, which rises to a landing and then continues upward in the reverse direction, was a favorite design of Holly's; his book shows several similar examples. Placing this doubled-back stairway along one side of a room adds decorative interest by emphasizing the stairs' paneled sides, wood balusters, and rail detailing. At Glenmont a stained-glass window on the landing provides an additional decorative element.

A second room that has changed little since 1882 is the library. In the Victorian era, before public libraries were common and before public high school education was widely available, a home library was considered of great importance. It clearly announced a family's interest in intellectual pursuits. Most pattern books of the day discussed the importance of a library, but Holly's was particularly explicit on the subject, citing the view of an unidentified expert:

> Give me a house furnished with books rather than furniture; both, if you can: but books at any rate. To spend several days in a friend's house and hunger for something to read, while you are treading on costly carpets, and sitting upon luxurious chairs, and sleeping upon down, is as if one were bribing your body for the sake of cheating your mind. . . . Books are the windows through which the soul looks out. A house without books is like a room without windows.

Small wonder, then, that Holly provided Glenmont with a fine library, which is the first room a visitor sees after entering the front door. Ironically, none of the books found today behind the room's glass-doored shelves were added by Edison—they were all part of the initial purchase from Pedder, and many still have uncut pages. Edison preferred to keep his own books on open shelves in the family room upstairs, well out of public view.

The original Glenmont interiors, although designed to Holly's general specifications, were actually planned and installed by the New York firm of Pottier and Stymus, which modern scholars have called "one of the most important cabinetmaking and decorating establishments of the 1870s and 1880s." Their library ceiling, with its multicolored, fifteen-part border, is particularly handsome. According to Holly: "Ceilings are especially susceptible to ornamentation, for the reason that their entire surface may be seen at once. If we wish to limit the decoration of our rooms, let us expend our efforts here, as the walls

The den, added in the late 1880s, features white mahogany wainscoting and a beautifully detailed cove ceiling. Victorian patterned wall coverings were removed in the early twentieth century.

The library (RIGHT) retains Pottier and Stymus's original finishes, furniture, fixtures, and even books. The plaster was allowed a lengthy drying period before the elaborate painted finishes were applied to the ceiling (ABOVE).

and floors can be relieved by pictures and furniture . . . borders on the ceiling are like the dado on the wall, and have the effect of breaking up its broad surface." The library ceiling features the muted tones that were replacing the brighter colors of mid-Victorian interiors—soft yellows, ochers, dulled reds, and medium shades of olive green.

The modifications Mina made over the years in other rooms at Glenmont make a fascinating statement about changing fashions in interior design. The drawing room and reception room were both redecorated about 1910, presumably after Mina had read Elsie de Wolfe's popular book *In Good Taste* (there are three copies of it in the Edisons' library). Miss de Wolfe was opposed to the somber paneling and dark upholstery fabrics preferred by the Victorians and advocated light-colored walls, brocades, and chintzes instead. Mina took de Wolfe's advice to heart and changed the walls and upholstery in both of these rooms, while retaining most of the original furnishings and decorative objects.

In the reception room the walls' original deep colors were replaced with a pinkish-beige brocade. The overmantel was removed and replaced with a gold Italian mirror. Ceiling decorations were also removed and replaced with a simpler ivory finish and a new light fixture. The original suite of Victorian furniture was retained but reupholstered in a light-colored fabric. The drawing room was similarly altered. Upholstery and wall coverings were lightened up, but the earlier furnishings and decorative objects were left intact. The

LEFT AND RIGHT *When the reception room was remodeled in 1909–10, its original brightly colored ceiling was covered in ivory paint. The Victorian overmantel was replaced with a low mirror; more restrained, solid-color draperies were added; and the walls and furnishings were covered with a light-colored fabric.*

Like the adjacent reception room, the drawing room was remodeled in 1909–10. Its former colorful ceiling was also painted a subtle "old ivory" highlighted with gold. Elaborate Victorian-era drapes and upholstery were replaced with lighter-colored brocade.

contrast between these two rooms and the entry hall and library with their dark, rich colors is striking.

The wood detailing Holly designed for the house differs from room to room. In the entry hall he used oak, and mahogany for the mantel; in the drawing room, rosewood; in the reception room, curly and bird's-eye maple; in the dining room, mahogany; and in the library, birch for the wainscoting and mahogany for the bookshelves and mantel. The styling of the mantelpieces is equally eclectic. The entry hall mantel is a Renaissance Revival design; the drawing room mantel has an Art Nouveau flair with pussy willow and lily pad ornamentation; and the dining room mantel is Colonial Revival with an Adamesque look.

As the Edison family expanded (Mina had three children between 1890 and 1898), so did the house and grounds. An early addition was a large den that opens off the dining room. A striking room with a high, coved ceiling, it probably first served as an informal family room. But it must not have fully satisfied the need for a family center because in 1905 a sitting room over the porte cochere was expanded to function as an upstairs living room and informal library where both Edison and Mina had their desks. Family books line the walls and these, unlike the books in the formal downstairs library, have seen much use. It is in this room that the family gathered in the evenings.

The downstairs gained additional living space sometime before 1900 when the side porch was enclosed, becoming a screened porch in summer and a glass-walled conservatory in winter. Later the room was permanently glassed in. The enclosure of this porch and the addition of a room over the front porte cochere changed the house's exterior appearance quite dramatically.

Many outbuildings were added to Glenmont's fourteen-acre grounds during the Edison years; while Mina oversaw the house Edison liked to tinker outside. A 1908 garage bears numerous Edison touches. It held six cars at a time when few families had even one, and it featured a turntable to help with parking. It also had its own gas pump and even a battery charger, which was added in 1912. Other Edison additions to the grounds included greenhouses, barns, a pump house, and a swimming pool.

All may be quiet at Glenmont today, but that was not the case when the large Edison family lived there. In a 1970 oral interview, Theodore Edison, the youngest son and an inventor in his own right, painted a lively picture:

> [Here we are up at the top of the stairs.] I used to be able to get up to the top and fall right over backwards and come down, somersault. I'd stagger, you know, kind of get up here, finally fall right over backwards. When I was coming down stairs, I used to jump that whole flight, down to there, without hitting the stairs.
>
> Now, we'll go up into the southwest room on the third floor, and this used to be my brother's room, Charles Edison's room. I played around in here myself too. And over in that . . . little dormer or whatever it is by the fireplace . . . I had knocked a hole in through the wall and made a little room in an L all clear around, over in back of the book cases. It goes way back in there. And this was a secret room. Even if you came here, you wouldn't see it, unless you went in far enough and looked back to see the hole in there, you see. And the hole was only big enough so I could get in. I had it wired with electric light and everything in there.
>
> Then another thing we did, it turned out that if you set the old electrics [autos] . . . backing up, there was a great tendency for the front

RIGHT *The upstairs family room was extended out over the porte cochere by the Edisons. Here the family spent their evenings and kept their working library.*

OPPOSITE TOP LEFT *Original plan of Llewellyn Park.*

OPPOSITE TOP RIGHT *Entrance to Llewellyn Park.*

OPPOSITE BOTTOM *Much of the original wraparound front porch was converted into a glass-enclosed conservatory.*

wheels to lock over into [a] hard turn. . . . You could put them out in the field and just let them run, and they would go round and round in a circle. . . . We used to play circus on [them].

These vignettes, only three of dozens, give a bit of the flavor of life at Glenmont with several imaginative kids, an incredibly inventive father, an understanding mother, and fourteen acres for outdoor fun.

Time has not been kind to most of the large Queen Anne houses throughout the United States. To facilitate commuting on electric trolleys, many of the grandest were built on the principal entry routes into larger cities. Ironically, in the early twentieth century, when these same routes became the cities' main automobile roads, the development of commercial strips hastened the destruction of the grand mansions that once lined them. Euclid Avenue in Cleveland, Woodward Avenue in Detroit, and Ross Avenue in Dallas are but three examples of this widespread phenomenon. In addition, the complex exteriors of large Queen Anne houses are extremely difficult and expensive to maintain, particularly those built entirely of wood. As a result, many fine examples deteriorated quickly. For these reasons the Edison house is a rare and unusually well-preserved survivor. It is also of unique value as one of the few remaining works by Henry Hudson Holly, the man who defined and popularized the Queen Anne style in America. Finally, Glenmont's location in one of the country's earliest planned suburbs and its long history as the home of the nation's preeminent inventor make it one of our truly priceless landmarks.

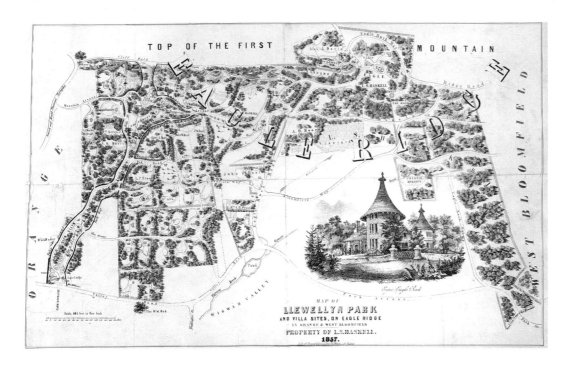

Queen Anne Style

(1880–1910)

The only thing that the American Queen Anne style has in common with its British counterpart is its name. The rambling and asymmetrical houses that we call Queen Anne in this country bear virtually no resemblance to the formal and balanced Renaissance designs that dominated British architecture during Queen Anne's reign (1702–14). The confusion stemmed from the appearance of two new architectural fashions in late-nineteenth-century Britain, both advocated by Richard Norman Shaw (1831–1912), one of the most influential British architects at the time.

IDENTIFYING FEATURES

1 STEEPLY PITCHED ROOF OF IRREGULAR SHAPE, USUALLY WITH DOMINANT FRONT-FACING GABLE

2 TEXTURED SHINGLES (AND/OR OTHER DEVICES) TO AVOID SMOOTH-WALLED APPEARANCE

3 PARTIAL OR FULL-WIDTH ASYMMETRICAL PORCH, USUALLY ONE STORY HIGH AND EXTENDED ALONG ONE OR BOTH SIDE WALLS

4 ASYMMETRICAL FAÇADE

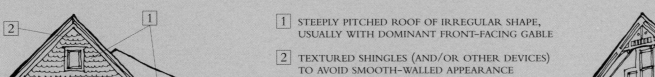

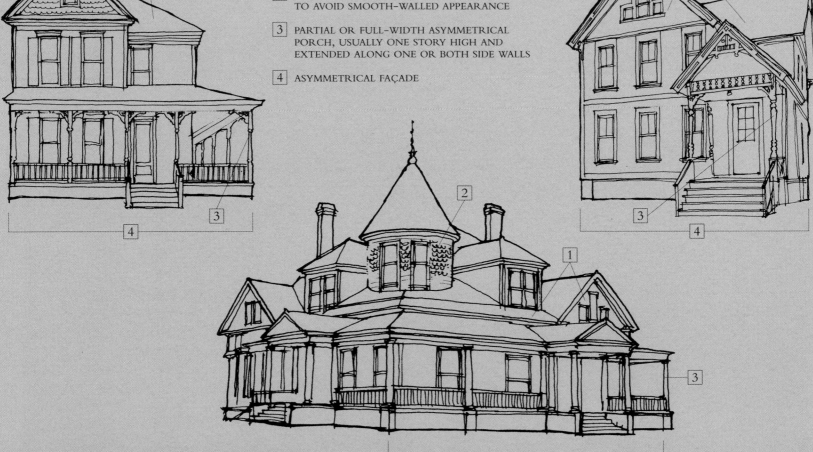

Shaw felt that the Gothic Revival designs that had dominated British building for several decades had become overly elaborate and artificially complex. To remedy this he advocated styles based on simpler historical models. One of these, the Old English style, harked back to medieval folk buildings with irregular façades and half-timbered walls—the smaller structures that surrounded the great Gothic churches of the Middle Ages. The other was based on the simple but symmetrical Renaissance designs that were popular somewhat later, during the reign of Queen Anne. It was the Old English style that found its way across the Atlantic and became the inspiration for much American architecture of the late nineteenth century. In the transition the Americans somehow dubbed these buildings Queen Anne. The name thus has a unique meaning when applied to Victorian buildings on this side of the Atlantic.

Much of the credit for popularizing this American revival of medieval English folk building goes to Henry Hudson Holly, the designer of Glenmont, whose influential 1878 pattern book *Modern Dwellings* provided models for what was to become the dominant style of American houses built during the last two decades of the century.

GLENMONT (BEFORE MODIFICATION)

13

Naumkeag

STOCKBRIDGE, MASSACHUSETTS

Shingle Style

This country house in the Berkshire Hills is one of the few grand survivors of the late Victorian Shingle style, an innovative and uncommon American architectural fashion that anticipated the first truly modern house designs of the early twentieth century. Completed in 1886 for the distinguished New York attorney Joseph H. Choate (1832–1917), Naumkeag was designed by the flamboyant Stanford White (1853–1906), a principal partner in the New York firm of McKim, Mead and White. Ironically, this architectural firm, which later became the world's largest, gained its reputation not as precursors of modernism but as the leading exponents of a return to the design ideals of ancient Rome (see Vanderbilt House, pages 246–57).

White, like the colorful Henry Hobson Richardson, under whom he apprenticed (see Glessner House, pages 178–89), was a larger-than-life figure. His multifaceted life is best known for its tragic end, an event that inspired the 1955 movie *The Girl in the Red Velvet Swing,* starring Ray Milland as the architect and Joan Collins as his former mistress Evelyn Nesbit. To summarize that over-sensationalized event, White was shot and killed by Nesbit's mentally unstable husband even though her affair with White had ended several years earlier and well before her marriage. The publicity, much of it false, that surrounded this bizarre event has long obscured appreciation of White's extraordinary contributions to American design. As Paul Baker succinctly notes in his recent biography of White, "By the mid-1890s, White was one of the best-known figures in New York, famous as architect, decorator, and designer of art objects—and well-known as art entrepreneur and private collector." In addition, it was largely White's innovative Shingle-style designs that led to his firm's early success and thus paved the way for its spectacular growth and influence.

White's half-dozen or so Shingle-style designs date from the period between 1879, when he went into partnership with McKim and Mead, and 1887, when the firm was chosen to design the new Boston Public Library. This building was so favorably received that the firm attracted an ever-increasing flood of commissions for large public buildings. Regarding White's earlier work, the Baker biography notes: "Culminating this romantic,

PAGE 166 *The Art Deco Blue Stairs, surrounded by a grove of white birches, was designed by Fletcher Steele for Mabel Choate in 1938.*

RIGHT *Naumkeag's brick-walled road façade is of Norman French inspiration, a surprising contrast to the Shingle style of the rest of the house.*

OPPOSITE TOP *This dormer window, which looks as if it is growing out of the shingle-covered roof, is typical of the Shingle style.*

OPPOSITE CENTER *A fanciful combination of fish-scale shingles, dentils, and a shell motif ornaments this gable peak.*

OPPOSITE BOTTOM *A decorative down spout records the year Naumkeag was built.*

country house mode for White was the Shingle style summer dwelling he created for Joseph H. Choate . . . near Stockbridge, Massachusetts, one of his most elegant early houses. . . . Not only did White design the house and superintend its construction but, as with so many of his houses, he also advised on its interior decoration and furnishings."

Conservative attorney Joseph Choate might seem an unlikely client for the ultra-fashionable White. A country doctor's son from Salem, Massachusetts, Choate studied law, moved to New York, and soon became one of that city's most respected and successful trial attorneys. By the 1870s he was among the most sought-after legal advocates in the country, and he and his large family began to spend occasional vacations in the quiet but fashionable resort town of Stockbridge, in western Massachusetts.

In 1884 Choate decided to build his own summer "cottage" just north of Stockbridge. He had met and become friends with White's older partner, Charles F. McKim (1847–1909), whose advice he sought about building his Stockbridge retreat. McKim recommended his younger partner, and White was soon busy planning what has been called "the last of the great Shingle-style cottages."

In memory of his boyhood a hundred miles to the east on the Massachusetts shore, Choate named his new home Naumkeag, the original Indian name for Salem. Naumkeag's exterior, one can only believe, reflects a compromise between the conservative attorney's vision of a proper country house and that of his modernist architect. The front façade, which was undoubtedly White's concession to Choate and which can be seen only from the adjacent public road, resembles a medieval French farmhouse, complete with simulated grain-storage towers, tall chimneys, rustic stone and brick walls, and a steep roofline broken by a group of small dormers along its lower edge. Behind the stone towers that punctuate each end of the front façade is where White's graceful shingle-dominated design begins. It culminates at the rear in a dramatic multichimneyed and many-gabled façade with porches overlooking the scenic valley below.

Inside the house White permitted no such compromises. One enters into a large living hall dominated by a massive fireplace, a trademark of innovative late Victorian designers (see Glenmont, page 155). The living hall extends through the entire house, opening onto a sweeping veranda at the other end. Along the way, wide doorways connect the living hall with the parlor, library, dining room, and stair hall. When all of the double doors to these rooms are fully opened, the effect is a marvelous sense of interconnected spaces flowing into one another. Beyond the stair hall, smaller doorways lead to a service wing that also includes Choate's simply furnished study at the northeast (right front) corner of the house.

Choate left the interior decor to his talented wife, Caroline Sterling Choate (1837–1929), who had met her future husband while studying art in Manhattan. Under White's expert guidance, Caroline and her two teenage daughters spent months combing New York shops for furnishings and decorative objects. Most of the pieces they chose were antiques, many of museum quality, representing an eclectic yet subtle mixture of styles and periods. The wood-paneled living hall, for example, is home to a sixteenth-century Flemish tapestry, an early American blanket chest, and an English grandfather clock.

The adjacent parlor, equally eclectic but dominated by French furniture and superb Chinese porcelains, is the most formal room in the house. Behind the parlor is the library, which, furnished with comfortable sofas and chairs, was also used as an informal family living room. The dining room hints at the differing tastes of architect and client. Elegantly simple English furnishings, typical of early New England, sit beneath an ornate silvered ceiling of Gilded Age inspiration.

Upstairs there are nine bedrooms, seven on the second floor and two on the third, designed to accommodate family members and summer guests alike. These rooms are also furnished with fine but understated antiques, including early four-poster beds, highboys, cabinets, tables, chests, and numerous pieces of rare and valuable china.

Although some details of Naumkeag's interiors have been changed over the years, the house's decor today is remarkably faithful to Stanford White and Caroline Choate's original plan. After the house was completed, Choate achieved ever-greater distinction as advisor to several presidents, longtime ambassador to Great Britain, and friend of both Queen Victoria and her successor, King Edward VII. Still active in the practice of law until his death, in later life he nevertheless found more time for his beloved Naumkeag. Caroline also loved Stockbridge and continued to use the house until her death, when it passed to her spinster daughter, Mabel (1871–1958). Having helped her mother assemble the original furnishings, Mabel wanted to preserve the house just as she remembered it as a teenager. On her death she left the house, all furniture, grounds, and a large endowment

to create a public museum and monument to her parents. In so doing she preserved a pricelessly intact example not only of Shingle-style design but also of the extraordinary talents of Stanford White.

As important a legacy as Naumkeag's house and furnishings are, the estate is perhaps even better known for another gift of Mabel Choate—the remarkable gardens that she created over the years. Mabel's parents bought the hillside acreage because they had come to admire the view of distant hills to the west as seen from the highest point of the fifty-acre tract. To design the grounds of the estate the Choates took McKim and White's

OPPOSITE TOP LEFT *Joseph Choate's study incorporates one of the round tower bays.*

OPPOSITE TOP RIGHT *The dining room combines understated antique furnishings with oriental porcelain. The usual chandelier is replaced by a silvered ceiling, which reflects the candlelight of the wall sconces.*

OPPOSITE CENTER LEFT *In the parlor a piano occupies the second tower bay. The room was primarily used for music recitals, after-dinner entertaining, and bridge parties.*

OPPOSITE CENTER RIGHT *With its comfortably upholstered furniture, the library served as a family room; it opens out onto the Afternoon Garden.*

OPPOSITE BOTTOM LEFT *Featuring a large sitting and study area, this is one of the nine inviting upstairs bedrooms.*

OPPOSITE BOTTOM RIGHT *Broad doorways connect the living hall to all the main first-floor rooms, creating a spacious feel.*

LEFT *View from the wood-paneled and -beamed stair hall through the living hall, with its large fireplace and massive entry door, and into the parlor beyond.*

The Shingle-style rear façade looks out over stately formal terraces and the valley beyond.

suggestion and employed the nation's most distinguished landscape architect, Boston's Frederick Law Olmsted, designer of Central Park, the Capitol Mall, and countless other important commissions (see Biltmore, pages 232–45). Olmsted was shocked when the Choates, with acres of hillside to choose from, insisted on siting their large house on the very spot where they had fallen in love with the view, which happened to be right next to a busy public road. Accustomed to having his advice heeded, Olmsted resigned from the project, and the difficult task of designing lawns and gardens around the hilltop homesite fell to a less-renowned Boston landscape architect, Nathan Barrett. Barrett worked out a series of formal terraces near the house but left most of the wooded slopes below intact to partially screen service areas and farm buildings. Olmsted, famed for his informal and natural-looking designs, would again have been appalled by the plants chosen to dominate the terraces—formal rows of yews meticulously trimmed into cones, cylinders, and globes. As a contemporary critic wrote: "Stately are these whimsical tributes to the efficacy of the shears of the gardener. . . . A garden of this type is at once an astonishment, a terror and a delight, as if designed by an artist in a spirit of wild adventure."

The Choates themselves must have been pleased with the results, however, because the garden and its demanding topiary were carefully maintained for many years. When her mother died, Mabel immediately set out to redesign the grounds. This project, which turned into a thirty-year mission, involved a close, almost symbiotic, relationship between the artistic, worldly, and intellectually adventurous Mabel and the like-minded, exceptionally talented landscape architect J. Fletcher Steele (1885–1971).

Mabel Choate and poodle at Naumkeag, c. 1900.

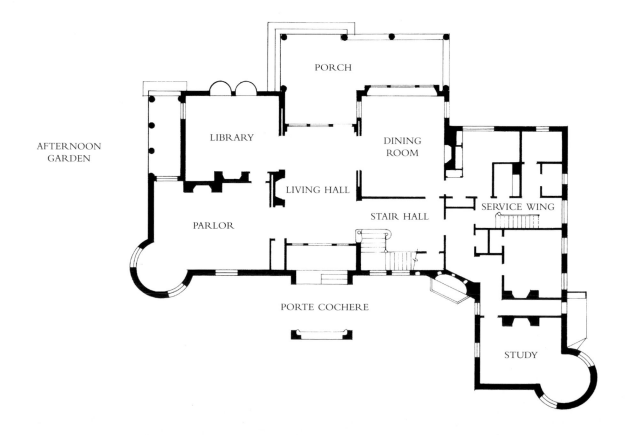

In the Afternoon Garden, the first of many designed by Fletcher Steele for Naumkeag, colorful gondola poles ring a small parterre.

Their association began in 1926 when Steele gave a lecture at the nearby Lenox Garden Club. Impressed with his credentials, Mabel asked him to design a sheltered outdoor seating area similar to those she had seen in California. The result was the delightfully eclectic Afternoon Garden with its Spanish-inspired central fountain, sunken French parterre, and surrounding "Venetian gondola posts." After that came Steele's redesigned top lawn and Perugino View (1931), Rond Pointe (1932), south lawn (1934), Chinese Garden (1937), and his acknowledged masterpiece, the Art Deco Blue Stairs (1938).

As she got older, Mabel found it increasingly difficult to negotiate the steep descent from her beloved Afternoon Garden to the large cutting garden far downslope. She asked Steele to design some sort of stairway to connect the two and his response was the Blue Stairs, an Italian-inspired series of stairs, fountain, and waterfalls cast in the then-fashionable idiom of French Art Deco. The grove of delicate white birches that unifies the design was a serendipitous afterthought by designer and client, who noticed how well a single native birch on the site accented the sinuous curves of the white stair railing.

Fletcher Steele's five hundred garden designs spanning more than half a century (1915–70) have been said to "contribute a link, arguably *the* link, between nineteenth-century Beaux Arts formalism and modern landscape design" (Robin Karson, *Fletcher Steele,* 1989). Naumkeag is among his finest works and one of only two that survive unaltered. Thus he and Mabel Choate have left a rare and delightful bonus for visitors to Stanford White's superb Shingle-style landmark.

ABOVE *The long and inviting Linden Walk.*

LEFT *Fletcher Steele began the walled Chinese Garden for Mabel Choate in 1937 and continued working on it until 1955.*

Shingle Style
(1880–1900)

Named for its characteristic shingle-covered exterior walls, this style is unusual for several reasons. Unlike most new building fashions, it was first intended only for the design of informal second homes, especially summer houses located in the coastal resort areas of New England, New York, and New Jersey. Its designers, freed from the usual demands of wealthy clients for more formal principal residences, began to experiment with simplified interpretations of traditional American Colonial designs (hence the emphasis on shingled walls), a trend that many historians believe set the stage for the more strikingly modern buildings of Frank Lloyd Wright and his followers two decades later (see Dana-Thomas House, pages 294–307). Architectural historian Vincent Scully, who first defined and named the style in the late 1940s, has noted that many Shingle-style houses also anticipated modernism in their interiors, where traditional room arrangements are replaced with more open and free-flowing multi-use spaces.

A number of prominent architects of the 1880s and 1890s designed Shingle-style "cottages" for their wealthy clients. Of these, Stanford White, the designer of Naumkeag, stands out as the acknowledged master of the style. These architect-designed Shingle-style landmarks were never plentiful but, publicized in the architectural magazines of the day, they inspired builder's and pattern-book imitations that are scattered around the country, mostly in late nineteenth-century suburban developments. Regrettably, only a handful of the grand originals have survived fire, flood, vandalism, or demolition, hazards to which seldom-occupied resort homes are particularly susceptible. Naumkeag is among the very finest of these survivors.

IDENTIFYING FEATURES

1. WALL CLADDING AND ROOFING OF CONTINUOUS WOOD SHINGLES

2. IRREGULAR, STEEPLY PITCHED ROOFLINE, USUALLY WITH CROSS GABLES

3. EXTENSIVE PORCHES

NAUMKEAG

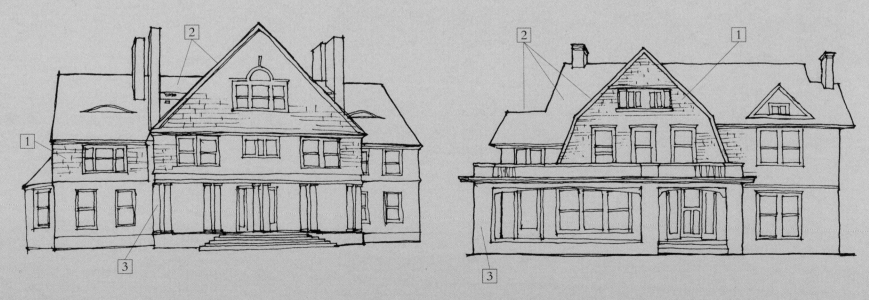

14
Glessner House

Richardsonian Romanesque Style

On his first visit to the future site of Chicago's Glessner House, Boston architect Henry Hobson Richardson (1838–1886) blurted out, "Have you the courage to build the house without windows on the street front?" His client later wrote that he "promptly . . . said 'Yes,' knowing that I could tear up the plan if I didn't like it." With this simple exchange the unusual plan of Glessner House was born, a design that inspired heated discussion in Chicago for many years after its completion and continues to intrigue architectural historians today.

Richardson, who rivals Frank Lloyd Wright (see Dana-Thomas House, pages 294–307) for the title of America's most creative and original architect, was born on a Louisiana plantation but spent most of each year in New Orleans. There his family lived in the newer, "American" section in one of a group of fine Greek Revival row houses known as the Thirteen Sisters. These houses were described by Eliza Ripley in her *Social Life in Old New Orleans* (1912) as being "occupied by the leading social element of the American colony . . . every one of them was tenanted by prominent citizens of New Orleans. . . . Even the well-known architect Henry Hobson Richardson lived on the Julia row [as it was then called] with his family. Ironic that the world-renowned architect whose work was a total rejection of classicism should have had as a boy, the most classic environment available in America."

Just eight blocks away, however, lay the Vieux Carré, heart of old French New Orleans, where an entirely different town-house plan—a tantalizingly familiar one to all who have visited the city—prevailed. The street façade of these houses abuts the sidewalk and usually features a carriage entrance, or porte cochere, that opens onto an enclosed interior courtyard. A stroll down Chartes or Rampart Street affords tempting glimpses of these romantic inner gardens through the openings in the porte cocheres. Their mysterious and beckoning quality must have held the same fascination for the young Richardson as it does for visitors today. Richardson later studied architecture in Paris, whose town houses are the precedents of the Vieux Carré versions. So it is perfectly understandable

The 1800 block of Prairie Avenue, Chicago, c. 1905. The Glessner House, out of view across the street, contrasted sharply with its ornate neighbors.

PAGE 178 *In a radical departure from traditional urban houses, the front entry to the Glessner House is flush with the ground.*

that on his first visit to Chicago's posh Prairie Avenue the architect conceived a large, porte cochere design. Here was a chance to do a truly grand town house in the French tradition he loved.

Prairie Avenue was then the "silk-stocking" district of Chicago, a several-block stretch that housed the city's wealthiest entrepreneurs, men with such familiar names as Marshall Field, George Pullman, and Philip Armour. Their houses were mostly traditional, freestanding urban mansions. Each sat squarely in the middle of its lot, surrounded by small front, side, and back yards. When the Glessners purchased their large corner tract, the adjacent lot had already been subdivided into several narrow row-house sites. One of these row houses was then under construction; its windowless side wall faced the Glessner site. This was a pattern Richardson instantly recognized and it must have triggered the thought of an L-shaped porte cochere design with an inner courtyard bounded on one side by the neighbor's solid brick wall.

It is also understandable that Chicagoans, who were used to grand houses with at least some yard around them, were shocked by the design. Richardson compounded the shock by creating a stern façade of massive stone that would have raised eyebrows in New Orleans, New York, and even Paris. The Glessners were not at all disturbed by the stir that accompanied the construction of their controversial dwelling. Mrs. Glessner even kept an amusing record of critical comments and a scrapbook of related newspaper clippings.

What was it about the house that made it such an object of notoriety? Primarily the same things that made it such an exemplary urban dwelling. First, there was its fortresslike "basement" story, which raises the base of the first-floor windows ten feet above the sidewalk. Second, the entry door itself was at ground level. No grand flight of steps topped by a front porch led up to it. No fancy wrought-iron or cast-iron balustrades guided the way. No pots or window boxes filled with flowers welcomed the visitor. It was just a strong and deceptively simple front door flush with the ground.

Third, most of the house's exterior appeared to have no windows. This is in part just a clever illusion. The front façade (Prairie Avenue) has ample windows, but they are inconspicuous because they are deep-set and lack the usual decorative surrounds. The long side façade (Eighteenth Street) has few windows but, unbeknownst to passersby, this wall adjoins a narrow service hall, not any of the main rooms of the house.

Finally, there were the massive, rough-faced stone walls of the exterior. The houses nearby were built of light, smoothly finished stone, with decorative ornamentation at doors, windows, and roofline in the classical manner. In the Glessner House, by contrast, the wall material itself was the main decorative element of the exterior. The way the stone was cut and laid imparts subtle organization and emphasis to the entire façade. Close inspection shows that the stone is patterned with three narrow ribbons of slightly more finished courses that encircle the house. The first runs over the porte cochere and front entry and under the first-floor windows to form an unusually low belt course. The second, a somewhat broader belt course, runs above the first-floor windows and doorway arch, and the third abuts the tops of the second-story windows. It is hard to think of

ABOVE *Henry Hobson Richardson, c. 1880.*

LEFT *A few small windows, service entrances, and an upstairs balcony are the only breaks in the massive stone side façade, behind which a service hall stretches the length of the house.*

heavy, rough-faced stonework as subtle, yet Richardson made it so. These understated variations give the house visual strength and unity.

In marked contrast to the street façades is the house's exterior as seen from the courtyard. After passing through the porte cochere the visitor is greeted by an entirely different house. Material, scale, and decorative detailing all change and soften. It is as dramatic as the passage from night to day. The massive stonework gives way to delicate brick with a light stone trim. The brick was originally pink but has been blackened by air

The window pattern of the front façade clearly indicates that the first floor of the house is about six feet above street level. The porte cochere leading to the courtyard is on the left.

pollution. Windows are everywhere and three rounded bays thrust into the sunlight. As we shall see, the interior of the house has an even warmer domesticity.

John J. Glessner (1843–1936) and his wife, Frances MacBeth Glessner (1848–1932), seem an unlikely couple to have stirred such controversy. They met in 1868 in Springfield, Ohio, where John was a promising young executive with Warder, Mitchell and Co., a manufacturer of mechanical reapers and other farm implements. By 1870 John was a partner in the firm, which had been renamed Warder, Mitchell and Glessner. In December of that year he and Frances were married and moved to Chicago, where John opened a branch of the firm to serve the rapidly expanding farmlands of the Corn Belt and Great Plains. He must have been a tough competitor because his company prospered during the reaper wars that were fought for the next thirty years among the country's many farm implement manufacturers. The wars ended in 1901 when the five industry leaders, including Warder, Mitchell and Glessner, merged to form the giant International Harvester Company. John Glessner was one of its original vice presidents.

Soon after their marriage, John and Frances developed what was to become a life-long interest in contemporary decorative art. In part this passion grew out of their association with a talented Chicago furniture maker and designer named Isaac Elwood Scott

Soot has blackened the pink brick of the interior courtyard. The three bays that project into it allow exterior light to pour inside.

(1845–1920), who provided many handcrafted pieces for their first Chicago home, purchased in 1874. By 1885 the increasingly affluent Glessners, now the parents of two young children, bought the site for their larger new home on elegant Prairie Avenue.

The Glessners interviewed several well-known architects, including New York's Stanford White (see Naumkeag, pages 166–77), for the job of designing the house but chose none of them. By chance they heard that Boston's renowned H. H. Richardson, then at the height of his career, was coming to Chicago to design a huge wholesale store for Marshall Field and Company. Fearing that Richardson now designed only large public and commercial buildings, they wrote him a tentative letter of inquiry. His reply almost boomed off the page: "I'll plan anything a man wants, from a cathedral to a chicken coop. That's the way I make my living."

Richardson soon arrived in Chicago and completely charmed the Glessners. John wrote: "He [Richardson] was the most versatile, interesting, ready, capable and confident of artists, the most genial and agreeable of companions. Everybody was attracted to him at sight." The architect, in turn, found the Glessners to be exceptionally rewarding clients. They were deeply interested in their new house and were anxious to learn more about "modern" developments in architecture and interior design. They visited Richardson in

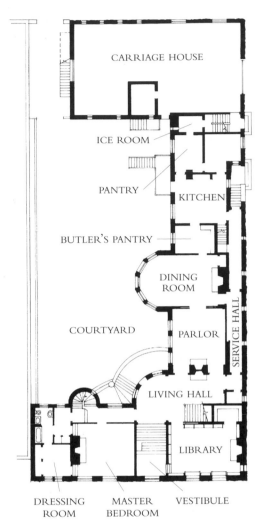

CARRIAGE HOUSE

ICE ROOM

PANTRY

KITCHEN

BUTLER'S PANTRY

DINING ROOM

SERVICE HALL

COURTYARD

PARLOR

LIVING HALL

LIBRARY

DRESSING ROOM

MASTER BEDROOM

VESTIBULE

TOP *View of the large living hall from the stair landing. Note the variety of spiral patterns used for the balusters, which are similar to those in the eighteenth-century Lee House (see page 27).*

BOTTOM *The library, with its beamed ceiling and massive desk, was modeled after Richardson's own study in Brookline, Massachusetts.*

Boston, dined with him, and joined the architect on shopping trips to choose appropriate furniture and decorative objects for their home. Realizing they were in the company of a genius who shared their own tastes, the couple allowed Richardson to create for them the house that "of all that he built he would have liked most to live in himself." Unfortunately, the architect would not live to see his finished masterpiece.

In April 1885 the Glessners again visited Richardson in Boston, where the architect reviewed final changes to the interior plans with them. Upon finishing Richardson declared, "There, Mr. Glessner, if I were to live five years longer, that is the last thing I would do on your house: my part is finished." Three weeks later the great architect was dead, felled by Bright's disease at age forty-seven.

Today a tour of the carefully restored Glessner House makes it clear why Richardson felt so much affection for this, his last house design. From the street-level entry one passes through an internal vestibule and then up a broad interior flight of steps to a large living hall. Richardson loved these friendly reception rooms, which his early Watts Sherman house in Newport, Rhode Island, had helped introduce to the United States. The Glessner version has a welcoming fireplace and functions as a bona fide room, not just as a passageway.

To the right of the living hall is the library, the heart of the house. Its design is closely modeled after the study in Richardson's own house in Brookline, Massachusetts. When the Glessners saw it, they were entranced with its beamed ceiling and huge double desk, and they asked Richardson to make a copy of this desk for their library. Once installed, it was so large and bulky that it was never removed from the house. The Glessners had wide intellectual interests and the library, filled with books and personal mementos, was their favorite room.

The long side of the L-shaped house contains the parlor, dining room, and kitchen. The parlor has a high picture rail, popular at the turn of the century for enabling pictures to be suspended without knocking holes in expensive wallpapers. Part of the Glessners' collection of early Dutch engravings hangs from the picture rail. The piano, originally designed for this room, was thought to have been lost forever. Some years ago, however, a visitor touring the house saw a photograph of the room with its original furnishings and recognized the distinctive piano; he remembered seeing it at Harvard. He turned out to be correct, and the piano was returned to its original home. Now the tour guides jokingly ask if anyone recognizes other furnishings in the photos.

The dining room features a wonderful bay window that overlooks the interior courtyard. Four of the chairs were originally designed for this room by Richardson's associate Charles Allerton Coolidge.

The other wing of the first floor contains a master bedroom suite featuring William Morris wallpapers and fabrics of the sort that became virtual trademarks of the British Arts and Crafts movement, whose designs were favored by both Richardson and the Glessners. Two unglazed and unfired ceramic flasks stand atop a mantelpiece; they were designed by Isaac Scott for the Glessners' earlier Chicago house, as were many of the furnishings in

The handsome case of the Steinway piano in the parlor was specially designed for the Glessners by Francis Bacon. The couple collected the engravings seen here and throughout the house. Tastefully framed by Isaac Scott, they hang from picture rails.

The marble-faced fireplace in the parlor has never been used. The small ebonized chairs to the left and right of the fireplace are original furnishings. The large windows overlook the interior courtyard. The doorway on the right leads to the living hall and library.

the suite. Richardson felt that Scott's furniture designs were a bit old-fashioned, so they were relegated to the master bedroom and the upstairs rooms, areas that consequently have a bit more of an Eastlake Victorian feel than do the house's principal rooms. Upstairs only a small guest room and the hall are open to visitors.

Realizing its architectural significance, the Glessners always wanted to preserve their unique home just as Richardson had designed it. To help ensure this they lived in the house long after the once-fashionable neighborhood had become dominated by light industry. In 1924 Mr. Glessner donated the house to the American Institute of Architects, Chicago Chapter, reserving life tenancy for himself and his wife. After their deaths in the depths of the 1930s Depression, the Chicago Chapter could not afford to keep up the large house so they gave it back to the Glessners' heirs, who in turn gave it to the Illinois Institute of Technology. The institute first used it for classrooms but later sold it to a private company for offices. When it was again put up for sale in 1966, a group of concerned citizens formed the Chicago Architectural Foundation to purchase and save the historic house. Only a few furnishings, such as the huge library desk, remained in the house through all these changes in ownership. Thanks to the generosity of Mr. Glessner's descendants, many of the house's original furnishings have now been returned to the house, helping to re-create the farsighted vision of Richardson and his unusually empathetic clients.

ABOVE *This view through the butler's pantry and into the dining room shows the original enunciator box, which was used to call servants.*

LEFT *The kitchen area features glazed white brick walls and a two-tone tile floor. The door leads to the ice room.*

Richardsonian Romanesque Style

(1880–1900)

As its name suggests, the Richardsonian Romanesque style was largely the creation of a single architectural genius—Henry Hobson Richardson (1838–1886). The son of Catherine Priestly, granddaughter of the great British chemist who discovered oxygen, Richardson was born on a prosperous plantation near New Orleans.

A three-hundred-pound giant of a man, he was larger than life in every sense. He attended Harvard, where he developed his interest in architecture, a subject then taught in America only by apprenticeship rather than as a formal academic discipline. Determined to pursue architecture as a career—and fluent in French thanks to his Louisiana childhood—he became only the second American to enroll in Paris's prestigious Ecole des Beaux Arts. The first was Richard Morris Hunt (see Château-sur-Mer, pages 126–37, and Biltmore, pages 232–45).

In 1867, after six years of study and apprenticeship in France, Richardson returned to the United States and opened an architectural practice in New York City. In 1872, when he entered a neo-Romanesque design in the competition for Boston's new Trinity Church and won, his success was assured. Soon he had so many New England commissions that in 1874 he moved his practice to the pastoral Boston suburb of Brookline. There, in a studio wing that he added to his house, he and a dozen assistants spent the next twelve years, until his early death in 1886, feverishly designing distinctive churches, train stations, public buildings, and houses—works that were to become the widely copied models for much of the nation's monumental architecture of the late 1880s and 1890s.

Most of Richardson's designs, including Glessner House, are built of rough-faced stone and feature round-topped, Romanesque-style arches as accents on porches, doors, or windows. Because such buildings are very expensive to construct they are limited primarily to architect-designed landmark houses. Richardson himself designed only a few houses in his signature style, and Glessner House is arguably the finest among them. Most surviving Richardsonian Romanesque houses were designed in the 1890s by his less inventive followers.

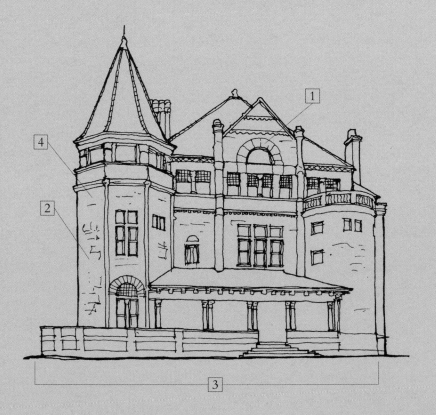

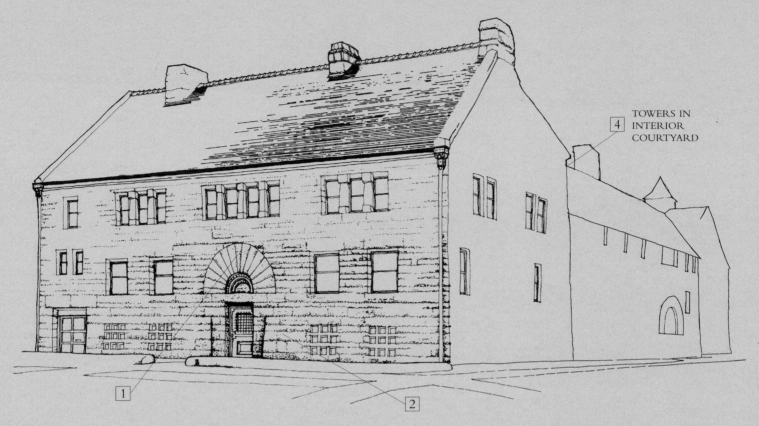

GLESSNER HOUSE

TOWERS IN
INTERIOR
COURTYARD

IDENTIFYING FEATURES

1 ROUND-TOPPED ARCHES OVER WINDOWS, ENTRANCE, OR
PORCH SUPPORTS

2 MASONRY WALLS, USUALLY WITH ROUGH-FACED, SQUARED
STONEWORK

3 FAÇADE USUALLY ASYMMETRICAL

4 MOST HAVE TOWERS, USUALLY ROUND WITH CONICAL ROOFS

Frank Lloyd Wright's finished drawing of the east elevation of the Dana-Thomas House, 1910.

Eclectic Houses

(1880–1940)

As the twentieth century began, the several competing house styles of the late Victorian era were rapidly being replaced by an even greater diversity of new housing fashions. New techniques for illustrating inexpensive books and magazines with photographs rather than drawings helped create this diversity. Now for the first time house builders could study countless accurate images of historic dwellings of all ages and styles. Thus began a taste for "period" houses that continues to this day.

This trend was sparked by the 1876 Philadelphia Exposition. Many of the smaller Exposition buildings were copies of long-unfashionable Colonial house designs and they touched a nerve of patriotic nostalgia. By the 1890s what had begun as a trickle of new houses in the Colonial Revival style (pages 204–5) had become a stream. By 1920 the stream had grown into a great flood that has ebbed only slightly since. By 1900 the taste for historic American designs had spread from Colonial-era houses to the Greek Revival houses of the early nineteenth century, which were re-revived as the Neoclassical style (pages 216–17).

The penchant for period houses also extended to European prototypes, the most popular of which were rustic English manor houses and cottages built in an Americanized interpretation known as the Tudor style (pages 230–31). A variety of French architectural precedents caught Americans' fancy as well. In the 1880s and 1890s Renaissance castles inspired the Châteauesque style (pages 244–45). From about 1900 to 1920 the Paris-based Neoclassical façades of the Beaux Arts style (pages 256–57) were most in vogue, only to be replaced in the 1920s and 1930s by the rustic country designs of the French Eclectic style (pages 266–67).

Mediterranean designs also competed for the favor of Eclectic-era home builders. The most popular were the Italian Renaissance style (pages 280–81), based on Italy's formal town houses and country villas, and the Spanish Eclectic style (pages 292–93), which incorporated Iberian decorative details from many eras into the picturesque shapes of simple Spanish farmhouses.

As in the Romantic and Victorian eras, technological advances facilitated Eclectic-era stylistic innovation. The inexpensive reproduction of photographs was one. Equally important was the perfection of techniques for adding a single decorative layer of brick or stone onto the exterior of traditional wood-framed houses. Whereas most European dwellings traditionally had massive masonry walls of brick or stone, as did some costly American landmark houses, the more affordable dwellings of typical American neighborhoods were wood-sided until the early 1920s. In that decade entire housing developments of masonry-veneered period cottages started to become a standard feature of suburban America.

Period houses make up only a part of the great stylistic diversity of Eclectic-era design. Early in the twentieth century several farsighted architects in Chicago and Los Angeles began creating truly "modern" houses without historic precedent. These efforts were so successful that pattern-book versions of their high-style landmarks dominated American housing from about 1905 until 1920. The Chicago-based fashion is called the Prairie style (pages 306–7), and the California-based fashion is the Craftsman style (pages 320–21). These innovative styles were replaced by mass-produced period house designs in the 1920s, but in the 1930s a more austere version of modernism was introduced by European émigrés fleeing Nazi terrorism. Known as the International style (pages 332–33), it was rare in the 1930s and 1940s, but was to become a principal theme of American design in the 1950s.

15
Westbury House

Colonial Revival Style

*W*estbury House is the kind of dwelling where one immediately feels at home, thanks to a rare combination of unpretentious elegance, intimately scaled rooms, and engagingly warm interior decor. Best known for the hundred acres of magnificent gardens that surround it, the house itself is a superb example of the Colonial Revival substyle known in this country as Georgian Revival.

In the 1880s a new fashion for reviving American Colonial architecture began to spread throughout the country. By the turn of the century new houses were mimicking the entire spectrum of Colonial-era design. First-Period English, Dutch Colonial, and Federal houses all served as models for the Colonial Revival movement, but Georgian-based designs were the most popular of all.

Compared to English "great houses," even the largest Georgian houses built in America during the Colonial period were quite modest in size and ornamentation. So Revival architects who wished to build truly grand Georgian country houses sometimes looked not to early American buildings for suitably elaborate models but directly to the English country houses that had inspired them. In the process they discovered that many of the fine houses built in the American colonies during the reigns of George I and George II (1715–60), the early part of our Georgian era, in fact more closely resembled the great houses of England built fifty years or so earlier, during the reigns of Charles I and Charles II (1625–49 and 1660–85), the English Caroline era. This is because in the seventeenth and eighteenth centuries it usually took at least several decades for new styles to spread from England to the distant colonies. Westbury House, directly based on English Carolinian models, is among the very finest examples of such English-inspired American "Georgian Revival" houses.

Westbury House was most likely modeled after direct English precedents for a more personal reason, however. The mistress of the house, Margarita Grace Phipps, called Dita (1876–1957), was from an old English family, owners of the Grace Steamship Company. In 1903 she married a wealthy young American, New Yorker John Shaffer

ABOVE *Two of the Phippses' sons at play on the south terrace.*

OPPOSITE *The magnificent south terrace is the only feature of the house about which Phipps and Crawley disagreed. According to* Halcyon Days, *Phipps felt it could be omitted or much simplified, while Crawley insisted it should be built as designed. Happily, Crawley prevailed. The terrace's first-floor colonnade has double doors that lead into the red ballroom.*

PAGE 192 *A formal allée lined with hemlock hedges and European lindens forms the main axis stretching south from Westbury House. The black iron and gilt ornamental gate, designed by George Crawley, adds a note of majesty.*

Phipps, known as Jay (1874–1958); the ceremony took place in historic Battle Abbey, the Grace family's English home. The groom promised to build his bride a fine American country house that would resemble those she had known in England. As the eldest son of Henry Phipps, Jr., whose holdings in the Carnegie Steel Company were second only to those of his close friend and partner Andrew Carnegie, Jay was in a good position to fulfill this promise.

Jay had already found the perfect setting for their home, a large tract in central Long Island known as Old Westbury. In the nineteenth century it had been a center of fox hunting for the New York elite, and as late as 1896 its rolling hills were still mostly Quaker farmland, although wealthy New Yorkers seeking rural retreats near the city were beginning to buy it up. Jay made his first land purchase there in 1901. His timing was good because by 1903 only three of the original fifty-odd Quaker farmsteads remained intact and grand manor houses were beginning to dot the countryside.

Jay and Dita occupied their completed dream home in 1907, only four years after their wedding; they were to live there for the rest of their long lives. When the couple moved in they already had three small children and a fourth on the way. Peggie Phipps Boegner, their third child and only daughter, has co-authored with Richard Gachot a charming reminiscence of growing up at Westbury with her three energetic brothers. Titled *Halcyon Days,* the book combines a delightful narrative with a treasure trove of vintage photographs found in long-forgotten attic trunks. The pages tell the story of a much-loved family home that was always bustling with activity.

The architect of Westbury House was a relatively unknown Englishman named George Crawley (1864–1926). An ardent antique collector and a meticulous student of design, Crawley had been an unsuccessful businessman early in his career and had never before planned an entire house from the ground up. He met the Phipps family when they rented a house near his home in England, and he became a good friend of Amy Phipps, Jay's sister. Amy found Crawley's artistic taste impeccable and in 1903 managed to persuade her parents to hire him to redecorate the interiors of several rooms in their Fifth Avenue town house. Crawley and his wife rented a New York apartment and he threw himself wholeheartedly into the first job he had ever loved.

Crawley's vast knowledge of all aspects of design, combined with his extreme attention to detail, greatly pleased his new clients. Soon he was offered a still greater opportunity—the design of Jay and Dita's new country house—and he met this challenge brilliantly. All of Westbury's many delights—buildings, rooms, furniture, and even the remarkable gardens—were planned and their construction supervised by the tireless and perfectionistic Crawley. Indeed, Westbury was to become his all-consuming masterpiece, a monument to one man's skill and energy focused on a single project over many years.

In the true spirit of early twentieth-century eclecticism, Crawley did not borrow large chunks of design directly from other houses. Instead, he carefully studied original Carolinian models and then modified and recombined individual elements into an organic whole that is highly evocative of that historic era. The unusual central chimney, the large

rounded central dormer, and the handsome front door are all examples of his original and skillfully crafted designs.

Halcyon Days describes Crawley's concern with quality workmanship. According to one of his craftsmen: "Mr. Crawley was so particular to get the right feeling into his work that he imported stone carvers from England, although it meant that the carvers would have to remain six months in the country and join a union before they could be allowed on the job. The American carvers at that time showed a strong French feeling in their work, while Mr. Crawley required eighteenth-century English and nothing 'there or thereabouts' would do." Concerning the front door, Crawley wrote Jay Phipps:

> I have got the front door underway at last. It has given me more trouble than anything I have ever done. I think I have made it 50 times without ever being satisfied. I wanted a very fine door which was completely out of the ordinary with lots of character. It was of course always open to me to do the simple commonplace thing, but I would not give it up. Yesterday morning, it all came right, the very thing I desired and if I tried ten years I could not do anything better. I hope and believe you will like it. I am completely happy about it. You may have thought of me as very lazy but it baffled me and has been on my mind for two years.

Visitors today enter the house through this same door, which has a motto carved above it: PAX INTROENTIBUS—SALUS EXEUNTIBUS ("Peace to Those Who Enter—Good Health to Those Who Depart"). The door opens onto a small vestibule, which in turn leads to a large entrance hall. This room is dominated by two imposing architectural features, one of stone and the other of wood. Both were carved by Frances Derwent Wood (1872–1926),

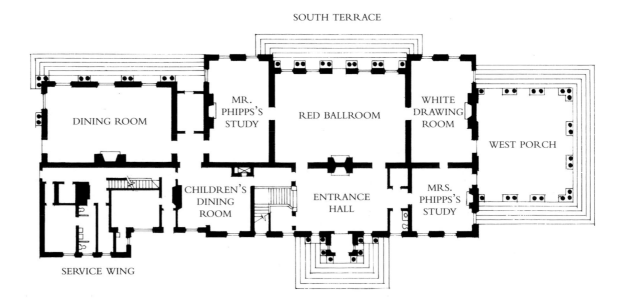

The White Drawing Room epitomizes the most popular decorating philosophy of the era. Light, solid-colored walls are broken into sections by panels framed with molding. Comfortable chairs and sofas are accentuated by elegant antiques, such as the white marble mantelpiece and the mahogany stool (c. 1760) in front of it. A table is set for afternoon tea with family silver, some pieces dating back to the eighteenth century. The floral-pattern carpet (c. 1760) is a rare English example woven in Frome, Somerset.

and feature segmental pediments (so called because the shape represents a segment of a circle). The first is a white marble chimney with cupids lolling on its pediment. To the right is a wooden "screen" supported by columns, its pediment adorned with carvings of angels. This screen serves to frame the handsome main stairway that ascends behind it.

Like its English prototypes, Westbury's original floor plan was rigidly symmetrical. The symmetry of the interior was slightly altered in 1924 when Crawley enlarged a porch on the west side and added a dining room and service wing on the east. But the exterior still retains a sense of symmetry.

The White Drawing Room exemplifies the gracious yet informal comfort of Westbury. The combination of inviting overstuffed sofas and chairs with various styles of antique tables, chests, mirrors, paintings, and other decorative objects is typical of the early twentieth-century penchant for eclectic interiors. Here one could sit comfortably and be surrounded by beautiful and valuable objects. The room features other typical design features of the period as well: moldings used to create rectangular wall panels; walls and panels painted in light colors; and boldly flowered chintz upholstery. The resulting "light" look was advocated by fashionable interior designers of the day, particularly Elsie de Wolfe (see Glenmont, page 159) and Ogden Codman (see Château-sur-Mer, page 131), both of whom deplored the dark Victorian interiors that had been in vogue just a few years earlier.

The Red Ballroom, made wider in Crawley's 1924 modifications, has five French doors that open onto what proved to be the most controversial feature of the house—a large rear terrace with spectacular views of the half-mile-long grand allée to the south. Crawley estimated the cost of the terrace at almost $50,000, and its construction was to begin just at a time when Henry Phipps had gently reminded his son that he was "spending money [he had] not yet earned." Jay suggested a simpler plan to Crawley, one he believed would be not only cheaper but also more appropriate to the house. Crawley disagreed strongly but was instructed to "prepare something less ambitious and to keep the cost as low as possible, of course having due regard to the effect." Crawley stalled and worried. According to *Halcyon Days,* "Somehow, eight months later, in a dramatic reversal Jay permitted Crawley to go ahead with the original design." Looking at the terrace today it is hard to imagine a more appropriate plan for integrating the house with the sloping rear gardens.

The original dining room, adjacent to the Red Ballroom, was converted into a study for Jay in 1924. The new dining room had originally been designed by Crawley for Henry Phipps's Fifth Avenue town house, but because that house was going to be demolished, the entire room was moved to Westbury—mantel, ceiling, and wood paneling. The lower mantel had been carved by Francis Derwent Wood, who also did the screen and mantel for Westbury's entry hall. Typical examples of the detail Crawley lavished on his interiors are the room's magnificent chandelier and silver door locks, all executed by skilled craftsmen following his designs. Crawley also had the rug specially woven for the room. All of these features are accented by carefully chosen antiques.

The upstairs hall is surrounded by bedrooms and guest rooms; the latter were converted from nurseries when the children were old enough to move to third-floor bedrooms. Each room has its own distinct character. The Adam Room is an early twentieth-century interpretation of Adam design with white walls rather than the more colorful surface finishes that we now know were typical of the originals. It has lovely 1790s

The elegant marble mantelpiece in the Red Ballroom was designed by Francis Derwent Wood. It is flanked by George II carved-mahogany side tables and carved- and gilded-wood pier mirrors.

The dining room, with its wood paneling, trompe l'oeil sky ceiling, and fine carved overmantel, was originally designed by Crawley in 1906 for Henry Phipps's Fifth Avenue home. It was brought to Westbury in 1924 when that town house was scheduled to be demolished.

The master bedroom's signature piece is a Chippendale mahogany tester bed (c. 1750). The window cornices were designed to echo it. The dressing table is of padouk wood and is almost identical to an engraving in Thomas Chippendale's Director.

The inviting master bath is of the school that bathrooms should look as much like sitting rooms as possible, with fixtures disguised. The "wicker chair" toilet is an original piece. The skirted dressing table sits in front of a door that once led to the sleeping porch; in the early twentieth century sleeping outdoors was considered healthful.

satinwood furniture. The comfortable master bedroom is dominated by a 1750 mahogany bed and pictures of the children.

It has been said that carefully designed "naturalistic" gardens are England's special gift to the fine arts. George Crawley designed Westbury's renowned gardens in this tradition, and Dita Phipps oversaw their planting. The large south terrace provides the principal transition between house and gardens and, as we have seen, it is over this terrace that Jay Phipps and George Crawley had their only recorded disagreement in designing the estate.

The gardens combine both formal and naturalistic design elements to great effect. There are three principal formal elements. The first is the north-south axis, which presents magnificent vistas as it stretches northward from the house's entry façade and southward from its garden façade. The axis is accentuated by a grand allée of trees that is less formally aligned on the south side than on the north.

The other two formal elements are a walled garden and rose garden. Both are situated in the southwest section of woodland so that while strolling along tree-lined paths one suddenly encounters a contrasting area of formal plantings (the English call these outdoor rooms). The rose garden is a summer delight. In the English manner, the roses are planted in formal sections, or parterres, outlined by low boxwood hedges.

The walled garden, surrounded by high brick walls and entered through decorative iron gates, has English-style mixed borders lining the walks that divide it into six large sections. A semicircular lotus pool with a walled pergola and statue forms an inviting terminus to this garden.

Mrs. Phipps's dressing table holds her monogrammed sterling silver grooming set and a small photograph of her grand-daughter and namesake, Dita Boegner.

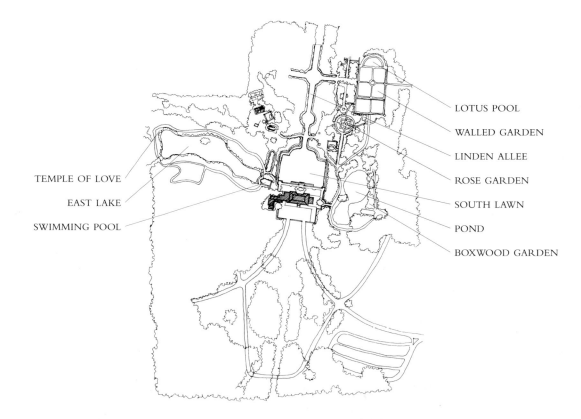

TEMPLE OF LOVE

EAST LAKE

SWIMMING POOL

LOTUS POOL

WALLED GARDEN

LINDEN ALLEE

ROSE GARDEN

SOUTH LAWN

POND

BOXWOOD GARDEN

ABOVE *Detail of the swimming pool's shell-mosaic ornamentation.*

TOP RIGHT *Capability Brown, an eighteenth-century pioneer of British naturalistic garden design, was fond of using formal garden structures, such as this pond and colonnade in Westbury's boxwood garden, as romantic accents.*

BOTTOM RIGHT *The formal swimming pool with its shell-mosaic details overlooks long, naturalistic East Lake.*

Westbury's largest naturalistic areas lie to either side of the main house. Water is the focal point of each, with a pond enhancing the west side and East Lake (with its Sand Island) anchoring the east. Such naturalistic lakes were a particular passion of eighteenth-century English landscape designers.

Surrounded on the north by dense woodland and to the south by a wildflower meadow, East Lake is appropriately picturesque in the English tradition. Nearby is Bluebell Walk, along which open woodlands are carpeted in spring with wild bluebells native to England. A classic Temple of Love rises up at the far end of the lake, while a handsome swimming pool ornamented with shell mosaics is positioned between the lake and the house. But for these two unexpected garden structures, one would be completely alone with nature when walking around East Lake.

Westbury is a modern example not only of the great English country houses that inspired much of our country's Georgian architecture but also of English period furnishings as adapted to early twentieth-century American interiors and of traditional English garden design transplanted to the New World. Much of its uniqueness stems from the fact that house, interior, and gardens were conceived as a unified whole by one exceptionally talented and dedicated man, George Crawley, who, like many earlier English aristocrats, oversaw every detail of the architecture, decor, and landscaping of this country estate.

We owe much to the farsightedness of the Phipps children in setting up a nonprofit foundation to preserve Westbury House and its gardens. Daughter Peggie Phipps Boegner was particularly generous; she and her children inherited the house, furnishings, and grounds and then made them into a permanent public monument to her visionary parents.

LEFT *The massive oak ceiling beams of the west porch are supported by paired Ionic-style columns.*

RIGHT *The walled garden has fruit trees in four of its six sections, a knowing reference to the earliest days of walled gardens, when they offered not only beauty but also food and were built to keep out hungry animals and other dangers of the surrounding wilderness.*

Colonial Revival Style
(1880–1940 AND LATER)

Through the middle years of the nineteenth century the United States was busily trying to forget its Colonial past and establish intellectual as well as political freedom from England. In architecture this is evidenced by Americans' taste for certain of the Romantic architectural fashions of that era. It was not until the centennial of American independence in 1876 that the country began to look back with nostalgia to the era when the Atlantic states were a part of England. Thus was born American Colonial Revival architecture—varying reinterpretations of the building styles exported to the colonies during the century and a half of British rule.

Many of the temporary buildings of the nation's 1876 Centennial celebration—a year-long exposition held in Philadelphia's Fairmont Park—were designed in "Colonial" style. Sensing the American public's new fascination with their Colonial roots, architects tentatively began designing Colonial Revival houses. By the 1890s this experimental trickle had become a flood that shows no signs of abating more than a century later. Colonial Revival houses have become an apparently irreplaceable staple of American domestic design.

Throughout this long period of popularity, Colonial Revival designs have varied principally in the degree to which they have attempted to be faithful to their early prototypes. Periods of "loose" interpretations, in which Colonial doorways or other details are applied to houses built in nontraditional shapes or materials, alternate with periods of stricter adherence to the early designs. This striving for authenticity reached its peak in the years from about 1910 to 1930.

Perhaps the grandest of all nostalgic Colonial Revival houses are those based not on the provincial buildings of the American colonies themselves, but on the original British designs that inspired them. Westbury House is a superb example of this trend. Designed by an English architect for a wealthy American client whose wife was from a distinguished English family, it represents a high point in America's architectural evocation of its British-ruled past.

IDENTIFYING FEATURES

1 FRONT DOOR ACCENTUATED WITH DECORATIVE CROWN AND/OR ENTRY PORCH

2 FAÇADES USUALLY HAVE SYMMETRICALLY BALANCED WINDOWS AND CENTERED DOOR

3 WINDOWS WITH DOUBLE-HUNG SASHES, USUALLY WITH MULTIPANE GLAZING IN ONE OR BOTH SASHES

4 WINDOWS FREQUENTLY IN ADJACENT PAIRS OR TRIPLES

AFTER 1920

WESTBURY HOUSE

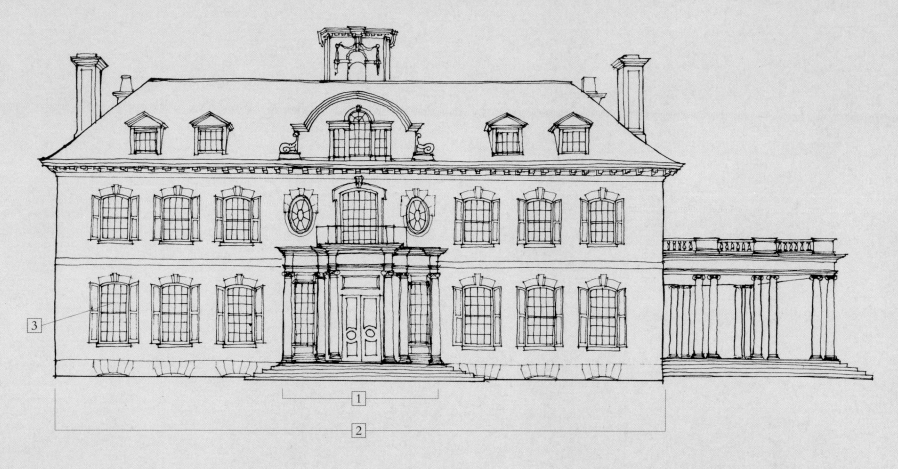

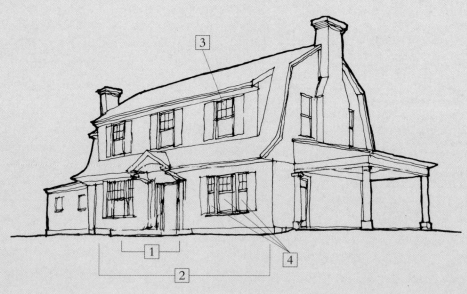

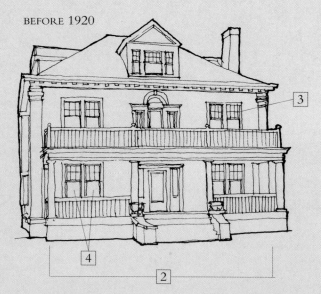

BEFORE 1920

The entrance walk and façade of Whitehall.

16

Whitehall

$\mathcal{M}$any of the entrepreneurs who amassed enormous fortunes during the period from 1870 to 1900, America's Gilded Age, have achieved legendary status. Such colorful figures as Andrew Carnegie, "Commodore" Vanderbilt, Jay Gould, J. Pierpont Morgan, and John D. Rockefeller are either hailed as builders of industrialized America or reviled as robber barons who ruthlessly disregarded the public welfare in their frantic quest for wealth and power. All but forgotten is one of their colleagues who spent the second half of his adult life, and most of his enormous fortune, on a visionary adventure in public service. That man was John D. Rockefeller's partner Henry F. Flagler (1830–1913), the mastermind behind the development of the fabled Standard Oil Trust, an extraordinarily profitable enterprise that by 1880 controlled most of the world's petroleum refining and marketing.

In 1884, at the age of fifty-four, Flagler turned over his day-to-day management duties at Standard Oil to a younger associate and took on what was to become a still greater challenge—converting the barren wilderness of subtropical Florida into a productive land of orange groves, truck farms, and winter resort communities. In this venture, as at Standard Oil, Flagler was so successful that he is justly called the founding father of modern Florida.

Flagler first visited the state in 1878 on the advice of his wife's doctor. Mary Flagler suffered from severe bronchitis, which made breathing difficult and greatly restricted her activities. For conditions such as hers physicians of the day often prescribed rest in a warm climate; the small northern Florida towns of Jacksonville and St. Augustine were favored locations. The Flaglers, who in spite of their wealth had always lived rather simply and were therefore not looking for grand luxury, found both towns depressingly primitive. The rundown hotels were filled with mosquitoes, the guests were mostly consumptives suffering from tuberculosis, and the food—northern canned meats and vegetables—was virtually inedible, even though lush fruits and vegetables as well as fresh seafood abounded in local markets. The Flaglers quickly returned to their New York home in disgust.

Henry and Mary Lily Flagler, c. 1910.

Mary Flagler died of her illness in 1881 and the next winter Henry was hospitalized with a liver ailment. During his recuperation his thoughts turned to the vast area of potentially productive but undeveloped land that he had seen in Florida, land that the state government had recently offered for sale at fifty cents an acre with few buyers. Henry decided to return to St. Augustine for a second look.

He found some welcome changes in the five years that had passed since his first visit. The town now had one comfortable hotel, though most of its guests were still convalescents. Believing that the picturesque town and its mild winter climate should also appeal to healthy travelers, he vowed to build a luxury hotel in St. Augustine to attract clients who, in his own words, "[had] plenty of money, but could find no satisfactory way of spending it," an apt description of Flagler himself. Opened in 1888 with much fanfare, the sumptuous Ponce de Leon was an immediate success. More important, Flagler correctly perceived that satisfied wealthy travelers would soon be followed by much larger numbers of middle-class tourists, some of whom might choose to become permanent residents as citrus growers, vegetable farmers, merchants, or just retirees. Flagler had found a new vision that would occupy the rest of his long life.

From the beginning Flagler saw the development of Florida in an entirely different light from the building of Standard Oil. Although he hoped that the vast sums he would have to spend—on undeveloped land; on railroads to make this land accessible; on hotels to attract visitors; and on towns, schools, hospitals, and churches to serve those who decided to become residents—would someday yield a fair return on his investment, monetary gain was clearly a secondary goal. He insisted that everything be planned to the highest standards with a view to permanence. In addition, Flagler would not participate in any local enterprise, no matter how profitable, that could function solely on its own capital and entrepreneurship. In short, he provided a vast infrastructure from which others could benefit. This costly approach, on such a grand scale, is sometimes practiced by enlightened governments but is almost unique in the history of private enterprise.

After the success of the Ponce de Leon Hotel, Flagler began to purchase and improve eastern Florida's primitive railroad system. Soon he was laying tracks southward to serve previously isolated coastal villages and newly planned towns—Daytona Beach, Palm Beach, Fort Lauderdale, and, finally, Miami. Each of these had a milder climate than its more northerly neighbor, so as the rails made their way south, a steady influx of new citrus growers, truck farmers, and winter visitors was assured.

The narrow island of Palm Beach, warmed in the winter by the Gulf Stream and cooled in the summer by breezes from the ocean to the east and narrow Lake Worth to the west, was planned as the crown jewel of Flagler's Florida empire. It was here that he built Whitehall, a palatial residence that is the most personal of the many landmarks he contributed to the state. In 1901 Flagler married thirty-four-year-old Mary Lily Kenan, who was from a distinguished North Carolina family. Whitehall, one of the few grand indulgences of Flagler's long life, was among his wedding gifts to his bride.

Mary Lily wanted a "marble palace" and to design it Flagler called on his favorite architects, New York partners John Carrère (1858–1911) and Thomas Hastings (1860–1929). Both men had studied at the Ecole des Beaux Arts in Paris in the early 1880s and then apprenticed as draftsmen for the distinguished New York firm of McKim, Mead and White (see Vanderbilt House, pages 246–57 and Naumkeag, pages 166–77). Hastings's father, a well-known Presbyterian minister and educator, was Flagler's New York pastor and a close family friend. In 1885 Flagler had asked the young Hastings and his friend Carrère to design the lavish Ponce de Leon Hotel, the first of his Florida ventures. The two architects jumped at the opportunity and resigned from McKim, Mead and White to establish their own firm. The Ponce de Leon sealed Carrère and Hastings's reputation. As historian Mark Alan Hewitt puts it, "The smashing success of their debut building presaged an association that would produce such acclaimed public edifices as the New York Public Library, won by competition in 1897, and the House and Senate Office Buildings in Washington, D.C. (1905–9)." The partners also designed many of Flagler's later Florida hotels and larger public buildings. They did not disappoint their first patron in planning Whitehall. Given virtual carte blanche to create a sumptuous landmark as quickly as possible, they completed the house in a breathtaking eighteen months at a cost of $4 million—$2.5 million for the building itself and $1.5 million for the interior decor and furnishings—a sum that in 1903 had the buying power of about $65 million today.

The house, sited on the western side of Palm Beach, overlooked Lake Worth, giving the Flaglers a spectacular view of the setting sun reflected in the lake. Henry placed his office and porches on this side of the house.

In designing the house's decor Carrère and Hastings were joined by the distinguished New York interior design firm of Pottier and Stymus. Buyers were sent to Europe to comb the Continent for appropriate antiques. Unlike Vizcaya, the great Italian Renaissance house in nearby Miami (pages 268–81), Whitehall's interior contains no sections or pieces of European houses; each molding, doorway, and ceiling was designed from scratch. This approach saved Whitehall's designers several years of searching, measuring, shipping, matching, and, finally, installing.

Flagler reportedly wanted the house modeled after a large but unpretentious Spanish Colonial dwelling in Cuba that he had long admired. With their Beaux Arts background, the architects had something more grand in mind. The only Spanish features ultimately woven into Whitehall were the interior courtyard and red tiled roof, which provides a striking contrast to the stark white façade dominated by classical columns. Why the Flaglers agreed to this formal, Neoclassical design is not known. One guess, however, is that it reflects Mary Lily's Southern heritage. Since Thomas Jefferson built Monticello (pages 46–59), white classical columns had come to symbolize the great houses of the South. Most large southern plantation houses featured either a colonnaded full-length porch or at least a tall-columned entry portico. Giving up this tradition may have been too much to ask of a wife from an old, established North Carolina family.

Visitors approach Whitehall through grounds planted with native Florida vegetation as well as with exotic tropical imports. The sight of palm trees growing in the middle

Monumental white marble urns sit in front of the columns along Whitehall's entry façade.

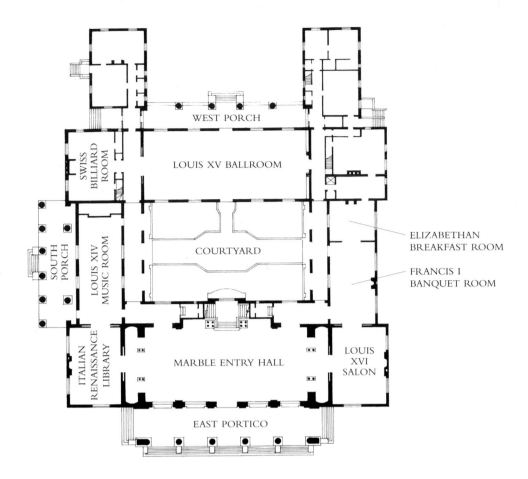

WEST PORCH

SWISS BILLIARD ROOM

LOUIS XV BALLROOM

SOUTH PORCH

LOUIS XIV MUSIC ROOM

COURTYARD

ELIZABETHAN BREAKFAST ROOM

FRANCIS I BANQUET ROOM

ITALIAN RENAISSANCE LIBRARY

MARBLE ENTRY HALL

LOUIS XVI SALON

EAST PORTICO

One of five small upstairs balconies on the front façade. Each has a surround of square window panes, or lights, similar to those in Greek Revival houses. Note the coffered ceiling.

of a meticulously tended green lawn is startling at first. It is the English savannah look—tall trees dotting large sweeps of mown grass—transported and adapted to the tropics.

The front door is at the top of a tier of steps that extends the entire length of the grand front porch with its six massive columns. For added emphasis, there is a huge urn set on a pedestal in front of each column. The entry door and all of the front windows of the main house are surrounded by additional "lights," or clear panes of glass. The lights around the first-floor windows are arranged in a rounded-arch pattern, similar to that found on Early Classical Revival houses, while those around the second-story windows are in a squared-off pattern reminiscent of the Greek Revival style. Each second-story window also has its own small wrought-iron balcony.

The magnificent bronze-grilled front door opens onto a stunning marble entry hall designed by Carrère and Hastings. It was a tradition of the day that architects handled the decor of grand entry halls and stairways, while interior design firms, in this case Pottier and Stymus, planned the decor of most other rooms.

Each of Pottier and Stymus's main rooms at Whitehall is designed in a different French decorative tradition. In historical terms the earliest is the large banquet room, which is decorated in the style of Francis I, who ruled from 1515 to 1547. As a result of an unsuccessful military campaign the king was held captive for a time in Italy, where he

observed some of the artistic fruits of the Renaissance. On his return to France he vowed to make his reign known for a similar devotion to the arts. A favorite decorative motif of Francis I designs was the salamander, fabled for its ability to withstand fire. In the White-hall banquet room salamanders are found in the gold cartouches over the doors, in the pattern of its Savonnerie carpet, and in the cast andirons of the massive fireplace. The ceiling's square pattern of wooden beams enlivened by ornament is typical of the Renaissance. A similar ceiling is found in Whitehall's library.

The music room reflects the next major decorative period in France, that of Louis XIV, the Sun King, who ruled from 1643 to 1715. During this era rooms tended to be very large because of the king's fondness for entertaining his countless courtiers on a lavish scale. Ceilings, walls, doors, and windows were ornately decorated, while furniture was of secondary importance. Often it was simply placed around the edges of the room to accentuate the sumptuously decorated walls and ceilings. Whitehall's music room, with its dramatic ceiling and coved cornice elaborated with almost life-sized figures holding

Whitehall's courtyard was inspired by one that Henry Flagler had seen in Havana.

The coffered ceiling in the Francis I dining room has papier mâché panels of dolphins made in Limoges, France.

musical instruments, adheres to this tradition. The central portion of the ceiling is a recessed dome crowned by a rendering of Guido Reni's *Aurora*. An innovation was the installation of hidden light bulbs around the perimeter of the dome to illuminate this painting.

The ballroom is decorated in the style of Louis XV, who reigned from 1715 to 1774. The ceiling, although also highly decorated, is much lighter and more delicate than in the music room. The tops of the windows are gracefully arched, rather than squared as in the music room. Even the pattern of the window panes incorporates the graceful curves associated with this later era.

The salon is decorated in the style of Louis XVI, who ruled from 1774 to 1793; this is the last French decorative era represented in the main rooms of Whitehall. The style is marked by a return to the aesthetics of Classicism, interest in which was stimulated

LEFT *The Louis XIV music room has a 24-rank organ and a heavy cornice decorated with almost life-size figures holding musical instruments.*

BELOW LEFT *Architects Carrère and Hastings designed the monumental marble entry hall; it is 110 feet long and 40 feet wide. The bases and capitals of the columns and the intricate stair rail are of bronze. The painted ceiling depicts the Crowning of Knowledge.*

BELOW RIGHT *The Louis XVI salon features a Savonnerie carpet, large overmantel mirror, and cornice molding carvings that are very restrained and flat compared to those in the music room.*

NEOCLASSICAL STYLE 213

The master suite (TOP RIGHT) has been restored with faithful reproductions of the original golden wall and upholstery fabrics. The Art Nouveau mirror on the dressing table (ABOVE) was made for Mary Lily by Tiffany and Company. The master bath (BOTTOM RIGHT) has a double "his and hers" onyx washstand.

by the excavations of Roman remains at Pompeii shortly before Louis XVI ascended the throne. In keeping with this style, the ceiling decoration in the salon is much less ornate, the primary adornment being simple swags and garlands. In contrast to the deep relief of the carvings in the Louis XIV music room, the carvings in the salon are quite flat. The large mirror over the fireplace, topped with a swag, is a typical overmantel decoration of the Louis XVI period. Large pieces of glass were still very expensive and difficult to manufacture at that time, so a mirror of this size was a technological triumph.

Other ground-floor rooms at Whitehall include the Swiss-style billiard room and an Elizabethan breakfast room; the latter features design elements borrowed from England's Warwick Castle. Upstairs there are fourteen guest bedrooms, all with a private or connecting bath. Each room has its own decorative motif, which is carried out in the furnishings, fixtures, woodwork, and even hardware. American Colonial, Arts and Crafts, and Art Nouveau are but a few of the styles used. In addition to the guest bedrooms there are thirteen servants' bedrooms on the second floor and five more on the third.

The Flaglers's master bedroom suite is decorated in Louis XV style, continuing the French decor that dominates the public rooms on the first floor. The silk damask curtains and the bed and wall coverings have recently been replaced by a faithful copy of the original fabric.

When the Flaglers married in 1901 Mary Lily was thirty-four and Henry seventy-one. Mary Lily loved giving parties, and for the first few years of their marriage the couple entertained countless guests at Whitehall. Later on, however, Henry usually retired early from his wife's parties. After Henry's death in 1913 Mary Lily seldom used the grand house, and after her untimely death in 1917, it passed to a niece, who sold it to an investment group. It served briefly as a clubhouse, and then a ten-story, three-hundred-room tower, the Whitehall Hotel, was erected, abutting the house on the west side. Some of the rooms in the house were used as hotel lobbies, lounges, and bars. Opened in 1925, the hotel was obsolete by 1959 and demolition of the entire complex was a distinct possibility. When Flagler's granddaughter Jean Flagler Matthews (1910–1979) heard that Whitehall was in danger of being torn down, she immediately formed the Henry Morrison Flagler Foundation to purchase the property and open it as a public museum. Thus began the house's restoration, which is still under way today. As a first step the nine upper stories of the hotel were demolished; the ground floor now houses the museum's offices and is used for charity balls, concerts, and other events.

After Mary Lily Flagler's death, Whitehall's furnishings had been distributed to various relatives. Mrs. Matthews set up a long-term program of returning them to the house. A number of pieces have been donated by Flagler's descendants and others have been bought so that today much of the original furniture is once again in place. A Memorial Room on the second floor commemorates Mrs. Matthews's twenty years of dedication to saving and restoring Whitehall for public enjoyment.

Neoclassical Style
(1895–1940 AND LATER)

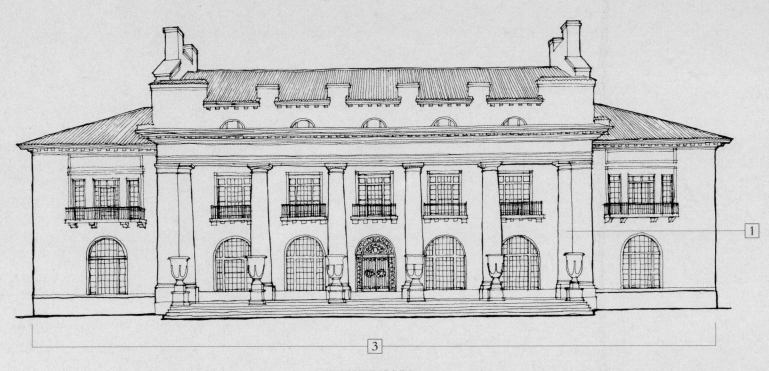

1

3

WHITEHALL

IDENTIFYING FEATURES

1

3

1 FAÇADE DOMINATED BY FULL-HEIGHT PORCH WITH
CLASSICAL COLUMNS

2 COLUMNS OFTEN HAVE IONIC OR CORINTHIAN
CAPITALS

3 FAÇADES USUALLY HAVE SYMMETRICALLY BALANCED
WINDOWS AND CENTERED DOORS

Façades dominated by classical columns were a central feature of the Early Classical Revival and Greek Revival styles of the early 1800s. By mid-century these styles had largely been replaced by styles based on medieval (Gothic Revival) or Renaissance (Italianate) prototypes. In 1893, however, there was a sudden rekindling of interest in Classical designs, sparked by Chicago's World Columbian Exposition, whose main attraction was a great White City featuring monumental, classically inspired buildings. Thus arose the Neoclassical movement, which, in its highly decorated Beaux Arts version (see pages 256–57), became for many decades the favored style for large public buildings and also inspired a renewed taste for column-dominated house façades that persists to this day.

Like the public buildings of the great White City, Neoclassical houses tend to magnify and elaborate the more subtle architectural detailing of their Early Classical Revival and Greek Revival American predecessors. A comparison of Whitehall's massive columns with the more restrained façades of Monticello (page 46) and Melrose (page 86) illustrates this tendency. The architects of the early classically based houses were faced with the complicated problem of constructing subtly shaped columns on site out of logs, brick, or stone. Most avoided the problem by using simple square "columns" or by opting for flat pilasters on the front wall. During the Neoclassical era, in contrast, columns of both wood and stone could be ordered in all sizes from the catalogs of large building-supply companies. These columns were topped by decorative capitals that were mass-produced in cast composite materials rather than painstakingly carved out of wood or stone. Elaborate Corinthian designs were particular favorites.

Whitehall is one of the country's rare monumental houses in the Neoclassical style; most examples are more modestly scaled neighborhood versions. But even Whitehall has an understated simplicity in comparison to its more elaborately decorated contemporaries in the closely related Beaux Arts style (see Vanderbilt House, pages 246–57).

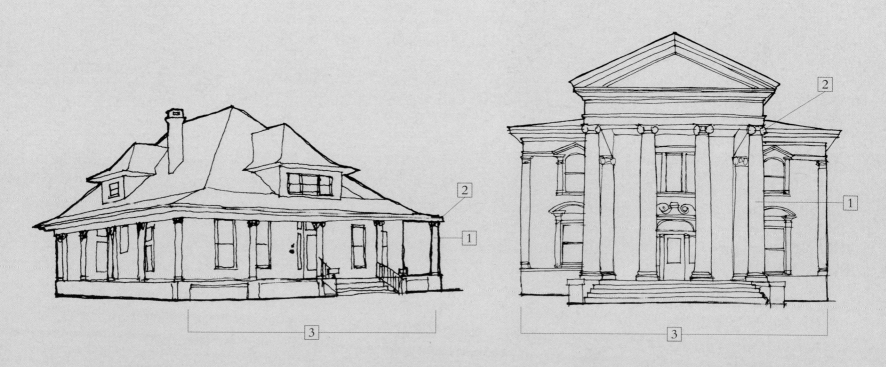

17

Stan Hywet Hall

AKRON, OHIO

Tudor Style

About 1910 Akron industrialist Frank A. Seiberling (1859–1955) and his wife, Gertrude Penfield Seiberling (1866–1946), decided to build a country house for their large family. In making this decision they were not alone. From about 1880 to 1930, thousands of wealthy Americans turned to large country estates as the ideal way to live.

Stan Hywet Hall, as the Seiberlings' called their house, is an almost perfect reflection of the country-house ideals of the day. First, it was on a sizable tract of land (three thousand acres) with extensive woodlands, fields, pastures, farm animals, orchards, and gardens—all important elements of the "country life." Second, it afforded a wide range of sporting activities—swimming, tennis, riding, golfing, bowling, fishing, and so on. Third, it was equipped with the latest technology, including central heating, an elevator, a telephone switchboard, a central vacuuming system, and electric refrigeration. Fourth, it was built in an appropriately picturesque style borrowed from sixteenth-century England and set amid English-style naturalistic gardens.

It is not an accident that the Seiberlings decided on such a grand lifestyle in 1911. When Frank founded the Goodyear Tire and Rubber Company in 1898, it was only one of several Akron enterprises that manufactured tires for horse-drawn carriages. Then in 1907 Henry Ford introduced his mass-produced Model T. It sold for $500, a fraction of the price of earlier automobiles, which had been little more than expensive toys for the affluent. Sensing the coming automotive revolution, Seiberling launched the first major advertising campaign for automobile tires, and sales soared. In 1909 he secured a contract to place Goodyear tires on all new General Motors cars. The preceding year Goodyear had sold 35,000 tires; by 1912 annual sales had topped a million, and the value of the company's stock—and Seiberling's wealth—had increased thirty-fold. By 1916 Goodyear was the world's largest rubber company.

To choose a designer for their new home the Seiberlings asked several architectural firms to submit preliminary plans in a sort of miniature design competition. The

winner, selected in January 1912 on the strength of a Tudor-style design, was New York's George B. Post and Sons. The firm's Ohio representative, Charles Sumner Schneider (1874–1932) of Cleveland, was assigned to the job. In April Schneider, the Seiberlings, and their twenty-two-year-old daughter, Irene, set sail for Europe to study English Tudor houses firsthand. Three of the houses they saw particularly influenced the final design of Stan Hywet Hall: Ockwells Manor in Berkshire (c. 1450), Compton Wynyates in Warwickshire (c. 1500), and Haddon Hall in Derbyshire (c. 1550). The main entrance, for instance, is modeled on that of Compton Wynyates. In a letter of July 1916, Schneider told the Seiberlings about a recent American Tudor house designed after Compton Wynyates by the well-known John Russell Pope: "Mr. Pope, the architect, has taken the main entrance straight, whereas I was only willing to be impressed by it when designing your house. Perhaps you will think that Mr. Pope is more successful and got more out of it than I did, but I prefer not to take things too straight." Schneider's position was characteristic of most Eclectic-era American architects; they were willing to be inspired by earlier models but changed and updated details as they pleased in planning their Americanized versions.

On his return from England, Schneider lost no time in drawing up the final plans for Stan Hywet Hall, which were completed and approved in December 1912. Construction began in the spring of 1913 and the exterior of the house was finished by Christmas. Two additional years were needed to complete and furnish the complex interior. The Seiberlings moved into the house in December 1915.

The siting of the house was determined by the eminent Boston landscape architect Warren Manning (1860–1938). Manning had worked for the renowned Frederick Law Olmsted (see Biltmore, pages 232–45). Skilled in the use of native American plants, he had been Olmsted's chief plant material specialist for a time. But by 1911, when he was engaged by the Seiberlings, Manning was practicing on his own.

ABOVE *Guests enter through a Tudor-arched, English-style enclosed front porch. The gable above is ornamented with a carved wooden verge board and half-timbering with brick infill.*

PAGE 218 *Stan Hywet Hall enjoys a sweeping vista to the west. The view can even be seen from the front door all the way through the house. This overlook terminates the strong west axis.*

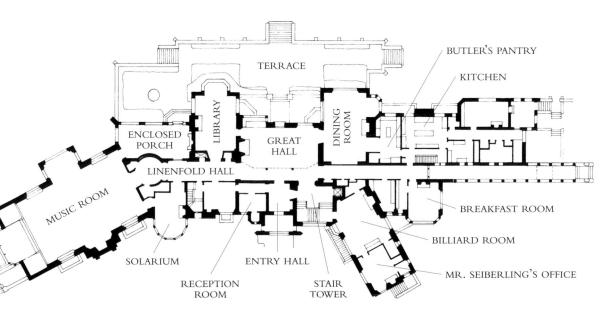

Manning ran the estate's long, sweeping entrance drive through an old apple orchard, now gone but slated for eventual restoration. This approach immediately indicated that the place was indeed a working country estate. The Great Meadow Lawn, which Manning called the Living Lawn, was visible beyond the apple trees. Manning also sited and helped plan the many outbuildings necessary for country life—gate lodge, stable (now the gift shop), paddock (now the main parking lot), poultry house (a two-story building that housed chickens, turkeys, and pheasants, now demolished), greenhouse, and so on. Moreover, he designed an elaborate cutting garden, which originally included a vegetable garden as well.

The task of adapting the grounds for the sporting activities that were a central focus of grand country living also fell to Manning. He provided a bowling green off the west terrace for croquet and lawn bowling, outdoor tennis courts near the lagoon, and a roque court, now gone. The family and their guests could engage in archery on the north meadow or go horseback riding along ten miles of trails. And of course they could play golf. A four-hole course stretched across the Great Meadow Lawn and there was a miniature "clock golf" course in the central circle in front of the house. A sunken area near the

The asymmetrical front façade has many typical Tudor features: numerous chimney flues, an entry porch framed by a Tudor arch, half-timbering, many small diamond-shaped window panes, and a large squared stair tower.

The naturalistic lagoon is in an old stone quarry; it was used for swimming, fishing, boating, and, in the winter, ice skating. The twin structures in the background are tea houses; beneath them are dressing rooms for swimmers.

OPPOSITE *The door of the garden façade is directly in line with the front door.*

house served as an amphitheater for theatrical performances. The lagoon provided still more activities—canoeing, fishing, swimming and, in winter, ice skating.

The devotion to sport continued inside the house as well. An indoor swimming pool was installed in the basement next to a two-story gymnasium in which tennis or basketball could be played. Upstairs, on the main floor, there was a game room (called the solarium) for such diversions as bridge, chess, and checkers, and a cozy, wooden-beamed billiard room, complete with built-in cigar humidor and drink cooler.

Lest this emphasis on games and athletics seem extreme, it should be kept in mind that the Seiberlings had six children, ranging in age from seven to twenty-seven when they moved into Stan Hywet Hall. In that pre-television and even pre-radio era, the more activities that could be devised for the children the better.

Stan Hywet Hall's superb gardens and interior design are largely a reflection of Gertrude Seiberling's many skills. A 1975 publication of the Stan Hywet Hall Foundation describes her as "a gracious, gentle lady of fine spirit and genuine charm . . . a devotee of beauty in all forms and greatly talented as a musician, poetess, and painter with a keen sensitivity to what constituted good taste."

The motto over the front door—NON NOBIS SOLUM—(Not for us alone) aptly describes the spirit in which the Seiberlings built and maintained Stan Hywet Hall. The house and gardens were the scene of frequent musical events, civic group meetings, family parties, and charity benefits. A community party the Seiberlings threw in 1928 is a case in point. They came up with the idea of fêting everyone who had lived in Akron for more than fifty years with a huge party on the front meadow. Outdoor stages, kitchens, dining tents, dance floors, and so on were set up. Advertisements were placed in the local paper, and more than four thousand people attended the day-long celebration.

Like the architectural plan, the interiors of the house are a fascinating combination of medieval English design and early twentieth-century American conveniences. The interior designer was New Yorker Hugo F. Huber. As the furnishings were being assembled, he wrote Gertrude, "I think if we adhere to a middle course by having all the comfortable pieces, such as divans, easy chairs, library furniture, dining room table and chairs and most of the bedroom furniture made new but subdued in effect, and then introduce here and there, cabinets, odd tables, etc., in the antique, I think we would arrive at the most successful and pleasing effect."

The visitor enters the house through what the English call a "porch," a roomlike enclosure in front of the main entry door. Beyond is the entry hall with a small reception room to the left. A nineteenth-century innovation, the reception room (see Morse-Libby House, page 115) was where visitors waited while servants informed the visitees of their arrival. The telephone rendered this type of room obsolete, as etiquette began to dictate that one call ahead and arrange a convenient time to visit, a courtesy not previously possible.

Straight ahead is the Great Hall, which was the principal room of original Tudor houses. These all-purpose "halls" were large enough to accommodate the entire household at meals and were also used as a general indoor living area. Usually they were a good two stories high with an open gabled space near the ceiling. The height was necessary because this room form evolved before the modern fireplace and chimney came into general use. To heat a great hall, a single fire would be built in an open pit right in the middle of the room. The smoke would simply waft up to the high ceiling and gradually escape outside through two "wind holes" in the gable ends. These wind holes eventually evolved into today's windows.

The prototypes of the modern fireplace and chimney were the most significant domestic innovations of the late Middle Ages. At first they were confined to grand dwellings and considered a status symbol. But when they began to appear even in modest dwellings, the indicator of status became the *number* of fireplaces and chimneys because every additional fireplace meant an additional heated room. Looking at the exterior of a house, one could determine how many fireplaces it had by the number of chimneys and chimney pots. One large chimney might serve several fireplaces through tile flues, which

In celebration of Stan Hywet Hall's opening, the Seiberlings held a Shakespearean costume ball, June 16, 1916.

projected above the chimney as "pots." Of course it was but a matter of time before people began to decorate their chimneys with any number of chimney pots. America's Tudor Revival designers adopted this practice, so the chimneys of most Tudor houses in this country sport multiple chimney pots. At Stan Hywet Hall there was no need to exaggerate the number of fireplaces since there are *twenty-three,* one in every major room except the enclosed porch, where the architect convinced the Seiberlings that a mantelpiece would detract from the room's decorative fountain.

Even though traditional Tudor fireplaces provided a focus for Stan Hywet Hall's room decor, in the best turn-of-the-century American fashion the house was heated by an up-to-date central steam system. Radiators are nowhere to be seen, however; they are artfully disguised throughout the house by walls, window seats, floors, or shelving. Despite the central heating, the fireplaces were often lit, and a special rope elevator was used to bring up logs and coal from the basement.

A long linenfold hallway, with beautiful paneling hand carved to resemble folds of cloth, leads from the entry area to the large music room. The paneling was not old but was specially carved for Stan Hywet Hall in medieval style. Ironically, this ancient-looking paneling also conceals entrances to both a modern elevator and a telephone room.

The music room at the end of the hallway is considered by one critic to be among America's most beautifully decorated rooms. Gertrude Seiberling was a highly trained contralto and might well have had a professional career had she so chosen. Her husband was also a music lover and played the flute as a young man. Unlike the music rooms of

The two-story Great Hall was used as a living room by the Seiberlings. Antique pieces include the large mid-sixteenth-century tapestry and the seventeenth-century oak table with joined stools.

ABOVE *An Arts and Crafts tile fountain designed by Mary Chase Stratton is the focal point of the enclosed porch.*

TOP RIGHT *Detail of the dining room frieze, a canvas mural by Robert Sewell depicting a procession of characters from Chaucer's* Canterbury Tales.

BOTTOM RIGHT *The dining room ceiling is ornamented with strapwork, a sixteenth-century decorative motif. The rug was woven for this room at the Beloochistan Rug Company in India.*

many grand country houses, the Seiberlings' saw a lot of use. Gertrude knew most of the prominent musicians of the day and often invited them to Stan Hywet Hall for private recitals. To facilitate this music making, the room was furnished with a Steinway concert grand piano, an eighteenth-century harpsichord, and a two thousand–pipe Aeolian organ.

Two other rooms open off the linenfold hallway near the music room. One is the enclosed porch, with a stunning Arts and Crafts tile fountain designed by Mary Chase Stratton, founder of Detroit's renowned Pewabic Pottery Company. A wall of windows floods this room with light from the west. The other is the solarium, which was used for cards and other table games. It is paneled in sandalwood and furnished with a combination of antiques and early twentieth-century reproductions.

At the other end of the house is a small breakfast room. A light, cheerful space, it faces east and overlooks a small garden. That the yellow, white, and blue of the room's Delft chandelier and sconces were reflected in the original planting scheme for the morning garden is but one example of the extraordinary attention to detail at Stan Hywet Hall.

Other first-floor rooms include the library and the dining room. The billiard room and Mr. Seiberling's private office are located in a wing with its own separate entrance. The second floor has bedrooms and more private living areas. The decor of the master bedroom is entirely antique. The walls and fireplace were purchased in England and transported to Ohio for restoration.

Unlike the rooms in original Tudor houses, most of Stan Hywet Hall's first-floor rooms are integrated with the surrounding gardens because they have large windows that offer beautiful views. The windows in the Great Hall, for instance, overlook a series of grand terraces that were used for outdoor entertaining.

Stan Hywet Hall stands today as a superb example of the American Country House movement; every aspect embodies the ideals of that era. The Seiberlings' six children understood its importance and, on their father's death, arranged to donate the house, furnishings, and about seventy surrounding acres to a nonprofit organization that was created to preserve the estate and keep both house and gardens open to the public.

The intimate breakfast room faces east to catch the morning sun. It is furnished with informal English antiques, including the Jacobean gate-legged table and country Chippendale chairs.

Tudor Style
(1890–1940)

The late Victorian Stick and Queen Anne styles, with their strongly asymmetrical façades, steeply pitched roofs, and wood walls, were loosely based on late medieval English buildings. But the 1890s saw the beginning of a trend toward more accurate copies of early English manor houses and farm cottages. Like their prototypes, these houses typically have walls of brick or stone instead of wood.

In America this style has come to be known as Tudor Revival, or simply Tudor, which is somewhat of a misnomer since few houses of this type resemble the transitional medieval-to-Renaissance designs of England's Tudor period (1500s). Rather, they draw on the entire spectrum of late medieval English building practices—half-timbered walls, high-pitched roofs of slate, thatch, or flat tiles, small-paned casement windows, massive multiflue chimneys, and so forth—resulting in picturesque composite designs. Tudor houses were relatively rare from the 1890s until about 1920. But for the next two decades they rivaled Colonial Revival houses as the dominant style in American housing design.

The perfection, about 1920, of techniques for adding a thin, single-layer "veneer" of brick or stone to the outside of inexpensive, wood-framed structures made mass production of Tudor houses possible. Previously, houses of brick or stone had required thick, multilayered supporting walls of solid masonry, which were far more expensive to

STAN HYWET HALL

230

construct. The result of these technological advances was that one-story, masonry-veneered Tudor "cottages" replaced Craftsman-style wooden "bungalows" (see Gamble House, pages 308–21) as the style of choice in most suburban developments of the 1920s.

Larger and more elaborate Tudor houses, with their suggestion of the elegant country life of the English aristocracy, were favored by wealthy Americans for country and suburban estates from the 1890s to the 1930s. Few of these were executed with more loving attention to detail than Stan Hywet Hall, which is also one of the rare examples that has been preserved intact for public enjoyment.

IDENTIFYING FEATURES

1 FAÇADE DOMINATED BY ONE OR MORE PROMINENT CROSS GABLES, SOMETIMES WITH HALF–TIMBERING

2 MASSIVE CHIMNEYS, COMMONLY CROWNED BY DECORATIVE CHIMNEY POTS

3 TALL, NARROW WINDOWS, COMMONLY IN MULTIPLE GROUPS AND WITH MULTIPANE GLAZING

4 STEEPLY PITCHED ROOF, USUALLY SIDE–GABLED

5 ENTRY HAS ROUND ARCH OR FLATTENED, POINTED (TUDOR) ARCH

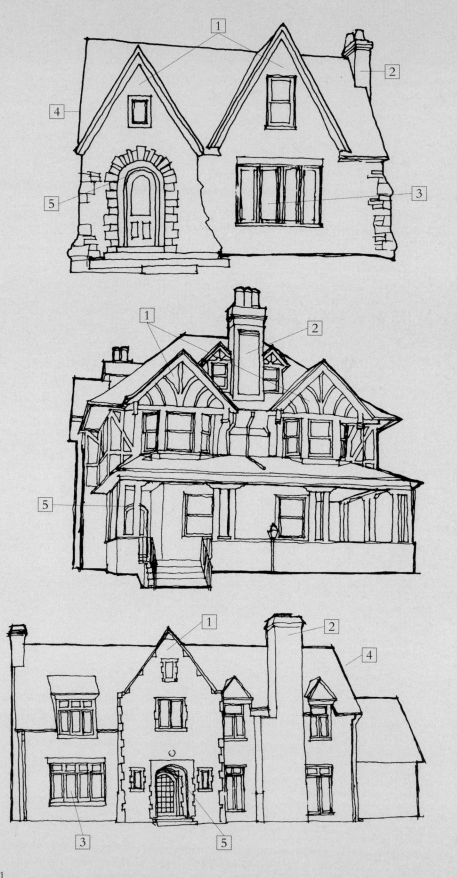

18
Biltmore

Châteauesque Style

Biltmore can only be described in superlatives. It is the largest private house ever constructed in the United States and was originally surrounded by one of the largest tracts of privately owned land in the eastern states—a 125,000-acre domain. To make one circuit around its forty-six-mile perimeter took a week on horseback. This monumental estate was the crowning achievement in the long careers of two of the nineteenth century's most distinguished designers—architect Richard Morris Hunt (1827–1895), who designed the house, and landscape architect Frederick Law Olmsted (1822–1903), who planned a multitude of farsighted uses for the land. Miraculously, the house and twelve square miles of land have survived to this day in almost exactly the same form as they were when planned and executed a century ago by Hunt, Olmsted, and their equally remarkable client—a shy and scholarly twenty-six-year-old bachelor who had recently inherited $10 million, much of which he spent on the creation of Biltmore.

George Washington Vanderbilt (1862–1914) was the youngest of the eight children of William Henry Vanderbilt (1821–1885), who was, in turn, the eldest son and principal heir of Cornelius Vanderbilt (1794–1877), the founder of the family fortune. Born to Dutch parents on a humble Staten Island farm, George's grandfather, who came to be called Commodore Vanderbilt, had by the age of forty used his brash aggressiveness and limitless energy to parlay a single small sailing vessel into a vast steamboat empire. He then shrewdly converted his shipping interests into controlling ownership of several small railroad lines that were beginning to link New York City with the steamboat traffic on the Great Lakes. The Commodore ultimately consolidated these holdings into the New York Central Railroad system, a vital transportation monopoly that was the cornerstone of the Vanderbilt family's wealth for four generations.

Not wishing to disperse his hard-won railroad empire, at his death the Commodore left the bulk of his $100 million estate to his eldest son, William Henry. A mild-mannered and unassuming man who was always considerate and fair to others, William was

Richard Morris Hunt (standing, center), George Vanderbilt (standing, right), and Frederick Law Olmsted (sitting, left) at Biltmore during its construction.

the virtual antithesis of his blustery, belligerent, and devious father. William did, however, inherit the Commodore's financial acumen. By the time he died, eight years after his father, he had increased his inheritance to about $200 million, a truly staggering sum in those days of no income taxes and modest inflation rates.

William's will was more generous toward his younger children than the Commodore's had been. Each of his four sons and four daughters received $10 million—five outright and five to be held in trust for them. Most of his remaining estate, valued at about $110 million, was then divided between his two eldest sons, Cornelius II and William K., who jointly managed the family railroad holdings.

Both the Commodore and his son William had lived quite modestly, given their large fortunes, although William did indulge a taste for art by assembling a collection of European paintings. After William died, however, his eight children, whose combined wealth then exceeded that of most of the world's kings and princes, quickly abandoned the unpretentious lifestyle of their forebears. For the next decade they went on a no-holds-barred spending spree, acquiring palatial town houses, grand country estates, ornate seaside villas, and sumptuous ocean-going yachts. By the end of their generation they had consumed most of their father's enormous legacy. Of all the third-generation Vanderbilt indulgences, Biltmore was the grandest, most visionary, and in many ways least typical.

Biltmore's creator, the introspective and bookish George Vanderbilt, was still unmarried and living at home when his father died. The large library he had assembled was filled with books in eight languages, all of which he could read, and he was a serious student of art, architecture, and the classics. He has aptly been called "the first Vanderbilt intellectual."

While his older brothers and sisters were busy building lavish town and country houses as settings for high-society entertaining, George developed a vision of something less frivolous and more lasting, if no less grand. As a student of art and architecture he made frequent trips to Europe, where he visited and came to admire the aristocratic country estates of England and France. Although centered around imposing manor houses, these estates were also vast agricultural enterprises that gave productive employment to entire villages of farmers and craftsmen. For his American version of these European baronies George Vanderbilt chose a remote and unlikely setting.

Sometime in the mid-1880s he and his mother visited the small but fashionable health resort of Asheville, North Carolina, which is situated in the clear and stimulating air of the Appalachian Mountains. On country walks and rides he became smitten with the region's beauty and soon purchased the first piece of land of what was to become Biltmore—the name derives from Bildt, the region of Holland from which the family took its name, and *more,* an ancient English word for rolling uplands. By 1888 George had assembled two thousand acres and hired Hunt and Olmsted, both of whom he knew and liked from their work on previous family projects. Together the three of them began to put some very substantial flesh onto the bare bones of George's dream.

PAGE 232 *Front façade of Biltmore.*

During the 1850s Richard Morris Hunt became the first American to complete architectural studies at France's world-renowned Ecole des Beaux Arts. In 1888 he was at the peak of a long and distinguished career (see Château-sur-Mer, pages 126–37). Among his most admired buildings was a magnificent Fifth Avenue town house that he had designed several years earlier for one of George's older brothers, William K. Vanderbilt. Alva, William K.'s socially ambitious wife, was particularly anxious for this new house to be a spectacular showplace. Hunt's Parisian education had made him partial to French designs and, with Alva's encouragement, he decided to model the town house after the early Renaissance châteaux of the Loire Valley. Built of white limestone, as are many of the French originals, Hunt's Château for Fifth Avenue was an instant landmark in a city then dominated by unspectacular buildings of drab brownstone.

Hunt's Châteauesque style was soon all the rage among wealthy Americans throughout the country. But the demand for these high-style dwellings had to be met by other architects because Hunt himself created only six more houses in the style. Biltmore is not only the largest of these but also the finest in terms of the mastery with which the architect incorporated French motifs into an original creation that is suited both to its site and to George's personal vision of aristocratic country life.

Although the house is enormous (it contains 255 rooms, many of which were originally servants' quarters and service areas), the focus of the interior is on four large first-floor rooms, each of which reflects a different aspect of George Vanderbilt's wide-ranging

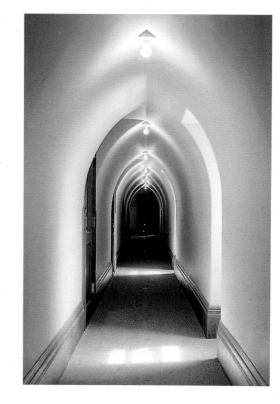

An upstairs servants' hallway has a pointed arched ceiling. The green wall color indicated that it was a service area of the house.

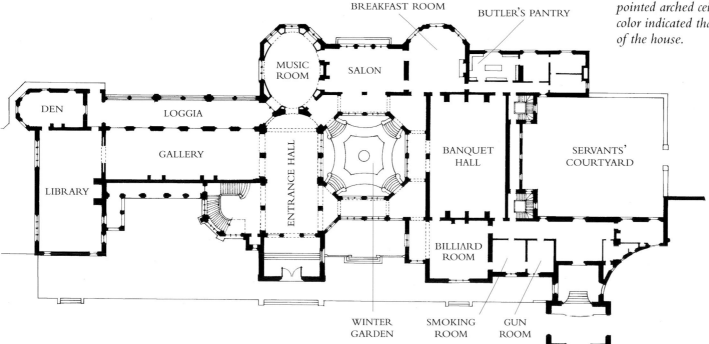

BREAKFAST ROOM

BUTLER'S PANTRY

MUSIC ROOM

SALON

DEN

LOGGIA

GALLERY

ENTRANCE HALL

BANQUET HALL

SERVANTS' COURTYARD

LIBRARY

BILLIARD ROOM

WINTER GARDEN

SMOKING ROOM

GUN ROOM

ABOVE *A three-story chandelier lights the towering four-story stair hall.*

RIGHT *The Winter Garden brought a bit of Biltmore's vast outdoor gardens inside. It is furnished with the original bamboo furniture purchased in Paris. The center fountain, depicting a boy with a goose, was sculpted by Karl Bitter, who immigrated to the United States from Vienna in 1889.*

interests. Most prominent is the greenhouselike Winter Garden that dominates and unifies the first-floor spaces and brings indoors a small sample of the estate's vast gardens, parks, and forests. The ornate library, Vanderbilt's favorite room, is more personal. It houses about 10,000 leather-bound volumes, featuring art, architecture, and gardening titles. These were selected from among George's personal collection of 23,000 books—the remainder are scattered throughout the house.

Connecting the Winter Garden with the library is a long gallery designed to display some of the art objects that Vanderbilt assembled for Biltmore. In the tradition of early French châteaux, whose interior stone walls were often covered with large, decorative tapestries, the gallery features a superb set of sixteenth-century Brussels tapestries illustrating the Triumph of Virtue. Decorative painting on the gallery's beamed ceiling and limestone fireplaces is carefully designed to harmonize with the tapestries. Among the other important works of art in the gallery are portraits of George Vanderbilt and his mother by his close friend John Singer Sargent (1856–1925).

The fourth principal room, the banquet hall, was used for formal entertaining and is the largest and most dramatic of all. Measuring 72 by 42 feet, it is crowned by an arched, 70-foot-high ceiling. At one end of the room is an enormous chimney, its three fireplace

The library (LEFT) contains more than ten thousand volumes. This magnificent room is dominated by an eighteenth-century ceiling painting by Giovanni Antonio Pelligrini (1675–1741); George Vanderbilt acquired it for Biltmore from the Pisani Palace in Venice. A handsome circular stair (RIGHT) leads to the walkway that provides access to the upper level of books.

openings topped by a massive frieze of carved limestone depicting the Return from the Chase. At the other end organ pipes stand on an elevated wooden gallery embellished with carvings of scenes from Wagner's *Tannhäuser.* As in the gallery, the two other walls are covered with antique Belgian tapestries, these depicting the mythological love triangle between Venus, Mars, and Vulcan.

A series of smaller public rooms, some of unusual shape, surround the arcaded Winter Garden. These include the entrance hall, a billiard room, a semi-octagonal breakfast room used for family dining, a salon with magnificent views of the mountains to the west, and an oval music room, which curiously remained unfinished and was kept closed during Vanderbilt's lifetime. It was finally decorated in 1976.

In an unusual departure from the prevailing practice of that period, much of Biltmore's original furniture and interior decoration was selected and planned by client and architect without the intervention of professional interior designers. George Vanderbilt had already accumulated a substantial collection of art and antiques before he conceived

LEFT *A seventeenth-century Spanish tester bed and many classical objects, including plaster copies of the Parthenon frieze, decorate Mr. Vanderbilt's bedroom.*

BELOW *The ninetenth-century English dressing table in Mrs. Vanderbilt's bedroom is decorated with a swag mirror, silver filigree toilet bottles, and family pictures.*

Biltmore. Then, from 1888 until the house was finished in 1895, he made several trips to Europe to gather still more treasures for his new manor house. On some of these trips he was accompanied by Hunt, who gave him authoritative advice on French decorative art. As a result, Biltmore's interiors reflect a rare and close collaboration between a superb designer and a discriminating client/collector.

Unlike its exterior design, which is a masterful compilation of details borrowed from a single architectural style, Biltmore's interiors follow the turn-of-the-century practice of mixing styles and periods. Some of the larger rooms are designed in one historical style, but others, particularly the smaller family rooms, reflect an eclectic mixture of stylistic influences. In addition, authentic antique furniture and decorative objects are freely mixed with reproductions made by the finest European craftsmen of the day.

The gallery and banquet hall, with their châteaulike fireplaces and tapestry-covered walls, would look most at home in a Loire Valley original, while the library, with its handsome carved-walnut paneling, is of Italian Baroque inspiration. The smaller downstairs public rooms, as well as most of the principal upstairs bedrooms and sitting rooms, feature combinations of various Latin decorative motifs and furniture—French, Italian, Spanish,

OPPOSITE TOP *The house's original copper pots and pans still hang from a metal rack downstairs in the main kitchen. There are also a pastry kitchen, a rotisserie kitchen, and numerous pantries and storage rooms.*

OPPOSITE BOTTOM *Despite its cavernous size (72 feet long, 42 feet wide, and 70 feet high) the banquet hall has almost perfect acoustics. The room was planned to display five sixteenth-century Flemish tapestries.*

TOP *The two-lane bowling alley was installed in 1895 and is probably the oldest one designed for a private home still in existence.*

BOTTOM *The indoor swimming pool has seventeen dressing rooms located on separate men's and women's hallways.*

and Portuguese. Hunt was not overly fond of English design; nor, apparently, was Vanderbilt. Only in three of the third-floor guest bedrooms (the Sheraton, Chippendale, and Old English rooms) do English themes dominate.

Almost as fascinating as Biltmore's superb public and family living rooms are its numerous carefully planned service rooms, which look virtually the same today as they did when installed a century ago. Most of these are concentrated in the basement, including kitchens, pantries, laundries, and servants' living rooms, dining rooms, and bedrooms. The enormous basement also contains a bowling alley, gymnasium, and indoor swimming pool. Adjoining the main house on the north side is a French-style service courtyard surrounded by a large stable and carriage house complex, which still displays some of its original furnishings and fittings.

Biltmore's vast acreage not only provided an idyllic setting for Vanderbilt's grand house but also played a seminal role in the founding of the American conservation movement. Much of the credit for this goes to landscape architect Frederick Law Olmsted, who, when first inspecting the site in 1888, remarked to his client that in Europe such land "would be made a forest; partly, if it belonged to a gentleman of large means, as a hunting preserve for game, mainly with a view to crops of timber. That would be a suitable and dignified business for you to engage in . . . and it would be of great value to the country to have a thoroughly well organized and systematically conducted attempt in forestry made on a large scale."

Biltmore was Olmsted's last project and his acknowledged favorite. The renowned planner of New York's Central Park, the grounds of the Capitol in Washington, D.C., the grounds of the World's Columbian Exposition in Chicago, and countless other important public spaces spent long periods in residence on the estate while it was being planned and constructed, supervising a small army of foremen and laborers as they transformed a ragged patchwork of cutover woodlands and worn-out subsistence farms into one of the grandest planned landscapes in the New World. Biltmore is the only example of Olmsted's large-scale works that has survived almost exactly as originally planned.

In many ways Hunt and Olmsted were unlikely collaborators. Hunt was partial to "formalistic" French designs, which featured large buildings surrounded by rigidly balanced and symmetrical gardens that made no attempt to look "natural." Olmsted, in contrast, was a dedicated proponent of the "naturalistic" approach to landscaping that had been favored in England since the eighteenth century. This type of design emphasized romantic simulations of natural landscapes.

Early in the planning of Biltmore the two designers reached an amiable compromise. Olmsted would design appropriate French-style formal gardens immediately around the house. Beyond these he would create transitional parks and gardens that graded into naturalistic pastures and woodlands in the distance. This plan can be seen as one goes along the entrance road Olmsted designed. It winds through three miles of picturesque streams and woodlands before merging into a vast formal courtyard with the château rising dramatically at its end to the west. Beyond the sheltered south side of this entry court is a

LEFT *In Italian gardens architectural elements tend to be more important than the plants themselves, and Biltmore's Italian garden is no exception. Its three formal pools are the dominant features.*

BELOW *A statue of Diana the Huntress stands atop a hill at the far end of Biltmore's entry garden.*

series of gardens—an Italian garden, shrub garden, walled garden, azalea garden, and arboretum—that decrease in formality the farther they are from the house. Only after entering the house and looking out its westward-facing (rear façade) windows does a visitor realize that it is sited on the edge of a high hill that affords a sweeping panorama of naturalistic parks, forests, and mountains. These forests were to become Biltmore's most important legacy to the nation.

In 1888 the concept of managing timberland for sustained, long-term yields, a centuries-old practice in lumber-scarce European countries, was virtually unknown in the United States, where there still were vast tracts of virgin forest. After clear-cutting a forest, it would be abandoned to natural second growth, a process that can take centuries. At Olmsted's urging, Vanderbilt turned Biltmore into the nation's first large-scale experiment in European-style forestry.

To manage his forests Vanderbilt hired Gifford Pinchot (1865–1946), a young Yale graduate whose enthusiasm for forestry had led him to postgraduate studies in Europe; he was one of the first Americans to receive such training. After overseeing Biltmore's forestry efforts for three years, Pinchot, who was independently wealthy and a close friend of president-to-be Theodore Roosevelt, went on to found both the U.S. Forest Service and the important Graduate School of Forestry at Yale. Pinchot was replaced at Biltmore by Carl A. Schenck (1868–1955), a superbly trained, idealistic young German forester whose Biltmore School of Forestry, operated from 1898 to 1913, became a principal training ground for the first generation of American foresters and conservationists.

Three years after Biltmore was completed George Vanderbilt married Edith Stuyvesant Dresser (d. 1958), a descendant of Peter Stuyvesant, the last Dutch governor of

ABOVE *A classical statue adorns the south terrace, which is set beside the house and affords a spectacular view of the mountains beyond.*

RIGHT *Landscape architect Frederick Law Olmsted created romantic naturalistic grounds for all but the areas nearest the house.*

LEFT *Two small butterfly gardens flank the path to the conservatory.*

RIGHT *One of the many carved-stone creatures that ornament Biltmore.*

New York. Edith also loved Biltmore, and although they maintained several other residences, the couple spent much time in the house. Here their only child, named Cornelia in honor of her great-grandfather, was born in 1900.

George died suddenly in 1914 following a seemingly routine appendectomy. Biltmore was left to Edith, who sold a hundred thousand acres of the estate's western woodlands to the federal government. This land, the first large private tract acquired as part of the nation's public forest system, became the nucleus of the Pisgah National Forest. By 1930, with the Great Depression under way, the enormous expense of maintaining Biltmore for private use had become prohibitive. Edith and Cornelia took the farsighted step of opening part of the house to the public. Today the estate is owned by Cornelia's son, William A. V. Cecil (b. 1928), who has worked tirelessly to restore Biltmore and preserve it as a public monument to the visionary dream of his grandfather George Vanderbilt.

Châteauesque Style
(1880–1910)

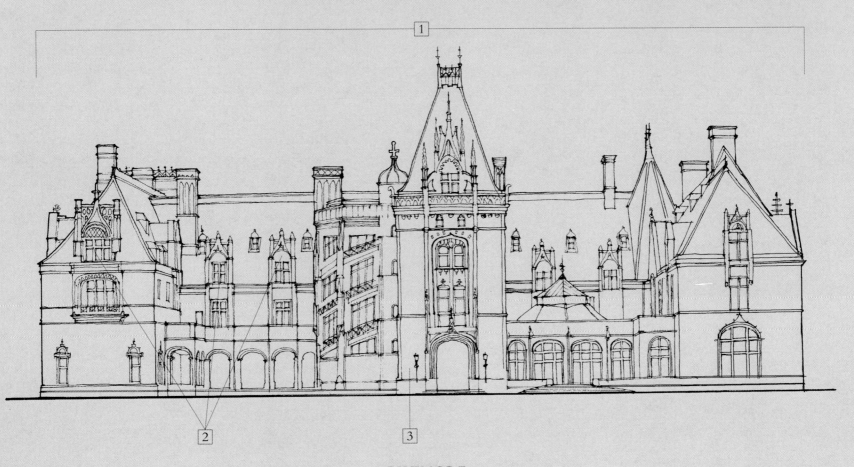

BILTMORE

IDENTIFYING FEATURES

1   STEEPLY PITCHED ROOF (USUALLY HIPPED) WITH MANY
VERTICAL ELEMENTS (SPIRES, PINNACLES, TURRETS,
GABLES, SHAPED CHIMNEYS)

2   MULTIPLE DORMERS, USUALLY WALL DORMERS
EXTENDING THROUGH THE CORNICE LINE

3   MASONRY WALLS, USUALLY OF STONE

The Châteauesque style, like the contemporary Richardsonian Romanesque, was conceived and popularized by one gifted architect—in this case Richard Morris Hunt, whose Biltmore is the masterpiece of the style. In fairness to Hunt, who never sought the public limelight as did his flamboyant rival H. H. Richardson (see Glessner House, pages 178–89), the Châteauesque style could well have been called Huntian French Renaissance, because, like Richardson, Hunt freely adapted historical precedents into a uniquely personal architectural fashion.

It took the rare combination of Hunt's comprehensive training at the Ecole des Beaux Arts, Alva Vanderbilt's equally francophile tastes, and her husband's bottomless pockets to create the first American example of the style, the now-demolished Château for Fifth Avenue that delighted both viewers and critics upon its completion in 1883. Soon wealthy clients elsewhere wanted similar houses and the Hunt/Vanderbilt original was imitated throughout the country.

For their Châteauesque designs architects had their choice of a vast array of details from grand French châteaux built over several centuries. Most American versions tended to focus on the steeply pitched hipped roofs and their rooftop detailing. Multiple dormers are common, as are other vertical elements such as spires, pinnacles crowned with finials, small turrets, shaped chimneys, and cresting along roof ridges or flat roof decks.

Appropriate only for high-style and expensive solid masonry buildings, the Châteauesque style is understandably uncommon. Most examples are also much smaller and less elaborately detailed than either Hunt's Fifth Avenue original or the still more splendid Biltmore, his last and grandest project, designed for Alva Vanderbilt's younger brother-in-law.

19
Vanderbilt House

HYDE PARK, NEW YORK

Beaux Arts Style

Two of the houses featured in this book were built by grandsons of the famous shipping and railroad magnate Cornelius, or "Commodore," Vanderbilt (1794–1877). Grandson George Vanderbilt, the youngest child of the Commodore's son William Henry, was an artistic and bookish man who spend most of his fortune on Biltmore, the enormous European-style country barony in rural North Carolina (see pages 232–45). His brother Frederick, builder of Vanderbilt House, a smaller but no less lavish estate on the Hudson River, had very different tastes and interests.

Frederick William Vanderbilt (1856–1938) earned a degree from Yale and had the distinction of being the first Vanderbilt to finish college. Despite his longer formal education, Frederick lacked his brother George's wide-ranging curiosity and artistic temperament; his interests lay in more practical matters. A private and unassuming man who shunned publicity, he quietly devoted his life to managing his inheritance, which, like that of his siblings, consisted primarily of stock in the New York Central and other Vanderbilt-controlled railroads. Fred apparently also inherited much of his father's and grandfather's financial genius, for when he died at age eighty-two, he had increased his wealth almost tenfold, to about $80 million.

Aside from his profitable dedication to his business interests, Fred appears to have had only two passions—yachting and horticulture. The splendid country house that he began building in 1896 on a large tract of land overlooking the Hudson River was to serve his second passion for more than forty years.

Like Biltmore, Fred's country house was not meant to be a temporary summer home occupied only a few weeks each year. For that purpose he and his wife, Louise Anthony Vanderbilt (1844–1926), owned or rented residences in Newport, Bar Harbor, Palm Beach, the Adirondacks, and elsewhere. They purchased the six-hundred-acre Hudson Valley tract, a prime part of the eighteenth-century Hyde Park Patent, from which the adjacent village took its name, as the site of a seasonal country house. Here they lived

William Rutherford Mead, Charles Follen McKim, and Stanford White, c. 1905.

for much of the fall and late spring seasons, as well as on weekends during the winter, when their principal residence was their New York town house.

Vanderbilt's Hyde Park site had previously been owned by a series of wealthy Dutchess County squires who had developed it into one of the most beautiful and renowned of the many large Hudson Valley estates (see also Lyndhurst, pages 98–111). A large Greek Revival house, the successor to an earlier dwelling, had been built overlooking the river in 1847, and the Vanderbilts first planned to remodel and expand this stately structure for their own use.

To design this remodeling Vanderbilt turned to Charles F. McKim (1847–1909), the principal partner in what was then the world's largest and most renowned architectural firm, McKim, Mead and White, headquartered in Manhattan (see also Naumkeag, pages 166–77). Fred may have had second thoughts about his choice of architect when McKim's engineers concluded that the foundation and principal supporting timbers of the 1847 house had deteriorated beyond repair. The only solution was to demolish the old house and build a new one. But the magnificent site and McKim's promise to design a classical portico overlooking the river, similar to that of the earlier house, which Fred and Louise greatly admired, finally won out. McKim didn't fail his client; the superb dwelling he produced is a refined distillation of the French-inspired Beaux Arts fashion that had made McKim, Mead and White the nation's premiere designers of important public buildings.

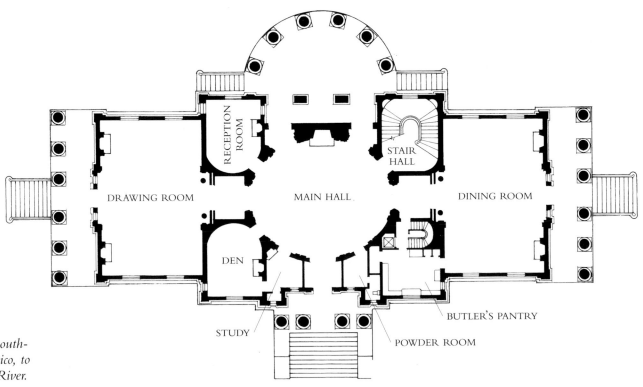

PAGE 246 *Vanderbilt House's south-facing side façade. The rear portico, to the left, overlooks the Hudson River.*

Fred and his wife had no children, and although they enjoyed entertaining family and friends, they did not go in for the frequent balls and week-long house parties that several of Fred's siblings relished. As a result, the house, even though designed for continuous occupancy, has relatively few rooms—only 54 compared, for example, to Biltmore's 255! Fred spared no expense, however, in making his country home a quietly elegant, even sumptuous, dwelling.

The first floor is dominated by three enormous rooms: an oval-shaped main hall in the center, flanked by a drawing room on one side and a dining room on the other. Smaller spaces around the oval hall include a reception room, den (used both as a library and informal family living room), study, and stair hall. On the second floor are two large adjacent master bedroom suites and four spacious guest bedrooms. There are additional guest bedrooms and servants' quarters on the third floor, while the kitchen, laundry, and numerous other service and storage rooms occupy the large basement.

Fred and Louise left most of the interior decoration up to three professional designers, who emphasized the prevailing penchant for historically based French interiors. Stanford White (see Naumkeag, pages 166–77) was responsible for the marble-dominated main hall and adjacent stair hall, as well as for the drawing room and dining room. Georges A. Glaenzer designed other main-floor rooms as well as Fred's second-floor bedroom; and the newly fashionable young designer Ogden Codman (see Château-sur-Mer, page 131) was entrusted with Louise's elaborate suite.

Judging from the styles of their bedrooms, Fred and Louise had widely divergent tastes in interior design, and these differences are reflected throughout the house. Like Fred's bedroom, most of the first-floor rooms are paneled in dark European walnut and have heavy, dark, French- or Italian-based furnishings. All of these rooms are infused with a powerful, masculine spirit. In contrast, Codman decorated Louise's bedroom in the delicately ornate style of Louis XV. On the first floor this French fashion appears only in the small reception room, which must have been Louise's downstairs favorite. Codman was noted for such feminine-spirited French designs.

The practice of using original antique furniture was not de rigueur in the 1890s, and many of the finest pieces in the mansion are reproductions from Paul Sormani's famous shop in Paris. These are case pieces of remarkable workmanship, indistinguishable from real antiques except for their newness. They may be seen in the drawing room and the reception room on the first floor and in Louise's bedroom and boudoir on the second. But many of the house's decorative details—mantels, carpets, wall hangings, lamps, porcelains, and so on—*are* superb antiques that add much character to the otherwise uniformly "new" interiors. Most of these objects were assembled by Stanford White. In 1897 Fred sent White to Europe on a monthlong buying trip with a budget of more than $150,000, an enormous sum in those days. White's impeccable taste is evident in the principal first-floor rooms, perhaps most conspicuously in the many antique rugs, the old Belgian and French tapestries, and the fine pieces of Renaissance furniture, which were his hallmark.

Fred's primary reason for purchasing the Hyde Park estate was to indulge his love

Detail of the battle scene that decorates the antique marble overmantel in Frederick Vanderbilt's bedroom.

ABOVE *This Carrara marble bust in the main hall represents Summer; a mate, Winter, faces it across the room. The pair were purchased from a catalog and are part of an original set of four.*

TOP RIGHT *The elliptical-shaped, formally balanced main hall, decorated by Stanford White, has cornice and pilasters of a soft green and cream Italian marble. A Medici tapestry hangs above the fireplace, which is flanked by high-backed Renaissance throne chairs and a pair of marble busts. A large Louis XIV table and clock occupy the middle of the room, dividing the hall into a seating area near the fireplace and a circulation area in front.*

BOTTOM RIGHT *The massive hall mantelpiece, supported by two female terms, originally graced a Renaissance palace.*

LEFT *A seventeenth-century coffered ceiling surmounts the elegant dining room. The large, three-hundred-year-old Ispahan rug and the Renaissance mantel (one of a pair) are typical of the purchases Stanford White made during his European buying trip.*

RIGHT *This corner of the living room boasts one of a pair of Italian marble fireplaces topped by carved-walnut paneling and a lamp with an antique Chinese vase as a base, French ormolu mounts, and an opaline glass shade.*

George A. Glaenzer of New York City decorated the library, which was used by the Vanderbilts as a family living room. The vaulted portion of the ceiling is of plaster grained to look like wood.

RIGHT *Designed by Glaenzer, the intricately carved bed, and all the other woodwork in Frederick Vanderbilt's bedroom, is of Circassian walnut. Seventeenth-century Flemish tapestries cover the walls and doors.*

*Ogden Codman designed Louise Vanderbilt's bedroom (*BELOW RIGHT*) to resemble an eighteenth-century French noblewoman's, complete with a rail outside of which the woman's courtiers would have gathered each morning. Louise's dressing table (*BELOW LEFT*), like the other case furniture in the room, is an outstanding reproduction from the Paris shop of Paul Sormani.*

The flower beds of the Italian gardens, as they look just after planting.

of gardening and farming, and he spared no expense to make it an agricultural and horticultural showplace. His loving attention to the estate may have stemmed in part from his appreciation of the important historical role it had played in establishing landscape gardening as a profession in this country. First developed in the 1790s, between 1828 and 1835 it became a Hudson Valley showplace. During this period it was owned by Dr. David Hosack (1769–1835), who was not only a prominent physician but also a professional botanist and founder of the Elgin Botanical Gardens in New York City, the first of its kind in the country.

To execute his grand plan for the Hyde Park property, Hosack enlisted the help of an equally gifted collaborator, a recent Belgian émigré named Andrew Parmentier (died c. 1830). Parmentier came from a family of distinguished nurserymen and garden designers who had long dominated those professions in his native country; he has been called America's first professional landscape gardener. Parmentier was particularly interested in the newly fashionable English, or naturalistic, approach to landscape design, which was then replacing the rigidly formal and symmetrical gardens that had been the European fashion for several centuries.

In only a few short years Hosack and Parmentier transformed Hyde Park into an innovative showplace that attracted a steady stream of local and international visitors. Andrew Jackson Downing noted that it was "justly celebrated as one of the finest specimens of the modern style of landscape gardening in America."

After Hosack's death the estate passed through several owners, and the landscaping suffered from neglect. Although no plan of Parmentier's original design survives, it is probable that its basic framework of plantings and roadways remained intact and that Fred respected the original concept and revitalized it. Many of the huge specimen trees that delight the eye today—beeches, oaks, elms, maples, and pines, as well as a fine specimen gingko—almost certainly date back more than a hundred and fifty years.

ABOVE *The east-facing entry façade.*

RIGHT *Pergolas and a classical-style pavilion are reflected in a pool in the Italian gardens.*

In sharp contrast to the estate's generally naturalistic and parklike grounds are the formal Italian gardens that descend a hillside to the south, out of view of the main house. These gardens were originally planted by Walter Langdon, who owned the property before the Vanderbilts purchased it. In 1902 Fred engaged landscape architect James L. Greenleaf to revise and enlarge them. The expanded gardens included large greenhouses (now demolished), as well as rose gardens, a cherry walk, and a pool garden, all of which have recently been restored.

Vanderbilt's Hyde Park acreage had long been bisected by the old New York-to-Albany Post Road, a principal north-south highway running parallel to the Hudson. The house is located on the two-hundred-acre tract between road and river. Like the previous owners of the property, Fred restricted this area to scenic parks and gardens with scattered outbuildings whose functions related directly to the main house. All of his agricultural enterprises were concentrated on the five hundred acres across the road. Here he raised prize-winning herds of Jersey dairy cattle, which supplied the estate with milk and butter, and Belgian draft horses for plowing and hauling in those pre-tractor days. The animals were housed in up-to-the-minute barns and stables and were fed on farm-grown hay, grain crops, and pasturage. Orchards, truck gardens, chicken houses, and hog pens also supplied food to the estate and its small army of workers, as well as to the Vanderbilt's Manhattan town house, which received regular shipments on the family's New York Central Railroad, whose main line conveniently borders the estate. This agricultural tract is no longer a part of the grounds, but all of the parks and gardens west of the highway survive intact, including such Vanderbilt-era outbuildings as a guest pavilion (now the Information Center), coach house and stable, powerhouse, and gatehouses. The only structures that remain from pre-Vanderbilt times are an Italianate gardener's cottage and adjacent tool house, built in 1875.

Louise died in 1926, and the seventy-year-old Fred, who had always enjoyed the quiet life of a country gentleman, spent his remaining years at the estate, where he occupied a small third-floor bedroom rather than the palatial second-floor suite that he had shared with his wife. To the great consternation of his many Vanderbilt relatives, Fred left about half of his vast estate to various charities and institutions, primarily Yale, his alma mater, and Vanderbilt University, founded by his grandfather. These bequests were the last in a long series of unpublicized philanthropic donations, many of them anonymous, that he and Louise had made over the years. He left the remaining half of the estate, including not only millions of dollars in cash and securities but also all of his valuable real estate and personal property, to Louise's niece, Mrs. Margaret Van Alen, who had long been a favorite of the couple. Already wealthy in her own right, Mrs. Van Alen was soon persuaded by her Hyde Park neighbor, President Franklin D. Roosevelt, to donate the house and grounds to the National Park Service as a house-museum and memorial to Fred, Louise, and the genteel lifestyle they had cherished.

Frederick William Vanderbilt, c. 1915.

Louise Vanderbilt, c. 1890.

Beaux Arts Style

(1885–1930)

The term *Beaux Arts,* French for "fine arts," derives from Paris's Ecole des Beaux Arts, which was the world's most prestigious center for education in the arts and architecture throughout much of the nineteenth century. Established in 1671, the Ecole advocated many architectural fashions over the years. In American architecture, however, the term usually refers to a single French-based style that peaked around the turn of the twentieth century. Rooted in the classicism of ancient Greece and Rome as well as in the modified classicism of the Italian Renaissance, this style embraced the principle of symmetrically balanced columns and arches but embellished it with sumptuous new patterns that emphasized paired columns and façades lavishly decorated with delicate floral swags, garlands, friezes, and panels.

In this country several Ecole-trained architects, including the masterful Richard Morris Hunt (see the Mark Twain House, page 150; Château-sur-Mer, pages 126–37; and Biltmore, pages 232–45), used Beaux Arts models in designing the principal buildings of the enormous World's Columbian Exposition in Chicago in 1893. The central attraction of the exposition was the great White City, a series of large, colonnaded buildings surrounding a huge reflecting basin; as a whole this monumental ensemble called up visions of ancient Greece and Rome. Soon Beaux Arts designs became the models for hundreds of large public buildings—courthouses, libraries, banks, and the like—scattered throughout the country. But only the wealthy could afford to commission private homes in this style because its highly decorated masonry façades were so expensive. Of the many fashionable architects who produced Beaux Arts buildings from about 1890 through the 1920s perhaps the most renowned was the New York partnership of McKim, Mead and White, which by 1890 had become the world's largest architectural firm. The splendid house that McKim designed for Frederick Vanderbilt is among the finest domestic examples of the style.

IDENTIFYING FEATURES

1. MASONRY WALLS (USUALLY OF LIGHT-COLORED STONE)

2. DECORATIVE GARLANDS, FLORAL PATTERNS, OR SHIELDS

3. FAÇADE WITH CLASSICAL PILASTERS OR COLUMNS, USUALLY PAIRED AND WITH IONIC OR CORINTHIAN CAPITALS

4. FAÇADES USUALLY HAVE SYMMETRICALLY BALANCED WINDOWS AND CENTERED DOOR

5. FIRST STORY OFTEN RUSTICATED

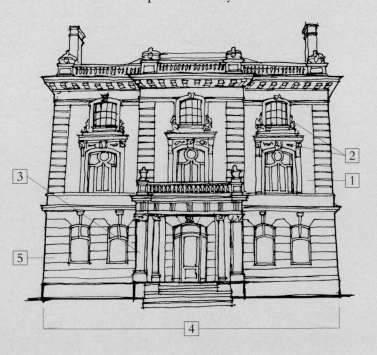

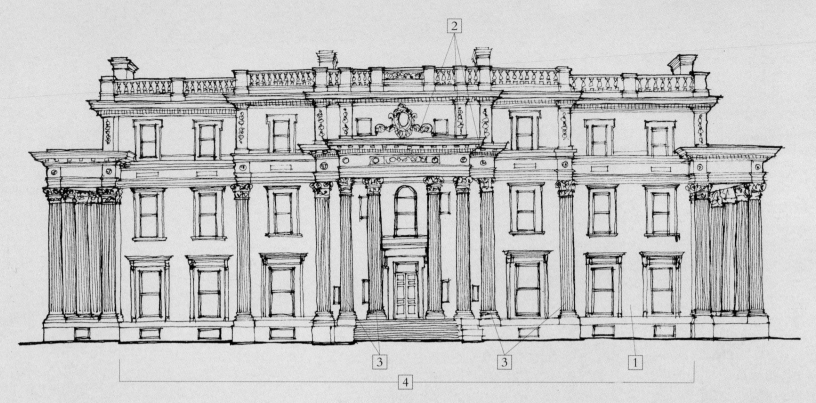

VANDERBILT HOUSE

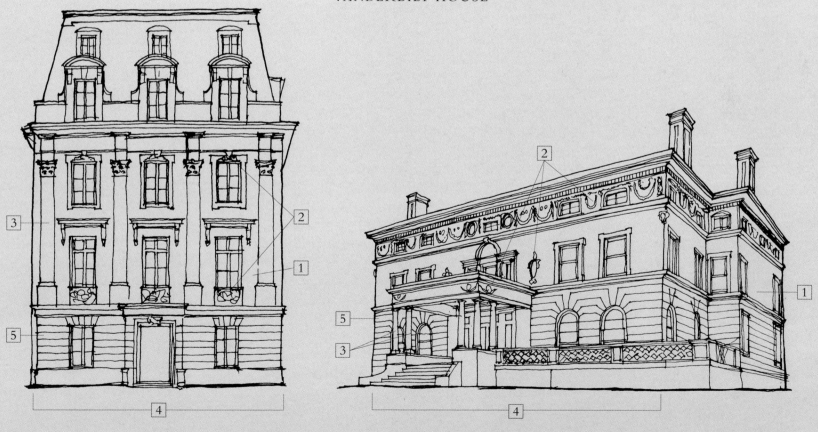

A casement window looks out over Falaise's high-pitched tile roof, dormers, and tower toward Long Island Sound.

20
Falaise

French Eclectic Style

From about 1900 to 1930 northwestern Long Island was a favored site among wealthy New Yorkers for large country houses. Most of these "Gold Coast" estates, with their countless acres of gardens, woodlands, golf courses, and hunting preserves, have since been transformed into suburban housing developments. And the grand country houses themselves, prohibitively expensive to maintain today, have been either demolished or converted into schools or other institutions. Among the rare survivors are Westbury House (see pages 192–205) toward the center of the island near Old Westbury, and Sands Point, a vast bluff-top estate overlooking Long Island Sound about eight miles northwest of Old Westbury. For half a century this complex of three large residences on 216 acres of lawns and woodlands was the country seat of one branch of New York's fabled Guggenheim family.

The founder of the family fortune was Meyer Guggenheim (1828–1905), who at age twenty emigrated to Philadelphia from his native Switzerland. Over the next twenty-five years he not only fathered a family of eleven children but also established a prosperous mercantile business that specialized in the import of fine Swiss lace and embroidery. The immense Guggenheim fortune, however, was not destined to be based on so delicate and fragile a material as lace but on mining and refining the basic raw materials of modern industry.

This unlikely turn of events began in 1881, shortly after Meyer's four oldest sons joined his thriving import business. Wanting to provide more challenges and opportunities for them and his three younger sons, then teenagers, Meyer started seeking other ways to put his substantial cash reserves to work. Among these was acting as a private banker to selected creditworthy borrowers with promising projects.

One prospective borrower was a Quaker friend, groceryman Charles Graham, whose hobby was speculating in western mining land. Graham had obtained an interest in two abandoned gold mines located near Leadville, the heart of a new silver-mining boom in the mountains of central Colorado. Graham somehow convinced the usually cautious

Falaise's roof and some wall surfaces are covered with heavy flat tiles. Those on the roof were applied with thick dabs of cement. Ridges are finished with rounded tiles.

Guggenheim to join this long-shot gamble by becoming a one-third partner and providing the $5,000 needed to clean out and reopen the old mines. As so often happens in such ventures, the costs escalated and an increasingly skeptical Meyer had to supply several times his initial investment before the first test loads of ore were mined. By the greatest of good fortune, not only did the ore turn out to be spectacularly rich in silver but, as later mining was to prove, it also indicated that an unexpected bonanza of gold lay beneath it.

Milton Lomask, a biographer of the Guggenheim family, succinctly summarized what happened next: "By 1888—the year in which the Guggenheims pulled stakes in Philadelphia, shifted their headquarters to No. 2 Wall Street in New York City and began liquidating their lace and embroidery business—Meyer had long since banked the first million of what was to become the largest fortune ever made from mining and its companion industries."

The development of this fortune was overseen by Meyer's seven sons, five of whom spent their entire working lives brilliantly managing their growing mining empire, which ultimately involved all phases of the industry—mining, smelting, refining, and marketing of copper, lead, silver, tin, and other industrial metals. The acknowledged leader of the brothers was Meyer's second son, Daniel Guggenheim (1856–1930). "Bold, dynamic, jovial, ebullient, full of ideas and restless energy" are the sort of terms biographers invariably apply to Mr. Dan, as he was called.

Like his father and uncles before him, Mr. Dan's son Harry F. Guggenheim (1890–1971), the builder of Falaise, spent his early years learning the family business from the ground up. After graduating from Cambridge University in 1913, he was sent first to Mexico and then to Chile, where rich copper deposits had recently been discovered. These duties were interrupted in 1917 by America's entry into World War I.

While still a student in England, Harry had been introduced to the infant field of aviation by a Cambridge friend. Wishing to join the war effort, he took flying lessons and then enlisted in the Navy for further training as a military pilot. When the war ended in 1918 he was a lieutenant commander and had served in both France and Italy. At the time Harry could scarcely have suspected that his personal love of flying would, within a decade, pave the way for our country's long dominance in the aeronautical and aerospace industries.

After the war Harry returned to Chile, where the family's Chile Copper Company soon proved to be the most profitable of the Guggenheims' many lucrative mining interests. In 1923 a rival company offered to buy a 53 percent controlling interest in Chile Copper for $70 million in cash, then an unprecedented sum with a buying power equal to about $600 million today. This offer precipitated one of the rare disagreements among members of the close-knit Guggenheim family. Mr. Dan, now the family patriarch, was sixty-seven and plagued by painful stomach ulcers. He and his aging brothers wanted to accept this cash bonanza, whereas Harry and his cousin Edmond, the only third-generation sons active in the business, argued heatedly for maintaining control of Chile Copper as the crown jewel of the family empire. Not surprisingly, Harry and

Edmond were overruled. Shortly afterward they resigned from active participation in the family business to pursue other activities with their already substantial fortunes. For Harry, one of these was the building of Falaise.

By coincidence, the year of the Chile Copper sale was also the year that Harry married his second wife, the artistic, highly cultured Carol Martin, daughter of a former secretary of the Navy. As a wedding present Mr. Dan gave the couple a prime ninety acres of the two-hundred-plus-acre Sands Point estate, which he had purchased six years earlier when his health began to fail. Months of frantic activity followed as the newlyweds planned their dream house, to be built on a high bluff overlooking Long Island Sound.

Harry must have had fond memories of the picturesque French dwellings he had seen during World War I because the couple instructed their architect, Frederick J. Sterner, to create a Norman-style country manor with a large, enclosed entry court similar to those of French farmhouses. Evidently Sterner, an Englishman by birth, felt a bit uncomfortable tackling a complex French design entirely on his own; as a result, the partners in the young firm of Polhemus & Coffin, specialists in French-style American dwellings, were employed as associate architects. Together they created a masterpiece in the French Eclectic style, which flourished in this country in the 1920s and 1930s.

In recognition of its dramatic site, Harry and Carol named their new house Falaise, French for "cliff." Viewed from Long Island Sound its tall foundation walls, steep tile roofs, and deliberately irregular placement of windows and roof dormers give the appearance of a large and imposing medieval fortress. In striking contrast, the landward approach to the house is carefully designed to create a sense of small-scale intimacy and informality, no mean feat in a structure with more than thirty rooms.

The roadway to the house winds through acres of dense woodland before ending abruptly at a narrow gate that leads into the brick-walled entrance court. Even from the courtyard the house appears relatively small, much of it being skillfully obscured by the walled enclosure, which incorporates a large "wagon shed" (used for parking) and a picturesque French-style tower (used as a gatehouse).

This feeling of intimacy continues as one enters the house through an antique doorway into a tall entry hall, whose true size is masked by subtle changes of level and overhanging balconies. As in its medieval French prototypes, the rooms of the house are arranged in a row, creating a long, narrow plan that is for the most part only one room wide. The entry hall leads, at varying levels, to a cozy dining room on the right and a large, sunken living room on the left. These rooms, furnished with an understated mixture of antique and contemporary pieces, contribute to the house's general mood of informal intimacy.

From the living room a narrow hallway leads to a study, trophy room, and library. The kitchens and service areas lie beyond the dining room at the other end of the house. All of the principal first-floor rooms open onto spacious rear porches or terraces with spectacular views across Long Island Sound to the Connecticut shore. On the several upstairs levels there are numerous picturesque bedrooms of varying size and shape.

The Guggenheims spent almost two years gathering French and Spanish antique furnishings and architectural pieces for the house. Among them was this fourteenth-century column from northern France, one of a group positioned near the front door.

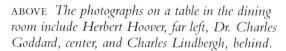

ABOVE *The photographs on a table in the dining room include Herbert Hoover, far left, Dr. Charles Goddard, center, and Charles Lindbergh, behind.*

TOP LEFT *The dining room's low ceiling lends it an intimate quality.*

CENTER LEFT *The trophy room displays the triumphs of Captain Guggenheim's racing stables.*

BOTTOM LEFT *The living room is sunk several steps below the entry hall level. An antique mantelpiece and tapestry provide the room's focal point.*

OPPOSITE TOP LEFT *Falaise's casement windows have medieval-style diamond-shaped panes, many of them inset with antique painted scenes. The interior sill is covered with tile.*

The intimate entry courtyard (OPPOSITE BOTTOM) is effective in disguising the true size of Falaise. A corner of the service courtyard (OPPOSITE TOP RIGHT) mimics a French wagon shed; in practice, it was used to shelter automobiles.

FRENCH ECLECTIC STYLE 263

Captain Guggenheim's library combines sections of old wood shelves with matching new sections. An eighteenth-century Italian walnut and fruitwood work table doubles as a desk.

Both Harry and Carol were Francophiles and spent most of the first two years of their marriage traveling around France collecting antique furnishings and architectural fragments for their new home. Their connoisseurship can still be admired today because the house remains much as it was in the mid-1920s.

Harry Guggenheim, a man of restless energy and many enthusiasms, was ill-suited to remain a semiretired country squire for long. Soon after Falaise was completed he embarked on a new career in public service, much of it centered around his interest in aviation. In 1926 he convinced his aging father that with intelligently applied "seed money," the then-struggling field of commercial aviation could play a dominant role in America's future. Mr. Dan contributed $2.5 million to establish the Daniel Guggenheim Fund for the Promotion of Aeronautics. Over the next decade Daniel's money and Harry's vision were to change the field forever. Among the many Guggenheim-inspired innovations were the first reliable instruments and techniques for all-weather flying; weather-reporting networks that became the nucleus of the United States Weather

Bureau; development of design principles that led to the famous Douglas DC-3, the first truly successful commercial airliner; and experiments on rockets and rocketry that paved the way for the Space Age. The seeds of many of these breakthroughs were planted at Falaise, where Harry and Carol entertained a steady stream of aviation pioneers, including Charles Lindbergh, who became a close friend. Shortly after his epoch-making solo flight across the Atlantic in 1927, Lindbergh wrote his best-selling autobiography, called simply *We,* while a guest at Falaise.

Too old to be a military pilot in World War II, Harry volunteered for naval duty in the South Pacific as an aerial gunner and later commanded Mercer Field in New Jersey. He left active duty as a captain, USNR. After the war he and his third wife, aviator and journalist Alicia Patterson, turned a small and struggling Long Island newspaper called *Newsday* into one of the nation's largest and most respected dailies. After the death of his Uncle Solomon in 1949, Harry painstakingly supervised the building of Frank Lloyd Wright's controversial design for the Guggenheim Museum, which was to house Solomon's priceless collection of modern art. Harry also found time to raise prize race horses, whose many trophies are displayed in two rooms at Falaise.

Harry died in 1971; under the terms of his will Falaise and its surrounding acreage were left to Nassau County as a public nature preserve and house-museum emphasizing the importance of Lindbergh and other aviation pioneers.

Captain Harry Guggenheim (center) with aviation pioneers Jimmy Doolittle (left) and Charles Lindbergh (right) at Falaise, 1960s.

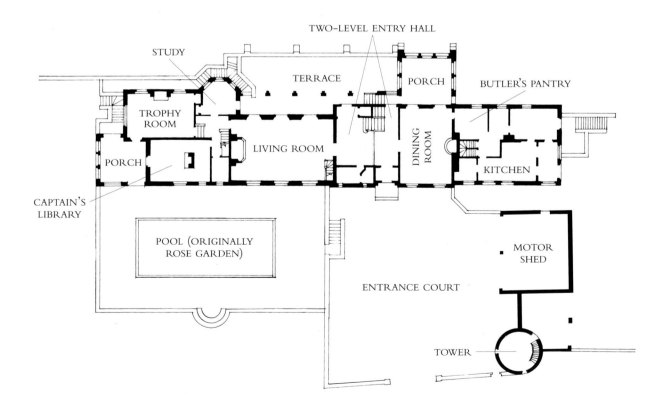

French Eclectic Style

(1915–1940)

French prototypes served as models for several American architectural styles, notably Second Empire, Beaux Arts, and Châteauesque (see Château-sur-Mer, pages 126–37; Vanderbilt House, pages 246–57; and Biltmore, pages 232–45). All of these were based on monumental French build-ings—elaborate Parisian palaces, grand public structures, or majestic Loire Valley châteaux. But after World War I, which exposed countless American soldiers to the more modest farm dwellings and manor houses of rural France, America began to develop a taste for these smaller-scaled

FALAISE

and more rustic French architectural traditions. Thus was born the French Eclectic style, which drew on a varied vocabulary of French country designs that were popularized in books of photographs published in the 1920s and 1930s.

Because its precedents encompass both formal symmetrical manor houses and informal asymmetrical farmhouses, the shapes of this style are unusually varied. Nevertheless, neighborhood examples based on both formal and informal models are united by a steep hipped roof, often with slightly flared eaves at the roofline.

Although never as common as the contemporaneous Tudor-style houses based on rural English dwellings (see Stan Hywet Hall, pages 218–31), French Eclectic houses can be found in most American suburbs developed between 1920 and 1940. Landmark examples of the style are quite rare, however; of these, Falaise is among the finest survivors. New York architects Henry M. Polhemus (1891–1970) and Louis A. Coffin, who collaborated on the design of Falaise, were early advocates of the French Eclectic style and helped popularize it with their 1921 book *Small French Buildings,* which features photographs and drawings of numerous picturesque examples.

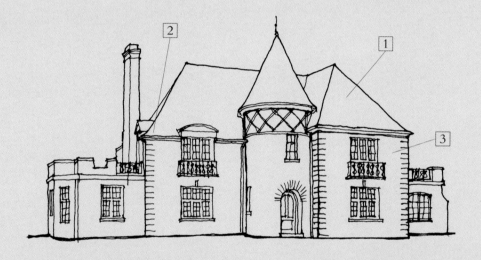

IDENTIFYING FEATURES

1 TALL, STEEPLY PITCHED, HIPPED ROOF WITHOUT DOMINANT FRONT-FACING CROSS GABLE

2 EAVES COMMONLY FLARED OUTWARD AT ROOF-WALL JUNCTION

3 BRICK, STONE, OR STUCCO WALLS, SOMETIMES WITH HALF-TIMBERING

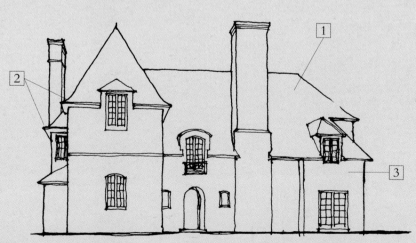

The east façade of Vizcaya overlooks Biscayne Bay.
Tall corner towers, a triple-arched entrance, and a sculptural central pediment lend distinction.

21

Vizcaya

MIAMI, FLORIDA

Italian Renaissance Style

*V*izcaya has always been a mysterious house—questions seem to hang in its tropical air. Who was James Deering, the quiet bachelor who in 1911 chose what was then a remote wilderness as the site of his winter retirement home? Why did he build such a grand monument when he professed to want only a simple country house and had no immediate family? Who was Paul Chalfin, the agent chosen to carry out the visionary plan that Deering never seemed fully to believe in? Eighty years later, despite a delightful book by Kathryn Chapman Harwood called *The Lives of Vizcaya,* the questions still remain. Perhaps the answers seem too simple for such a magnificent house.

James Deering (1859–1925) was only fifty-one years old when he retired as executive vice president of Chicago's International Harvester Company. No ordinary executive, he owned much stock in this very profitable farm-machinery enterprise that had resulted from the 1902 merger between the McCormick Harvesting Machine Company in Chicago and several of its former competitors. One of these was the Deering Harvester Company in Portland, Maine, an enterprise that had been founded and built by James's father, William Deering (for another grand dwelling built by an International Harvester vice president see Glessner House, pages 178–89).

When he retired James Deering wanted to leave Chicago for a milder winter climate. Like many retirees after him he chose Miami, which was then a small town of only two thousand inhabitants. To help him plan his country house Deering hired a New York designer named Paul Chalfin (1873–1959). Chalfin had unusual credentials. A graduate of Harvard, he had lived in Rome for three years as a Prix de Rome student at the American Academy, studied painting under the renowned James McNeill Whistler in France, and been a curator at the Boston Museum of Fine Arts, all before coming to New York, where he lectured on art and design at Columbia University and the Metropolitan Museum of Art. Eventually he became an associate of the influential interior designer Elsie de Wolfe, who sent him to help install a wall fountain in James Deering's Chicago

house. That project went well, and Deering remembered Chalfin when he was looking for a designer to help him with his Florida home.

Surviving letters between Chalfin in New York and Deering in Chicago reveal that the designer soon emerged as the one in charge of the Florida house. He made the project so large, and himself so indispensable, that Deering let him plan everything. He was even allowed to choose and supervise the house's architect, and he decided upon F. Burrell Hoffman, Jr. (1882–1980), then a young man in his twenties whom Chalfin thought could be easily "guided." Hoffman also met Chalfin's other criterion—he had attended France's Ecole des Beaux Arts and therefore had the European experience Chalfin deemed necessary for his grand plan.

Chalfin personally handled all of the house's elaborate decorative details, right down to the monograms on the linens. Deering himself may not have understood how it all happened. He wanted a house, he hired Chalfin, and the next thing he knew they were off on buying trips to Italy, where they purchased elaborate furnishings and even whole parts of ancient villas—cornices, antique gates, wall paneling, doors, and so on. The house then had to be of a scale to accommodate these acquisitions and the die was cast. Deering had serious concerns about the size of the house, its cost, and particularly the length of time it took to build. The art of creation was not important to him; he simply wanted a finished house to live in. Construction, begun in 1913, ended up taking four years, far longer than it should have, primarily because shipments from Europe were interrupted during World War I and also because most able-bodied men were then helping the war effort, not building grand retirement homes.

Chalfin wanted Vizcaya to be a re-creation of a three-hundred-year-old Italian villa whose rooms had not been finished all at once but evolved over several centuries. This is, in fact, how most grand European dwellings were built. In many of England's great country houses, for example, a medieval hall might be the oldest room, to which dozens of others were gradually added. As a result, they are veritable museums of decorative history.

Vizcaya emulates this tradition; one of its earliest rooms, decoratively speaking, is a large Renaissance Hall. Chalfin designed it in the form of what is known as a double-cube room. During the early Renaissance, cubes were thought to make particularly pleasing interior spaces, with their equal width, length, and height. Larger rooms could comprise two or three cubes, in this case two.

Vizcaya differs from most grand turn-of-the-century American houses in its emphasis on antique architectural elements and furnishings. The room detailing and most of the furniture in typical Eclectic-era houses, including such monumental ones as George Vanderbilt's Biltmore (see pages 232–45), were created from scratch, even if they were patterned on earlier European styles. Vizcaya, in contrast, has wall elements and fittings removed from early European houses and each room is furnished with European antiques whose style and spirit are appropriate to it.

For example, much of the Renaissance Hall's cornice is an original sixteenth-century creation. The stone fireplace is from an early French château, and the massive black wrought-iron candlesticks are early handmade Spanish pieces. The rug is a miraculously preserved fifteenth-century Moorish example woven for the ruler of Castille. The room's dominant piece of furniture is an enormous table with decorative sea horses entwined in its legs. Such tables were among the few items of permanent furniture in early Renaissance halls, which tended to be a bit somber, and this one is no exception. Vizcaya's banquet hall—with its antique wall tapestries, ceiling copied from a sixteenth-century Italian palace, and sixteenth-century refectory table—evokes the same era.

Such understatement did not last long in early Renaissance Italy and decorative objects soon became increasingly elaborate and ornate. This trend culminated in the mid-eighteenth century with the flamboyant curvilinear designs of the Rococo style. Vizcaya's music room is an example of this exuberant fashion. The wall and ceiling were painted in Milan at the height of the Rococo era, the chandelier is Venetian, and the French-inspired

Ancient columns and a seventeenth-century Venetian fountain grace the large central courtyard.

A sixteenth-century French chimneypiece presides over one end of the Renaissance Hall (TOP RIGHT). A small cherub (ABOVE) sits beneath the hall's beamed ceiling, its back to the hand-carved cornice. The Rococo-style reception room (BOTTOM RIGHT) has silk-covered walls, an eighteenth-century Portuguese needlework rug, and a mixture of French and Italian furniture.

furnishings and harpsichord case are in the same spirit. The reception room's walls, lined with a rare silk in a palm-tree motif; antique ceiling, purchased from its original setting, the Rossi Palace on Venice's Grand Canal; and French Louis XV furnishings capture much the same Rococo mood, as does the Espagnolette bedroom on the second floor. Only slightly more restrained is the nearby Galleon bedroom.

Two other upstairs rooms celebrate the Oriental design fashions that first became popular in the Western world in the mid-1700s. As large sailing ships opened up trade with the Far East, exotic screens, wallpapers, porcelains, and statuary began to make their way into Europe. These objects were incorporated directly into interiors and inspired European furniture makers to capture Oriental influences in their designs. The elegant second-floor

Like the reception room, the music room is in the Rococo style. The walls and ceiling were painted in Milan in the eighteenth century. The harpsichord, made of cypress, is signed and dated 1619.

With its exotic tasseled bed canopy, silk wall panels, and delicately colored chinoiserie screen and secretary, the Cathay bedroom (ABOVE AND RIGHT) captures the fantasy of the East.

breakfast room's hand-painted canvas murals depict great sailing ships; its furnishings include imported Chinese screens and porcelains as well as a chinoiserie, or Chinese-influenced, mantel and carved figures. The Cathay bedroom uses chinoiserie elements in a playful manner; the mood is set by a bed that looks like it comes straight out of the Arabian Nights. The location of this exotic bedroom next to Deering's private study, coupled with rumors that famous women, such as actress Marion Davies, may have slept there, helped contribute to the Vizcaya legend. Local gossip conjured up images of incense burning, opium smoking, and Far Eastern intrigue, rather than the gentle, quiet, and often sickly James Deering.

Because of its extraordinary interiors Vizcaya is as much a museum of the decora-

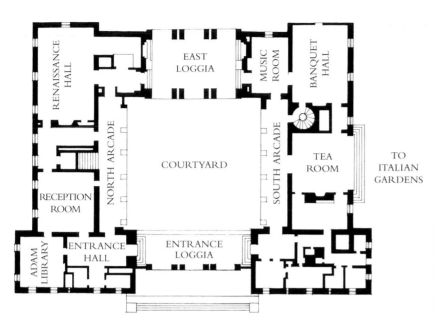

tive arts as it is a grand architectural landmark. Its rooms and furnishings were planned to reflect several periods in the European decorative arts seldom seen in this country, beginning with early Renaissance fashions and ending with Neoclassical designs.

The Neoclassical style was inspired by mid-eighteenth century archaeological work, particularly in Italy, where large ancient Roman sites such as Herculaneum and Pompeii were being excavated. Architects and designers, among them England's renowned Robert Adam (see Russell House, pages 32–45), visited these excavations and were much impressed by the delicacy and restraint of the artifacts they saw. Soon these discoveries were being incorporated into all of the arts of the day. As a consequence, the unrestrained, ornately curvilinear fashions of the Rococo era came to an abrupt end in the late 1700s. Following close on the heels of the Roman excavations was Napoleon's Egyptian campaign of 1798, and the many examples of Egyptian design motifs that the members of the expedition brought back with them became favorites of the future French emperor. These Egyptian and Roman influences combined to make up the Neoclassical movement.

Neoclassical designs are used at Vizcaya in James Deering's elegant private study, bedroom, and bath. The downstairs tea room and entrance hall are also in the Neoclassical mode; both have extraordinary walls, ceiling fixtures, and geometrically patterned marble floors. The wood-blocked French wallpapers in the entrance hall, dating from about 1814, are particularly fine and rare.

In contrast to the varied styles of its interior decor, Vizcaya's exterior and gardens are all designed in the style of the late Italian Renaissance. The concrete walls, which simulate the stucco-covered stone of the Italian originals, are accentuated by lighter-colored stone detailing and a red tile roof. The exterior stone, as well as the stone in the house,

TOP *In James Deering's Empire-style bedroom the dark mahogany furniture is enhanced with gilt-bronze decoration. The bed and walls are covered with silk and the floor with an Aubusson rug.*

BOTTOM *The walls of the Empire-style master bathroom are inlaid with rare marble. The shaving stand, made especially for the room, even has running water.*

Decorative statuary is an integral part of Italian gardens. At Vizcaya it ranges from elegant classical figures (ABOVE) to a sculpted frog (BELOW) that clings to the top of the sarcophagus fountain on the south terrace.

came from quarries in several locations near Miami and in Cuba, the use of the different types depending on the strength and effect needed. Much of the house's original interrelationship with its gardens (open atrium courtyard, arches open to the exterior) has been lost because the openings are now sealed with transparent panels to keep the warm and salty sea air from damaging Vizcaya's priceless interiors. Today it requires some imagination to visualize how organically the indoors and outdoors once interacted. These panels were severely tested in 1992 by Hurricane Andrew; fortunately, they did protect the interior from irreparable damage.

Vizcaya's gardens today are but a fraction, perhaps one-twentieth, of the estate's original grounds. To the south, beyond the formal Italian gardens, which have been preserved, there used to be a huge informal garden criss-crossed with canals and planted with hundreds of palm trees, including 265 royal palms that were imported full-grown from Cuba to line a causeway leading to a large boathouse. Now destroyed, this garden had been planned to complement the native jungle "hammock" immediately surrounding the house.

Consisting primarily of low, broad-leafed evergreen trees, the hammock was originally almost impenetrable. James Deering, who was deeply interested in conservation, insisted that the house, roads, and gardens be sited in such a way as to cause minimal disturbance to this natural setting. He was once so distressed that an ancient tree was about to be cut down to make way for a new Miami road that he had it dug up and transplanted to Vizcaya. On another occasion his design team realized that the main entrance to Vizcaya required removal of a very large tree. No one had the nerve to tell Deering about this, so the tree was taken down in the dead of night, the stump removed, and the ground care-

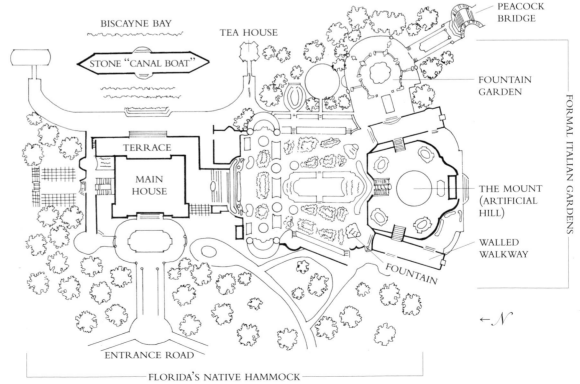

fully smoothed over before morning. Deering either didn't notice the removal or had the tact not to mention it.

Another section of the original grounds—across the road from the main house—was given over to a large working farm and kitchen gardens that fed not only Deering but the small army needed to build Vizcaya and then to keep it running. More than a thousand workmen helped build the house, and the permanent staff numbered over a hundred.

Of all the gardens on the estate, the formal Italian gardens relate most closely to the architecture of the house. Originally they provided a transition to the informal garden areas beyond. Developed over many years by Paul Chalfin, they are probably the most authentic Italian-based landscapes ever done in the United States.

Because of Italy's dry climate, water is a central theme in Italian garden design. Fountains, pools, streams, and waterfalls dominate the landscaping of Italian villas; the venerable Villa d'Este near Rome is perhaps the most renowned example. A second important theme is the liberal use of stone masonry for garden screening walls, for pools

This fountain and walled walkway exemplify two of the main themes of Italian gardens: water and architectural stone work. No flowers are visible, and the greenery plays mainly a supportive role.

and other water features, for steps leading from level to level in hillside gardens, and, of course, for decorative statuary. It was also used for myriad exterior architectural details, including freestanding columns, small bridges, shapely balustrades along terraces, and small garden houses. Italian gardens are thus often said to be architectonic; that is, the plants seem to be mere decorative elements in a man-made environment.

A third theme in more formal Italian gardens is the use of parterres, which are planting beds shaped into decorative patterns, usually bounded by dense low hedges. Italian parterres tend to be laid out in geometric shapes, whereas the forms of their French counterparts are often intricately curved and sinuous, like a giant floral carpet.

For the most part, the plantings in Italian parterres are low green hedges. Flowers may be used to fill a pair of urns or accent a dark corner, but they are rarely the central focus. For formal floral parterres one must look to France and Germany. With their preponderance of green foliage, stone masonry, and running water, the formal gardens of Vizcaya, like their Italian prototypes, offer a cooling retreat from the often blistering southern Florida heat.

ABOVE *A view of the fountain garden, which features a seventeenth-century baroque travertine fountain that once graced the main square of the small Italian town of Sutri.*

RIGHT *Each end of the Biscayne Bay sea wall culminates in a bridge. The south one leads to this latticed tea house.*

The "canal boat" was created to solve the problem of an unsightly island that appeared when the bay was dredged. The eye-catching structure was badly damaged by Hurricane Andrew in 1992.

One of the most appealing features of Vizcaya's grounds was created as a solution to a formidable problem. When a navigation channel in front of the house was dredged, a small rocky island appeared. Everyone involved wondered what to do with this eyesore. The inspired solution was to use the island as a base for constructing a concrete and limestone "canal boat," thus creating a focal point that intrigues everyone who visits Vizcaya. The island and other parts of the grounds were damaged by Hurricane Andrew, and donations are still being sought to restore the estate's extraordinary gardens.

Deering moved into Vizcaya during the winter of 1916, even though the estate was not yet complete. He was able to enjoy his grand creation for only a few years, however, because he died in 1925 on a transatlantic crossing. Vizcaya was left to his two nieces, both of whom lived elsewhere. In deference to Deering's dream they struggled to keep up with the enormous expenditures required to maintain the vast estate. To make matters worse, in 1926 a hurricane damaged both the house and the gardens. Although only the most necessary cleanup and repairs were done, this entailed the long-term efforts of more than a hundred workmen.

In 1933, at the depth of the Great Depression, Deering's heirs appealed to the Miami Chamber of Commerce for help. They offered to operate the property as a house-museum, if the annual taxes could be reduced, but the city and county preferred to continue collecting $30,000 a year in property taxes. The heirs' efforts to preserve the entire estate intact for the public continued until 1945, when they were forced to sell 130 of its 180 acres. Finally, in 1952 the county Park and Recreation Department agreed to purchase the house and remaining grounds at a bargain-basement price. When the heirs were convinced that the property was being well managed as a public museum, they generously donated the house's priceless furnishings so that now this remarkable architectural and artistic monument can be enjoyed and appreciated by all.

Italian Renaissance Style

(1890–1935)

The Italian Renaissance provided the inspiration for several styles of American architecture. During the 1700s the Georgian and Federal styles, both imported to the American colonies from England, were among the last *original* architectural fashions of the artistic Renaissance that began in Italy in the 1400s and spread slowly northward through Europe over the next two centuries. The first American *revival* of Renaissance themes came in the mid-nineteenth century. Loosely based on Italian rather than British prototypes, it is known as the Italianate style (see Morse-Libby House, pages 112–23).

A later revival of Renaissance-inspired design in American houses occurred from about 1890 to 1930 and was the purest in its resemblance to the Italian originals. For this reason it is called the Italian Renaissance Revival, or simply Italian Renaissance style. Like their Mediterranean prototypes, these houses have stone or light-colored brick masonry exterior walls that are sometimes covered with a uniform layer of stucco. Roofs are usually covered with tile or metal shaped to look like tile. They are typically low-pitched and hipped, with a broad, sheltering eave overhang and decorative brackets below.

At first this style was relatively rare, found mostly in architect-designed landmark houses with solid masonry walls. By about 1920, however, the technique of veneering a single layer of brick or stone onto the outside of wood-framed walls had been perfected. This development led to smaller and less costly Italian Renaissance designs that were popular in suburban neighborhoods until they were superseded by other fashions in the mid-1930s.

Vizcaya is perhaps the finest, most authentic Italian Renaissance dwelling in America. Its creator, Paul Chalfin, went to extraordinary lengths to transplant seventeenth-century Italy to this masterpiece in subtropical Florida.

IDENTIFYING FEATURES

1. HIPPED ROOF OF LOW PITCH, USUALLY COVERED WITH TILE

2. WIDELY OVERHANGING EAVES, OFTEN SUPPORTED BY DECORATIVE BRACKETS

3. UPPER-STORY WINDOWS SMALLER AND LESS ELABORATE THAN WINDOWS BELOW

4. COMMONLY WITH ARCHES ABOVE DOORS, FIRST-STORY WINDOWS, OR PORCHES

5. FAÇADE USUALLY SYMMETRICAL

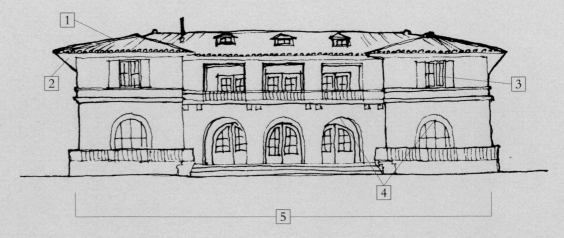

VIZCAYA

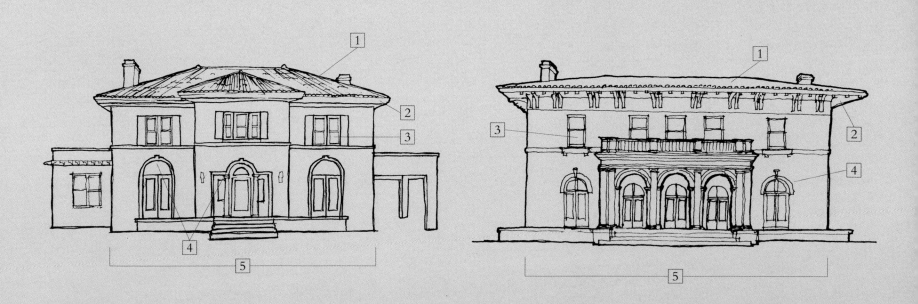

22

Casa del Herrero

SANTA BARBARA, CALIFORNIA

Spanish Eclectic Style

The Santa Barbara area received its name in 1602 after a storm at sea threatened the lives of Spanish explorer Sebastian Vizcaino and his crew on St. Barbara's Day Eve. They prayed to the saint to protect them and survived the night. When they sailed into a beautiful harbor the next morning they gratefully named it Santa Barbara. She is also the patron saint of architects, builders, and spire workers and has obviously watched over her namesake city for four centuries because modern Santa Barbara is among the most architecturally unified towns in the entire country.

In 1782 Santa Barbara harbor was selected as the site for one of a series of Spanish fort-missions established along the California coast; an 1820 rebuilding of the early mission survives to this day. Modern Santa Barbara began as a Victorian resort town. Its picturesque but inaccessible location, squeezed between ocean and mountains, precluded the pell-mell real estate development that was soon to cover much of southern California. The first great resort hotel on the West Coast, the Arlington, was built in Santa Barbara in 1875 and helped to establish the city's destiny. By the late nineteenth century travel guides were extolling the town's lovely climate and pleasant vacation possibilities. Nearby hot springs became the location of the unimaginatively named Hot Springs Hotel, which quickly gained a reputation as an exclusive resort.

At first, wealthy northern and midwestern industrialists came to the area to enjoy the mild winters or soak in the warm springs. In time, some built winter residences and many ultimately decided to make it their year-round home. Suitable land for building was always scarce and therefore expensive, so Santa Barbara tended to have an affluent population, as did adjacent Montecito, or "little hills." Montecito had originally been considered as the location for the early Spanish mission, but its hilly, shrub-covered topography was deemed too wild and rugged. As the flatter, oceanside core of Santa Barbara became developed, those seeking large homesites turned to Montecito, whose rolling hills provided an even sunnier and drier climate than Santa Barbara's.

The Casa del Herrero crest. The inscription reads: "Casa del Herrero is built on outer pueblo lands of Santa Barbara bought by Jose De Jesus Cota for ninety two cents an acre in 1868, twenty two years after General Fremont captured the town presidio. This house was first occupied on the morning of the great earthquake, June twenty ninth, 1925."

PAGE 282 *The East Garden axis extends from the entry hall through the living room, the walled Spanish Patio, and the East Garden and terminates in the Rose Garden, which has an outdoor seating area with a high, tiled back wall.*

The architectural unity of modern Santa Barbara was born out of disaster—a massive earthquake in 1925 that destroyed most of the city's downtown buildings. In response its citizens quickly formed a City Plans and Planning Committee to oversee the building and rebuilding of almost two thousand structures. The committee encouraged construction in "Mediterranean" style with low-pitched tile roofs, plaster walls, arched façade openings, and wrought-iron decorative detailing. Spanish-inspired architecture was already an established Santa Barbara tradition both for public buildings, including the city hall, which survived the earthquake, and for many of its fine residences.

The acknowledged leader in designing these Santa Barbara buildings was Pennsylvanian George Washington Smith (1876–1930), a soft-spoken, Harvard-educated architect who had abandoned that profession to become an award-winning painter. In 1915, after a three-year stay in France, Smith and his wife traveled to California to see the Panama-Pacific Exposition in San Diego and the Golden Gate Exposition in San Francisco. They also spent some time in Santa Barbara looking for appealing landscapes to paint and soon decided to settle there. As Smith explained in an interview given near the end of his life:

I came back to this country and went out to California in search of picturesque landscape for painting, and there became filled with the local Spanish tradition—I was just ripe to settle down and build a house after my Paris ideas. This took the form of an Andaluz white-walled and tile-roofed house, which I later sold to Mr. and Mrs. Heberton. . . . I soon found that people were not really as eager to buy my paintings, which I was laboring over, as they were to have a white-washed house like mine. So I put away the brushes and have not yet had a moment to take them up again, although I am always looking forward to doing so.

Among Smith's finest designs is Casa del Herrero ("House of the Blacksmith") in Montecito, a Spanish-style villa commissioned by St. Louis industrialist George F. Steedman (1871–1940) and his wife, Carrie Howard Steedman (d. 1963). The couple moved into the completed house on the day of the great Santa Barbara earthquake of June 29, 1925. Mercifully the structure survived the tragic event without serious damage.

George Steedman was an avid architecture buff. He had endowed a traveling fellowship in architecture at Washington University and founded the Steedman Architectural Collection in the St. Louis Public Library. When planning his new home he made two trips to Spain, where he studied all that he saw and purchased antiques and architectural artifacts for the house.

Steedman had no qualms about pushing for what he wanted. As he noted in a letter to Smith: "I sincerely hope you will be just as frank and stubborn as I am. . . . I have certainly been an awful client—let us hope the results may be good." The Steedmans' daughter, Medora Bass, elaborates further in a chapter on Casa del Herrero that she contributed to a book called *The American Woman's Garden* (1984):

The house and garden were begun in 1922, and my perfectionist father wanted both to be authentically Spanish. I remember hearing the names of Ralph Stevens, Peter Riedel, and Lockwood de Forest in connection with the garden, and over and over again, the name of the architect, George Washington Smith. My father worked constantly on the blueprints. He made a trip to Spain, accompanied by Arthur Byne and his wife Mildred Stapley, authorities on Spanish gardens and antiques, and in five weeks was able to buy tiles, grilles, Moorish doors, furniture, tapestries, stone carvings, and even a fifteenth-century ceiling from a monastery. He took photographs and made sketches in Seville, Granada, Ronda and Majorca. Then it was back to the blueprints to incorporate all these into the plans.

One approaches Casa del Herrero through a walled fountain court paved with pebbles in an ornamental pattern and accented by a raised, hexagonal reflecting pool surrounded by low, tiled walls. Both paving and pool are typical Spanish enhancements for an interior courtyard, here neatly converted into an automobile entry court. The house's entry façade shows Smith's ease with picturesque asymmetry and his ability to suggest the gradual accumulation of informal additions and modifications so typical of Spanish folk dwellings. How many architects would have dared to place a small shed-roofed room next to an elaborate Spanish doorway or design three different roof levels above that doorway?

LEFT *The walled Spanish Patio culminates in a three-arched structure, behind which the octagonal book tower is visible. Mr. Steedman himself made the metal patio furniture. In the center is a low octagonal fountain with tiled sides.*

RIGHT *A small grilled window and a one-story extension lend a picturesque asymmetry to the entry.*

The curved stairway is subtly ornamented with a metal balustrade and decorative tiles on the stair risers (ABOVE). A wide opening onto the stair hall (TOP LEFT) gives the dining room a spacious feeling. A beamed ceiling and family portraits (TOP RIGHT) add distinction to the living room.

Stepping from the California sunlight into the dim, cool entrance hall, visitors encounter one of the house's many treasures—an ancient beamed ceiling intricately painted with religious figures. It was purchased in Spain and is described in a 1923 letter to Smith from antiquarian Arthur Byne: "The Monastic house from which your XV century ceiling came is, or rather was, El Convento de San Francisco, near the town of Naranco, in the Province of Teruel, once part of the old Kingdom of Aragon. . . . Your ceiling is all that remains of the covering to the old claustral walk."

To the left of the entrance hall is the large living room with its Spanish-style beamed ceiling and handsome Spanish furnishings. A door in the far corner leads to a small octagonal book tower, an addition designed by Smith's architectural partner Lutah Maria Riggs in 1931, the year after Smith's death. This delightful room may have been added in lieu of a study that, according to the original plans, was supposed to occupy the northern third of the living room area.

To the right of the entrance hall is the dining room, the focal point of which is a Spanish-style angled corner fireplace. A wide arched opening allows the room to open onto a stair hall with an elegantly curved staircase featuring decorative tile risers and a wrought-metal balustrade. A tall wrought-iron candle holder nestles in the curve of the stair.

A charming surprise is the downstairs powder room, exuberantly decorated with ornamental tilework and metal detail. Extensive use of Spanish-style wrought-metal hardware and fixtures is typical of many Spanish Eclectic houses, but it is particularly appropriate here. According to Steedman's daughter, "Casa del Herrero means the House of the Blacksmith. Our place got its name because manufacturing metal products was my father's business and he jokingly referred to himself as a blacksmith."

LEFT *Details of the fifteenth-century ceiling in the entry hall; this ceiling was once part of a covered cloistral walk in an ancient Spanish convent.*

*The small octagonal book tower (*LEFT*) was added in 1931 by Lutah Maria Riggs, Smith's partner until his death in 1930. A close-up (*ABOVE*) shows the stenciled and painted shelf supports, ceiling, and cornice detail.*

With its hand-wrought metal detailing and decorative tilework, the downstairs powder room is a delightful surprise.

Steedman and Smith paid almost as much attention to the Spanish-style landscaping of Casa del Herrero's eleven-acre site as they did to the house itself. A modern scholar considers the Steedman-Smith garden "one of the finest surviving gardens of the 1920s in California." On their 1923 visit to Spain with decorative arts experts Arthur Byne and his wife, Mildred Stapley, the Steedmans visited many classic Spanish gardens. The trip provided Stapley and Byne with material for a series of articles that began appearing in *The Architectural Record* in December 1923 and featured photographs and drawings from the trip. The Steedmans' garden adheres closely to the "lessons" on Spanish gardens outlined in the Stapley-Byne articles. The first is that Spanish gardens are enclosed, private, and sheltering rather than broad, expansive, and open to the entire countryside as are many of the great garden parks of western Europe. Because lawn-type grasses are not indigenous to the dry climate of southern Spain, large English-style expanses of clipped grasses are not a viable landscape option.

Second, the Muslim Moors, whose influence is still prominent in southern Spain, did not allow sculpture for religious reasons. Thus, Spanish gardens have none of the sculptural focal points found in Italian, French, or English gardens. Instead, fountains, arches, or tiled walls serve as focal points.

Third, water was scarce in southern Spain, so cooling pools, streams, and fountains were dominant features of garden design. But because water was such a precious com-

Round-arched doors are a common theme in Spanish Eclectic houses. A single-door version (LEFT) connects two outdoor "rooms." A double-door interpretation (RIGHT) leads between the Spanish Patio and the living room. Both incorporate typical Spanish wooden grills.

modity these features are usually small-scale in comparison to the large open lakes of England or the huge, gushing fountains of Italy.

Fourth, Spanish gardens were divided into "rooms" separated by sheltering walls or tall hedges. The rooms' "floors," and their connecting paths, were usually paved with flat, unglazed tiles or patterned pebbles or were merely surfaced with hand-compacted clay soil. The walls and floors were adorned with flowers grown in pots rather than planted in beds. These could be quickly and easily changed throughout the year in southern Spain's year-round growing season.

In the garden at Casa del Herrero, an axis leading eastward from the living room bisects three garden rooms. The first, the walled Spanish Patio, is tile floored and features a small octagonal tile fountain. Next is the East Garden with pergolas at each end. Arches along the back wall are covered with creeping fig, effectively simulating the cypress arches found in Spain. A broad expanse of lawn flanked by perennial beds adds an English note.

The focal point of this axis is a tiled wall fountain, or exhedra, that screens the third room, a rose garden featuring tree roses surrounded by low hedges, another northern European feature.

The equally prominent south garden axis has less clearly defined rooms and is more eclectic in design. Spanish-style terraces and fountains at each end are connected by an

The scarcity of water in Spain ruled out English-style lakes and ponds and even Italian-style fountains. Instead, water features were small reflecting pools or narrow channels inspired by Moorish irrigation systems (TOP LEFT). Polychrome decorative tiles with stylized and geometric designs were a common feature of Muslim architecture, often used to cover wall surfaces and fountains (TOP RIGHT, BOTTOM LEFT). Small figurative tiles, such as these inset into a floor surface (BOTTOM CENTER AND RIGHT), were less typical.

The tiling on the wall that terminates the East Garden axis (LEFT) and on the stone seats in front of the wall (BELOW) is typical of Moorish non-figurative decoration.

English-style grassy lawn with shrub borders. Beyond these two formal axes lie less structured orange groves and naturalistic areas.

George Steedman died in 1940, his wife in 1963. After her death their grand house passed to their daughter, Medora Bass, who lovingly preserved both house and gardens until her recent death. Her heirs have generously agreed to donate the entire estate to a private foundation that will preserve it intact as a memorial to the Steedmans and the creative adventure they shared with their Montecito neighbor George Washington Smith.

BOTTOM LEFT *The South Garden axis begins with an upper terrace incorporating a flat, Spanish-style pool. The lower section beyond features a Moorish water channel. Finally, a long, non-Spanish, grassy walk terminates in a raised fountain.*

Spanish Eclectic Style
(1915–1940)

The wave of nostalgia for America's Colonial past that followed the 1876 Philadelphia Centennial celebration (see Westbury House, pages 192–205) was at first centered on the English Colonial styles found along the Atlantic seaboard. Soon there was a complementary California-based revival of interest in the Spanish Colonial heritage of the southwestern states. Abstracted architectural details based on the picturesque Spanish missions of the region began to be incorporated into southwestern public and commercial buildings about 1895, and the trend continued until about 1920. This Mission Revival, or simply Mission, style was also used occasionally for vernacular dwellings around the country, but few landmark examples survive.

By 1920 the Mission style was being replaced by a more broadly based and historically accurate Hispanic fashion sometimes known as the Spanish Colonial Revival style. Because many architects designing in the style sought precedents for it in Spain itself rather than in Spanish colonies, we prefer to call it the Spanish Eclectic style.

Although it is an extremely varied style, drawing on a wide range of Hispanic designs for its details, most of its variants have certain features in common. Walls tend to be of stucco or light-colored brick, and roofs are usually covered with red tiles. Unlike the red tile roofs of Italian Renaissance or Mission-style houses, which have broad overhanging eaves, the roofs of most Spanish Eclectic-style houses stop near the wall line.

A more popular style for dwellings than the Mission style, Spanish Eclectic houses are found throughout the country in suburban developments built during the 1920s and 1930s. Santa Barbara–based George Washington Smith was one of the country's most talented designers of Spanish Eclectic houses, and Casa del Herrero is among his small number of landmark masterpieces.

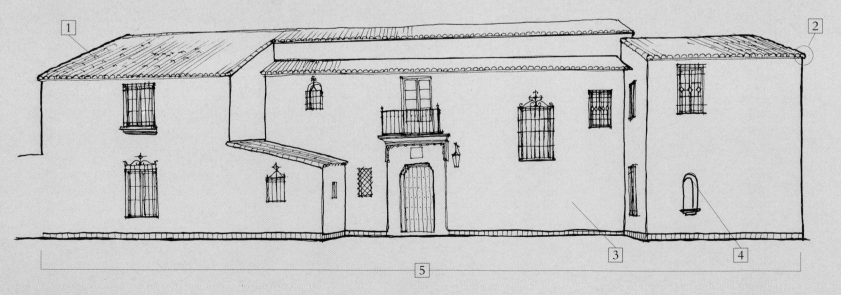

CASA DEL HERRERO

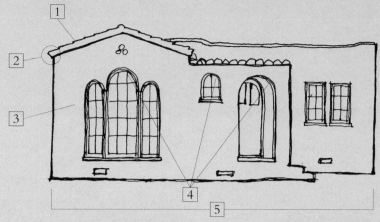

IDENTIFYING FEATURES

1. LOW-PITCHED ROOF, USUALLY WITH RED TILE COVERING

2. EAVES USUALLY WITH LITTLE OR NO OVERHANG

3. WALL SURFACE USUALLY STUCCO

4. ARCHES ABOVE DOORS, PRINCIPAL WINDOWS, OR BENEATH PORCH ROOFS

5. ASYMMETRICAL FAÇADE

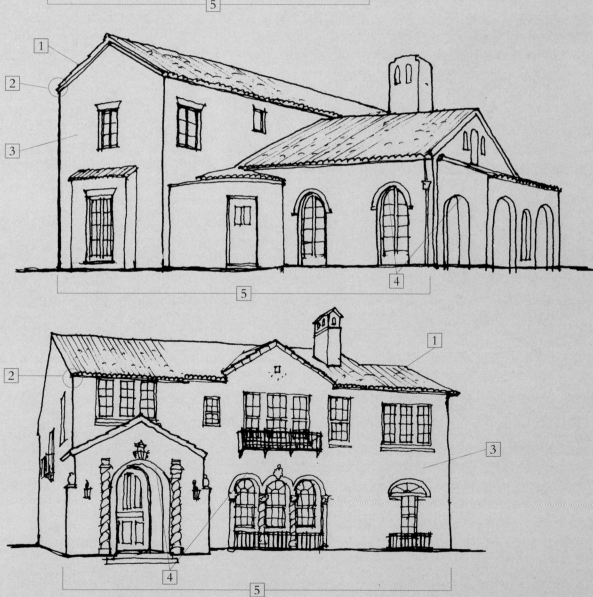

View of the round-arched main entry.
The projecting eaves, wall copings, and brick joints combine
to give the façade a strong horizontal emphasis.

23

Dana-Thomas House

SPRINGFIELD, ILLINOIS

Prairie Style

Magnificent multilevel spaces and subtly changing natural light are hallmarks of the Dana-Thomas House, designed in 1902 by the renowned architect Frank Lloyd Wright (1867–1959). One of his innovative "Prairie" houses, this project was Wright's first commission with an unlimited budget, and he used this financial freedom to create a unified masterpiece of modern design. His client was Susan Lawrence Dana (1862–1946), a young widow whose father, Rheuna Lawrence, had died in 1901, just six months after the death of her husband. Left with an enormous fortune from her father's many investments, chief among them large blocks of stock in rich western gold and silver mines, Susan decided to build a grand house to serve as a base for her new role as a wealthy civic leader and socialite.

Susan had grown up in the world of politics. The Dana-Thomas House, built on the site of her childhood home, is but a few blocks from the state capitol in Springfield, Illinois. Rheuna Lawrence had once served as mayor of Springfield but for most of his career operated behind the scenes in the inner circles of the Republican Party. After his death an associate wrote, "It is safe to say that within the past thirty years few, if any, important political moves have been made affecting the interests of the state, without his counsel and advice." Susan shared her father's interest in politics, so she planned the house to facilitate entertaining, which was the primary means for the women of her generation to exert political influence. Charles Deneen, governor of Illinois from 1905 to 1913, and his wife were two of Susan's closest friends, and she frequently entertained on their behalf during his governorship.

Susan was also fond of other kinds of entertaining—women's club meetings, musical events, lectures, and so on. Whether for social, political, or educational purposes, entertaining was one of the few avenues intelligent middle- and upper-class women in the early twentieth century had to improve their minds or develop skills.

It is not known how Susan Dana learned about the then-little-known Frank Lloyd Wright, but once they met they became close friends. The architect's son, John

Susan Lawrence Dana, c. 1893.

Lloyd Wright, states in his book *My Father Who Is on Earth:* "Papa liked Mrs. Dana! Mrs. Dana liked Papa! I liked to smell her Chanel. So did Paa-pa." In any event, Susan gave Wright virtual carte blanche to construct a grand house in his new style. The only constraint was that for sentimental reasons it had to incorporate parts of the original Lawrence house, which it was replacing. In the end Wright managed to cover all traces of this house except for Susan's father's study, which was left intact in his honor.

In his book *Modern Architecture* (1931), Wright expressed his antipathy for the Victorian houses that preceded his Prairie-style designs:

> Dwellings of that period were "cut-up," advisedly and completely, with the grim determination that should go with any cutting process. The "interiors" consisted of boxes beside or inside other boxes, called *rooms*. All boxes inside a complicated boxing. Each domestic "function" was properly box to box. I could see little sense in this inhibition, this cellular sequestration that implied ancestors familiar with the cells of penal institutions, except for the privacy of bedrooms on the upper floor. They were perhaps all right as "sleeping boxes." So I declared the whole lower floor as one room, cutting off the kitchen as a laboratory . . . screening various portions in the big room, for certain domestic purposes—like dining or reading, or receiving a formal caller. There were no plans like these in existence at the time and my clients were pushed toward these ideas as helpful to a solution of the vexed servant-problem. They liked it. . . . The house became more free as "space" and more liveable, too. Interior spaciousness began to dawn.

Wright's determination to "open up the box" is clearly evident in the Dana-Thomas House. Some fifteen different floor levels are found throughout the house. Balconies, elevated walkways, and overlooks are emphasized at every turn, creating many unusual and interlocking spaces.

The house's freewheeling spatial pattern is apparent as soon as one steps into the entry hall. In the center of the room is a large terra-cotta sculpture by Richard W. Bock. Behind it is a huge opening carved out of the upper two-thirds of the rear wall. Through this opening one sees, at about chest height, the floor of the reception area, which terminates in an imposing arched fireplace. Also visible through the opening are two levels of balconies that overlook the reception area. In all, five different floor levels can be seen from this one vantage point.

To reach the reception-area level one turns to the left and climbs up a narrow, enclosed stairway. A large space, the reception area has ceilings of varying height; a dramatic high-ceilinged section, opening the reception area to the upstairs walkways, contrasts with a much lower-ceilinged, more sheltering section. A fountain provides the focal point for the cavelike sheltered section, while the arched fireplace anchors the soaring portion of the room.

In accord with Wright's conviction that rooms should flow into one another, the reception area opens into the dining room. Here, too, the architect plays with height. The main section of the dining room has a high, barrel-vaulted ceiling. Its semicylindrical shape rises above a hand-painted frieze of sumac, asters, and goldenrod. At the end of the room is a low-ceilinged inglenook, a cozy space just right for an intimate breakfast or luncheon. In this room, as throughout the house, Wright made effective use of patterned glass, whose role he defined in a 1928 *Architectural Record* article:

> In the openings of my buildings, the glass plays the effect the jewel plays in the category of materials. The element of pattern is made more cheaply and beautifully effective when introduced into the glass of the windows

The high-ceilinged portion of the reception area opens to the entry hall below, the musician's balcony just above, and a second-floor open walkway, above left.

than in the use of any other medium that architecture has to offer. The metal divisions become a metal screen of any pattern—heavy or light, plated in any metal, even gold or silver—the glass a subordinate, rhythmical accent of any emotional significance whatever, or vice versa. The pattern may be calculated with reference to the scale of the interior and the scheme of decoration given by, or kept by, the motif of the glass pattern.

I have used opalescent, opaque, white and gold in the geometrical groups of spots fixed in the clear glass. I have used, preferably, clear primary colors, like the German flashed-glass, to get decorative effects, believing the

ABOVE *The Moonchildren fountain in front of a wall of Wright's jewel-like art glass is the focal point of the low-ceilinged portion of the reception area.*

TOP LEFT *Seen from the vantage point of its second-floor balcony, the two-story dining room's barrel-vaulted ceiling appears to spring from a somewhat faded mural of native wildflowers. The octagonal one-story inglenook beyond is perfect for more intimate dining.*

BOTTOM LEFT *This view of the dining room emphasizes the butterfly chandeliers and the alternating tall and short chair arrangement that Mrs. Dana was fond of.*

ABOVE *One of a pair of decorative glass-doored cabinets that are built into the passage between the reception area and the dining room.*

OPPOSITE TOP LEFT *The fifty-foot-long conservatory hallway leads from the reception area to the Gallery Wing. The design themes found here were widely copied in high-quality commercial interiors of the 1950s.*

OPPOSITE BOTTOM LEFT *Wright designed innovative double-sided stacks for the low-ceilinged library in the Gallery Wing. He also designed the lamp, library table, and chairs.*

*Wright designed all of the light fixtures in the house. The chandelier in the Gallery Wing landing (*OPPOSITE TOP RIGHT*) is in the same stylized butterfly design as the ones in the dining room. The large double-pedestal lamp on the living room table (*OPPOSITE BOTTOM RIGHT*) is similar in design to the single-pedestal lamp in the library.*

clear emphasis of the primitive color interferes less with the function of the window and adds a higher architectural note to the effect of *light* itself. The kinder-symphony in the windows in the Coonley play-house is a case in point. The sumac windows in the Dana dining-room another.

The Gallery Wing of the house was designed for large-scale entertaining. It is reached through a fifty-foot-long conservatory hallway lined with ribbon windows on either side and a long, low planting box along one side. The wing itself has one large room on each of two levels. The snug, low-ceilinged area below is furnished with library stacks and seating—a cozy place in which to curl up and read. The space above has a high, light-flooded, barrel-vaulted ceiling.

The semicircular arched openings found throughout the Dana-Thomas House are atypical for Wright. This particular kind of arch was a favorite of Wright's early mentor, the famed Chicago architect Louis Sullivan (1856–1924). In the Dana-Thomas House it is used for the entry door, the main fireplace, the bowling alley ceiling, and, most prominently, the barrel-vaulted ceilings in the dining room and gallery.

The exterior of the Dana-Thomas House provides a fitting introduction to the interior. As in most landmark Prairie-style houses, low horizontal lines predominate. The exterior brick walls rest upon a low foundation capped by a stained concrete coping, whose line gives the house its first horizontal emphasis. The bricks themselves are much longer than average, thereby adding to the horizontality, which is further reinforced by Wright's unique method of shaping the mortar joints between the bricks. He had his masons carefully recess the horizontal lines of mortar while leaving all the vertical ones

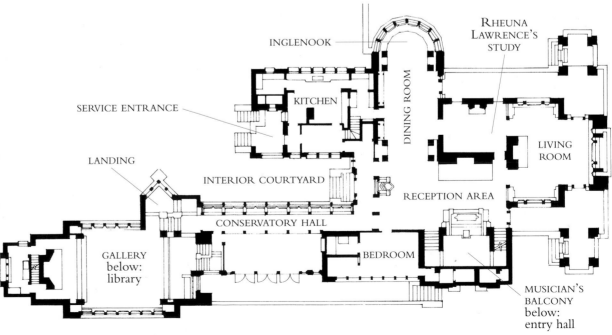

The gallery was designed for both entertaining and exhibiting art; the large tables were meant to display and examine art prints. The barrel-vaulted ceiling here is wider than the one in the dining room and springs from a ledge that provides display niches for pottery, statuary, and dried-flower arrangements.

flush with the face of the brick. This technique results in long, horizontal shadow lines that create the effect of narrow ribbons of brick encircling the house, a look quite different from that of traditional brickwork.

At the base of the upper-story windows the walls terminate in another horizontal band of concrete coping. The space between this coping and the roofline introduces a second design element: the windows are inset into a geometrically patterned green frieze. Together, windows and frieze read as a dark band that contrasts sharply with the lighter brick walls below. The overall effect is of a roof that appears to float several feet above the walls.

The entrance to the house is accentuated by a massive brick semicircular arch, beneath which Wright inserted not one but two complementary semicircles of decorative stained glass. Most of the entrances to Wright's Prairie houses were far more understated—

located on a side porch or obscured by a small entry court—as if to emphasize not the doorway but the overall horizontality of the façade. But because Susan Dana's principal reason for building the house was to entertain others, she may have requested a prominent front door.

Wright always tried to integrate his houses into their surroundings. At this early stage in his career he achieved this integration by building long planting boxes into the walls and placing large, squat planting pots atop lower-level copings. These pots held plants that cascaded down the walls toward the ground. This close union of architecture and nature was a striking innovation in 1902.

Over the years, most of Frank Lloyd Wright's grand Prairie-style houses have been dismantled, subdivided, or remodeled. At the very least, their original, Wright-designed furnishings have been removed. The Dana-Thomas House, its original art glass, fixtures, and furniture still intact, is thus a rare treasure that documents the seminal early work of the man considered by many to be our country's most creative architect.

The house barely escaped the same fate as its Wright-designed cousins. In 1942 Susan Dana was hospitalized, and over the next few years most of her personal property was sold at auction to pay her debts. Her house, now deteriorating and long out of fashion, was appraised at $5,000, "mostly for scrap." It was saved by the farsighted

The interior courtyard (LEFT) is overlooked by the windows of the Gallery Wing landing to the right and the long conservatory hall beyond, which leads to the main house. The service entrance is to the left. This view shows the brick wall surface, which continues without a break to the bottom of the upstairs windows, where it terminates in a buff-colored concrete coping. Dark green–stained plaster in a geometric design (RIGHT) fills the space from the coping to the copper-guttered roof.

An early proponent of blending architecture with nature, Wright used low, broad planting pots and urns and also integrated long planters into the ledges of his houses. Here greenery cascades from a planter over the entry area.

LEFT *For this window in the dining room Wright designed a geometric interpretation of fall sumac.*

intervention of Mr. and Mrs. Charles C. Thomas, who purchased it with most of its original furnishings intact, restored it, and then used it for many years with few modifications as the headquarters of their Springfield-based publishing business. In 1981 the house and furnishings were purchased by the State of Illinois as a public museum devoted to Wright and Susan Dana. The state has exercised extraordinary care and attention in restoring the house to its original appearance, thus assuring that at least one of Wright's early landmark works, which laid the foundation for much of twentieth-century architectural modernism, will be preserved intact for future generations to appreciate.

Frank Lloyd Wright, c. 1909.

Prairie Style
(1900–1920)

All of the housing styles discussed so far in this book were inspired by earlier building traditions, whether those of ancient Greece and Rome, medieval western Europe, or Renaissance Italy. The final three styles represent the beginnings of yet a fourth great architectural tradition, one that rejects direct borrowings from buildings of the past and attempts instead to create entirely new, "modern" designs.

The roots of this twentieth-century modernism can be detected in the stylized exteriors and open interior planning of the American Shingle style (see Naumkeag, pages 166–77) as well as in some turn-of-the-century British Arts and Crafts designs. It remained for a young Chicago architect, Frank Lloyd Wright, to synthesize these trends in his Prairie-style houses, which, with their ground-hugging emphasis on long, horizontal lines and muted, earth-tone color schemes, are aptly named. These houses are considered by many scholars to be the first truly modern architectural designs.

Wright went on to make many other contributions to architectural modernism during his career, yet none was to have the impact of his early Prairie houses, which, in a more modest "American four-square" form popularized by imitative pattern books, became widespread in American suburban developments built between about 1905 and 1915. Still more important, Wright's landmark Prairie designs were meticulously documented in a multivolume German monograph published in 1910. This work, all but ignored in the United States, was to have a seminal influence on the architectural modernism that spread throughout Europe in the 1920s (see Gropius House, pages 322–33).

Regrettably, most of Wright's dozen or so landmark Prairie houses have been either demolished, remodeled, or stripped of their valuable architectural details and Wright-designed furnishings. This makes the intact Dana-Thomas House, one of Wright's first landmark designs, a unique architectural treasure.

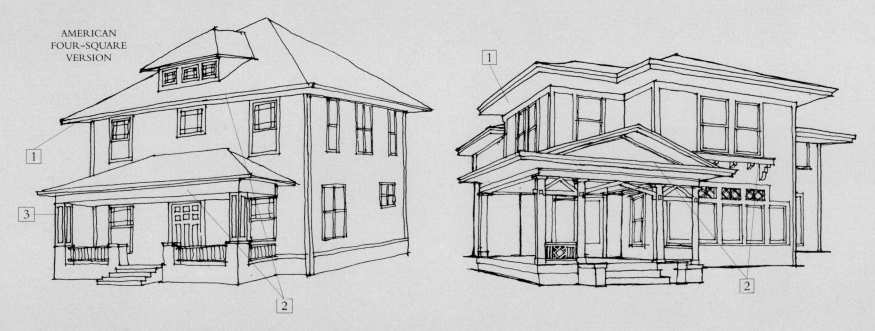

AMERICAN
FOUR–SQUARE
VERSION

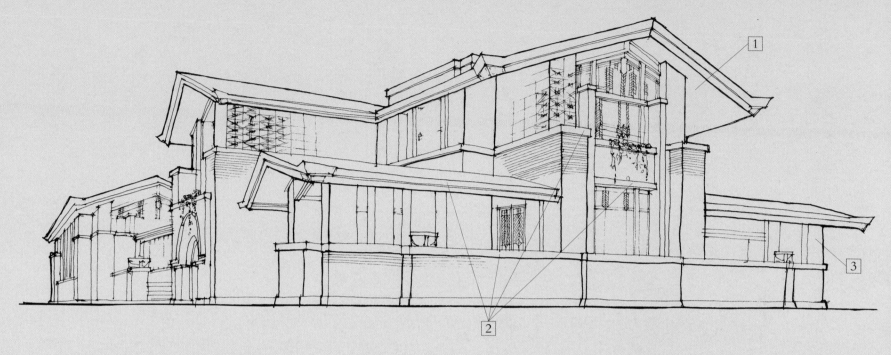

DANA-THOMAS HOUSE

IDENTIFYING FEATURES

1 LOW-PITCHED ROOF, USUALLY HIPPED AND WITH WIDELY OVERHANGING EAVES

2 DETAILING EMPHASIZES HORIZONTAL LINES

3 MASSIVE SQUARE PORCH SUPPORTS

A side view of the Gamble House shows the back terrace "growing"
out of the ground to the right and three upstairs sleeping porches.

24
Gamble House

PASADENA, CALIFORNIA

Craftsman Style

*T*he design of the Gamble House, with its large windows, sheltering eaves, and multiple porches and terraces, was shaped by the mild and sunny southern California weather. Pasadena, California, located near Los Angeles and the Pacific coast, lies at about the same latitude as Charleston, South Carolina, on the Atlantic, yet the prevailing temperate winds off the Pacific give Pasadena a far more moderate climate. In Los Angeles the temperature almost never dips below freezing, while Charleston averages thirty-seven subfreezing days each year. Summer nights in Pasadena are about ten degrees cooler than in Charleston; winter nights, about ten degrees warmer.

The Gamble House's pioneering designers, the brothers Charles S. (1868–1957) and Henry M. (1870–1954) Greene, positioned its many outdoor terraces, upstairs porches, and large windows to take full advantage of the mild climate and prevailing winds. Wide, overhanging eaves shade the windows from the bright southern California sun. Each main bedroom has its own open sleeping porch, and the indoor and outdoor living areas flow smoothly together.

The Pacific winds that bestow such balmy weather on southern California are also responsible for bringing the heavy rains that nurture the towering forests of the Pacific Northwest, which is the source of all the fine woods used throughout the Gamble House. The house's massive roof-support timbers are of Oregon pine; redwood and oak also serve as basic structural materials. The exterior walls are covered with three-foot-long, hand-split redwood shakes that were soaked in stain for three days and then applied with eleven inches exposed to the elements to provide a thick layer of natural wood insulation.

The Greene brothers were tireless perfectionists and the Gamble House is among their crowning achievements. They designed the house *and* the landscaping (for which they could have called in a landscape designer), the interior finishes (for which they could have used an interior designer), and even much of the furniture. They oversaw every last detail, which meant, for instance, spending several hours a day at the furniture studio and having the rugs custom woven to produce the exact colors they wanted.

Heavy wood beams are held fast with elaborate metal straps.

ABOVE *Many of the windows and screens are ornamented with a cloudlike "lift line," here pierced by three "rays" of sunlight.*

RIGHT *The rear terrace, built of brick and natural rock, is bordered by an intriguing fish pond.*

In doing all this the Greenes did not use the long-established vocabulary of building design but invented a totally new architectural style virtually from scratch. Every light fixture, wood joint, tile inlay, clinker brick, and stone pathway presented new design problems that they solved with extraordinary skill. For allowing the Greenes the freedom to create what was then an unprecedentedly modern house, the credit goes to their farsighted clients, David Berry Gamble (1847–1923) and his wife, Mary Huggins Gamble (d. 1929), of Cincinnati, Ohio. David Gamble, whose father was a co-founder of the Procter and Gamble Company, had recently retired as an officer of the company. According to historian Randell Makinson, when the Gambles were seeking an architect to build a suitable permanent residence in Pasadena they "responded to the recommendation of a close friend and met with the architects Charles and Henry Greene. During this one brief discussion the Gambles discovered that the Brothers' ideals and philosophies expressed their own beliefs. From this single meeting came the commission for the Gamble House."

Once given the commission, the Greenes' first order of business was to decide where to site the house on the Gambles' hilltop lot. They chose a spot near the crest of the hill and then reshaped the front lawn area to allow a large circular driveway to be built into a subtly lowered area so that its brick paving could not be seen from the street. Three huge eucalyptus trees on the site became the focus of the house's back terrace.

The Gamble House interior is a symphony of natural woods, with each room composed in different combinations of texture, color, and grain. Leaded stained glass, decorative Arts and Crafts–movement tiles, and specially woven carpets provide the primary accents.

The Greene brothers' training in woodworking and the other building crafts began early. Their father, a St. Louis physician, enrolled them in a special high school, the Manual Training School of Washington University, one of the first such programs in the United States. In addition to their academic subjects, students spent two hours a day working with their hands—one year on wood, another on metals, and a third on tools. The school's motto was "The Cultured Mind—The Skillful Hand." After graduation the brothers attended a two-year architecture program at the Massachusetts Institute of Technology. Later, in an unpublished novel, Charles expressed his feelings about programs, like MIT's, that were slanted toward the European Beaux Arts tradition and its emphasis on historic architecture as the basis for new designs: "Why is it we are taught that it is impossible to invent anything worth while in architectural art? . . . Isn't invention the life of science? Don't men of science do it every day? And science has not had the last word yet. Why not art?" Prescient words for one who would later become renowned for his architectural innovations.

The brothers completed their MIT studies in 1891 and were hired as apprentices in separate Boston architectural firms. In 1893 they were encouraged by their parents, now retired and ailing, to join them in "the little country town" of Pasadena, California. Reluctant to leave New England, the brothers nevertheless agreed and on the trip west visited the World's Columbian Exposition in Chicago, where the Japanese exhibit, a half-scale

Charles Sumner Greene, c. 1906.

Henry Mather Greene, c. 1906.

A striking Greene-designed lantern, mounted on the wall surrounding the terrace, presides over the rear lawn with its stepping-stone path of native rock.

replica of a Buddhist temple, so impressed them that the following year they attended an exposition in San Francisco featuring Japanese gardens. Later they began collecting and studying books on Japanese architecture and design. In California the brothers also became interested in the new Arts and Crafts movement, which stressed a return to the kind of handcrafted design they had learned in high school.

When they arrived in Pasadena, Charles and Henry found not a sleepy country town but a prosperous young city in the midst of a building boom. Soon a friend of their father's hired them to design a small cottage, and their career as California architects was launched. For the next ten years they designed houses in the popular late Victorian styles of the day but always with an emphasis on fine craftsmanship. About 1903, however, they began experimenting with their own building style, which combined elements of both Japanese and Arts and Crafts design. Thus was born the Greenes' California bungalow, which, popularized by countless house pattern books, became the dominant fashion for American houses from about 1910 to 1925.

As their California bungalow caught the public's fancy, the Greenes began receiving commissions from wealthy clients who wanted larger and more expensively detailed

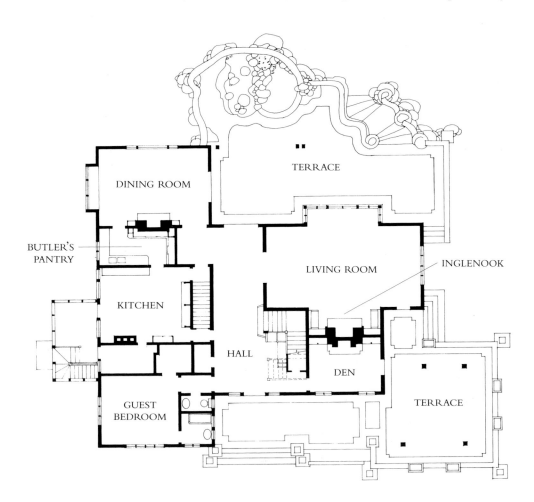

An elaborate tree-of-life design in stained glass fills the front entry. Most stained-glass work has static, uniform-width leading between the panes. The Greenes' innovative use of varying widths of leading became an important element in the overall design.

versions of the new style. The result was a series of "ultimate bungalows" of which the Gamble House, completed in 1909, is among the finest.

A masterful art-glass entryway provides a dramatic introduction to the house. Based on a gnarled tree-of-life design by Charles Greene, the doorway's subtly colored art-glass panels are held together by an innovative leading process that widens and narrows as needed to become an integral part of the overall design. The large, heavy central door is flanked by two smaller side doors with corresponding screens to allow for ventilation even when the main door is closed.

Beyond the entryway is a broad stair hall. Oriental rugs cover the floor, walls are of warmly stained Burmese teak, and natural-finish wooden beams support the ceiling.

ABOVE *This corner of the living room reveals the same intricate wood detailing as is found on the exterior of the house.*

*The downstairs stair hall (*TOP LEFT*) is paneled in Burmese teak and has a low, subtly beamed ceiling. Accent color is provided only by the entry-door glass and Oriental rugs. The stairway (*BOTTOM LEFT*) is one of the most innovative features in the house.*

The fireplace inglenook in the living room (RIGHT) incorporates the cloud-like lift line in the overhead beam. Tiles with a specially incised design surround the fireplace, which is flanked by cabinets; this arrangement is found in many Craftsman and Prairie houses. A hand-carved frieze of stylized scenes from nature (ABOVE) encircles the room.

The Greene-designed dining room furnishings (RIGHT) include a striking art-glass light fixture, an expandable mahogany pedestal table, and a built-in sideboard topped by a stained-glass window. Note the use of the same Oriental lift line in the wood portion of the window (ABOVE).

A large maple table is the main work surface in the kitchen, which is detailed in maple throughout. The sink is typical of those found in kitchens of all sizes in the early twentieth century.

The stairway, one of the most original domestic stairways ever designed, leads upward on the right. Meticulously crafted in dark teak, its rich sheen and rounded edges invite one to touch it.

The downstairs of the house has four interconnected living "zones": Mr. Gamble's den, a guest room, the living room area, and the dining-kitchen area. Upstairs there are family bedrooms and an additional guest room.

The living room has a cross-shaped plan. An inglenook, complete with an Arts and Crafts tile fireplace and built-in banquettes and cabinets, forms one end of the "cross-bar" and a window-surrounded alcove the other. The attention to detail in the room is extraordinary. The rug was hand woven from a design by Charles Greene; it had to be partially rewoven to replace an imprecise color before being laid down for the first time. Hand-carved redwood panels featuring bas-relief trees, flowers, bats, and birds form a frieze along the upper walls. Such carved friezes are typical of both traditional Japanese and turn-of-the-century English Arts and Crafts designs. The living room fireplace tiles are embellished with a mosaic vine pattern that appears to be growing through the square background tiles. An Oriental, cloudlike "lift line" ornaments the upper windows, the beam over the fireplace nook, the window alcove, the piano case, the stained glass of the bookshelf doors, and even the light-switch plates. The fireplace andirons were also specially designed by the Greenes.

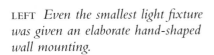

LEFT *Even the smallest light fixture was given an elaborate hand-shaped wall mounting.*

RIGHT *In the large master bedroom the walnut furniture, inlaid with ebony and semiprecious stones, was designed by the architects, as were the light fixtures, which hang from leather straps. The partially open door leads to a sleeping porch.*

The dining room features Honduras mahogany paneling and a handsome fixed-pedestal table that extends to seat fourteen. Over it hangs a coordinated art-glass light fixture. Above a built-in sideboard is a large window of sinuously lined art glass. During the day the glass gives off a warm glow and at night it comes magically alive with iridescent mother-of-pearl accents that reflect the light from the central fixture.

The upstairs bedrooms show a similar attention to detail. Indeed, every room in the house is somewhat different in tone, wood, or style, yet the distinctive detailing of each contributes to the house's overall decorative unity.

The interrelationship between the house and the outdoors is as harmonious as that among its interior spaces. Low-walled, tile-surfaced terraces connect the house with the surrounding garden. Built up of boulders of gradually decreasing size, the walls of these terraces appear to grow out of the lawn. They are topped by clinker bricks, which are bricks placed too close to the hardening fire, causing them to become slightly misshapen and miscolored but giving them great character.

The genius of the Gamble House is that it manages to convey a sense of calm and repose even though it is absolutely crammed with architectural and decorative detail. Decorative glass, wood, metal, carpets, and ceiling beams cover every interior surface yet the house seems understated and "homey"—a very rare accomplishment in interior design.

Of the seven "ultimate bungalows" designed by the Greene Brothers between 1907 and 1909—the high point of their professional career—the Gamble House is the only one to have survived with its original Greene-designed furnishings intact. After Mr. and Mrs. Gamble's deaths the house passed to their eldest son, Cecil H. Gamble, who along with his wife, Louise, appreciated its great significance and preserved its original character. When Louise died in 1963 their son, James N. Gamble, acting on behalf of the Gamble heirs, deeded the property to the City of Pasadena, which, in conjunction with the University of Southern California, maintains it as a permanent memorial to the Gambles, to the brothers Greene, and to their innovative California bungalows.

The master bathroom (BOTTOM LEFT) is of the airy, white, easy-to-clean school. Exposed pipe was considered more hygienic than pipe concealed in an enclosure that might harbor germs. The architects allowed the wood detailing in this room to be painted white for the sake of "cleanliness" (TOP RIGHT). Gamble's father was a co-founder of Procter and Gamble; a glass shelf in the kitchen displays some of the company's early products (TOP LEFT).

Craftsman Style
(1905–1930)

Like their contemporary Frank Lloyd Wright (see Dana-Thomas House, pages 294–307), the Greene brothers broke with centuries of architectural tradition and created an entirely new style that did not borrow directly from Classical, medieval, or Renaissance predecessors. Their Craftsman-style houses shared Wright's concern for hand-crafted workmanship, unified interior design, and free-flowing spaces, yet differed in overall shape, architectural detailing, and an emphasis on wood-framed rather than masonry construction. The Greene brothers' themes were to have an even greater impact on the design of American vernacular housing than Wright's did.

Turn-of-the-century Los Angeles was a boomtown. As its suburban neighborhoods mushroomed, local builders and developers were quick to adopt many of the Greenes' innovative design details—low-pitched gabled roofs with overhanging eaves, exposed rafters, and wide porches supported by pyramidal cobblestone or decorative wood pillars that rose directly from ground level. Soon entire neighborhoods were made up of these one-story "California bungalows." Enterprising Los Angeles–area architects also produced numerous house pattern books that spread the new style throughout the country, and building service companies began selling entire sets of building plans for Craftsman houses. Some even offered do-it-yourself kits, complete with precut lumber and all necessary hardware. These kits were shipped crated and ready for on-site assembly. As a result, most American cities of that era have neighborhoods dominated by pattern-book–inspired Craftsman designs.

After their own expensive, handcrafted houses passed from fashion about 1915, the unassuming Greene brothers—unlike the flamboyant Wright, who was a lifelong master of self-promotion—lived quietly productive lives designing and building fine furnishings and domestic interiors. The Gamble House, a still-intact modern masterpiece built at the apex of their career, is among the most warmly appealing American dwellings ever designed.

GAMBLE HOUSE

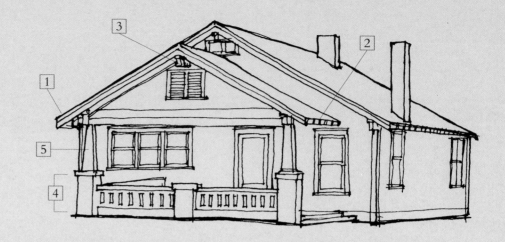

IDENTIFYING FEATURES

1. LOW-PITCHED GABLED ROOF (OCCASIONALLY HIPPED) WITH WIDE, UNENCLOSED EAVE OVERHANG

2. ROOF RAFTERS USUALLY EXPOSED

3. DECORATIVE BEAMS OR BRACES UNDER GABLES

4. PORCH SUPPORT BASES EXTENDING TO GROUND LEVEL (WITHOUT BREAK AT LEVEL OF PORCH FLOOR)

5. PORCH SUPPORTS USUALLY SQUARED AND SOMETIMES SLANTING INWARD

25
Gropius House

LINCOLN, MASSACHUSETTS

International Style

Only when architects build houses for themselves do they have the opportunity to demonstrate the full range of their talents, unfettered by client demands. One such house stands today as a fitting monument to the worldwide influence of Walter Gropius (1883–1969), founder of Germany's fabled Bauhaus school of design and a father of modern architecture. In a pure and simple way the Gropius House incorporates all the principles its designer held dear—principles that were to revolutionize architectural designs throughout the world in the mid-twentieth century.

Born in Berlin, Gropius studied at the universities of Berlin and Munich and then became chief assistant to Peter Behrens, a Berlin architect who pioneered modern designs for factories. After serving on the Western Front during World War I, Gropius was asked to take over the School of Arts and Crafts at the Grand Ducal Saxon Academy of Art in Weimar, which he reorganized into the Staatliches Bauhaus. At the Bauhaus (which literally means "house of building"), Gropius put equal stress on the artistry of the design process and the craftsmanship necessary to construct innovative buildings. He also established a set of basic precepts for modern design, which his biographer, James Marston Fitch, has summarized as follows:

1. "The Bauhaus believes the machine to be our modern medium of design and seeks to come to terms with it."
2. All design must recognize this fact of life and distill a new set of esthetic criteria from it. Such a process would, for architecture, lead to "clear, organic [form] whose inner logic will be radiant and naked, unencumbered by lying facades and trickeries."
3. The Bauhaus teaches "the common citizenship of all forms of creative work and their logical interdependence upon one another."
4. The scale and complexity of modern problems necessitates collaborative design. "Any industrially produced object is the result of countless

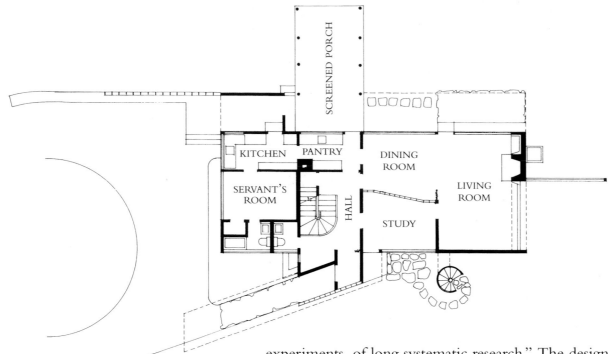

experiments, of long systematic research." The design school must recognize this and equip the student with "the common basis on which many individuals are able to create together a superior unit of work."

5. The education of the designer "must include a thorough, practical manual training in workshops actively engaged in production, coupled with sound theoretical instruction in the laws of design."

In 1919 these were radical concepts. By 1925 the Bauhaus had left Weimar because of growing community antagonism toward the school and moved to Dessau, where greater financial support was promised. In Dessau Gropius applied his revolutionary architectural philosophy to the design of new buildings for the school. Seven years later, however, the Bauhaus was closed by the Nazis, who disliked its avant-garde, communal approach to design. They denounced it as "art-bolshevism which must be wiped out."

Perhaps the greatest innovation of Gropius's Bauhaus was that it brought together in a cooperative setting many talented artists, architects, and craftsmen, most of whom were then relatively unknown. Among the artists and sculptors the Bauhaus attracted were László Moholy-Nagy, Paul Klee, Lyonel Feininger, and Wassily Kandinsky. Architect Marcel Breuer (1902–1981) headed the Bauhaus furniture workshop, where he designed and produced much of the furniture seen today in the Gropius House. Through these talented colleagues, and many others, the influence of the Bauhaus school was multiplied manyfold.

Gropius's personal interest in designing housing for the masses, at times in prefabricated form, was deemed "communistic" by some, and in 1934 he left Germany rather than live under Hitler. At first he settled in London, but in 1937 he was invited to join the faculty of the Harvard Graduate School of Design, where he became chairman of the Department of Architecture one year later.

Gropius had great difficulties getting his personal belongings, and the Bauhaus archives, out of Germany and into the United States. The main stumbling block was none other than Hitler's propaganda minister, Joseph Goebbels, who was in charge of, and hated, Gropius. But as the architect's widow, Ise Frank Gropius, recalls in her memoir, *Gropius House: A History* (1977), a friend in Berlin came up with the following strategy for convincing Goebbels to release Gropius's possessions:

> For the first time in the history of German-American relations, a German instead of a French Beaux Arts architect had been engaged for the Harvard School of Design. Therefore, it would be advisable to let Gropius go without unpleasant remarks in the press and with the permission to take all his possessions like furniture, books, office files etc. to the U.S.A. Göbbels, in spite of his intense dislike for Gropius and all he stood for, took this advice and we were able to return briefly to Germany to have all our things packed and put on the boat which was to take us to New York.

Walter Gropius at home, 1960.

Arriving at Harvard with nothing but these few possessions, the Gropius family rented a small house in suburban Lincoln, near Concord. Not surprisingly, their Bauhaus furnishings looked a bit strange in this Colonial-style dwelling. But fate soon smiled on them. The distinguished Boston architect Henry Shepley of the firm of Shepley, Bulfinch, Richardson and Abbot, approached Mrs. James Storrow, a wealthy local philanthropist, and suggested that she offer Gropius a building site on a large tract of rural land she owned in Lincoln. Shepley also encouraged Mrs. Storrow to finance the building of Gropius's new house and then rent it back to him. Mrs. Storrow agreed, and Gropius began planning his new home.

According to Mrs. Gropius's memoir, she and her husband then spent months looking at Colonial houses in New England; Gropius focused on how America had adapted England's Georgian style. He was particularly fascinated by the use of painted wood instead of stone or brick for the exterior walls and by the ubiquitous porches. Central halls with doors at each end for ventilation also impressed him, as did the speed and ease with which American wood-framed houses could be erected.

Gropius decided to cover the exterior of his new house with the traditional wooden siding he had seen and admired around the New England countryside, but he applied the boards vertically rather than in the usual horizontal fashion. The boards were painted white; for accent, the exterior circular staircase, window framing, and roof coping were painted a contrasting gray. In shape the house is a simple rectangular block but with cutouts and additions: an added covered entry and staircase on the north; a cut-out sun deck with a protective screen on the west; and an added screened porch on the south.

In designing the house, Gropius paid special attention to heating, ventilation, and drainage. The almost flat roof, a startling innovation in 1930s New England, drains water to an interior downpipe that leads to a dry well. The advantages of this scheme

This view of the south-facing rear façade (BOTTOM RIGHT) shows the screened-in porch and the roof-level sun visor to the left. The west façade (TOP RIGHT) includes a gray-painted brick fireplace and chimney; the projecting sun visor is visible beyond. To the left is the cut-out deck built for the Gropiuses' daughter. It has a private entrance reached by an industrial circular stairway. An ancient vine, just beginning to leaf, ornaments the chimney wall and sun deck (ABOVE).

over exterior drainage are that the interior downpipe never freezes during cold weather, no gutters are needed, and no downspouts are required on the outside of the house. This drainage system has worked well for more than fifty years.

For heating Gropius installed three separate systems. Built-in hot-water radiators under most windows emit warm air through grills in the windowsills; a ducted hot-air system is available for quick heating when needed; and a fireplace can supply emergency heat during power or fuel shortages.

Summer cooling is facilitated by an overhanging sun visor across much of the south side. The large west window has an exterior aluminum venetian blind that is controlled from inside the house. Unlike interior blinds, this exterior blind deflects heat *before* it can be absorbed through the window. These antiheat devices, in addition to the many windows and the cross-ventilation generated by having doors at either end of the same corridor, proved so effective that air-conditioning was never considered necessary.

On his New England tours Gropius had noticed many screened-in *side* porches but decided upon a more private, less noisy rear location for his own screened porch. The view from it is delightful, with a picturesque white pine and small Japanese-inspired garden in the foreground and rural countryside beyond. And because it faces south, both sunsets and sunrises can be seen. The screening, which allows gentle breezes in and keeps insects out, was much appreciated by the Gropiuses. An unscreened upstairs sun deck with its own exterior staircase was provided for their daughter, who was twelve when the house was built and wanted to be able to come and go with her friends without encountering any adults.

One of Gropius's most sacred principles was using mass-produced parts in his designs. The hardware, light fixtures, and interior fittings throughout the house were all standard items found in 1937 building-supply catalogs. As a rule Gropius chose the simpler designs made of high-grade materials found in commercial catalogs rather than those intended for domestic use. The only fixture in the house that is not a stock catalog item is the inside stairway banister, which had to be custom-made on the site.

The house conserves space by having only one hall, a central area that opens onto all the rooms except the living room, which can be entered only through the study or the dining room. The Gropiuses, however, considered the entire downstairs to be one large living area, of which the study, with its large, two-person desk, was but a section. Indeed, a close look at the furnishings of the living room reveals that it was generally used as an extension of the study. Two comfortable reading places occupy much of the living room's sitting area: a daybed with headrest and a shaped plywood long chair. Each has a lamp designed for reading. Wooden bookshelves line one end of the room, which was clearly intended for long hours of reading and contemplation, not just for entertaining. Carefully avoided is the cliché of a central sofa with side chairs.

Lighting was meticulously planned throughout the house. For example, the single down light over the dining room table is masked so that it sheds its light only on the table surface. A single upstairs switch turns on all of the exterior lights, as protection against

prowlers. Like all the other systems in the house, the lighting consists entirely of standard parts readily available at that time.

As Ise Gropius explains, "Gropius wanted to prove that the mass produced output of American industry was quite capable of producing a sophisticated house of contemporary design though it had never been tried before in this manner." She goes on to quote the house's contractor, a Mr. Jenney:

> During several meetings we had . . . we checked the various items from stock catalogues to see what items we could use for the construction of this house, because he was limited as to how much money he could spend, since the house was financed by Mrs. James Storrow, and Dr. Gropius was going to rent it from her. We found about everything we needed for the house in stock. His ideas were most unusual. Although he used stock items,

The comfortable reading end of the living room (ABOVE LEFT) also functions as part of the adjacent study. The fireplace end of the living room (ABOVE RIGHT) features a Breuer-designed tubular-steel table with black lami-nated top, a Saarinen womb chair, and a pair of Yanagi stools. The painted and etched lucite piece above the fireplace is by László Moholy-Nagy, and the mobile to the left was constructed for Gropius by students.

Marcel Breuer designed the dining room table and its tubular-steel chairs (BELOW LEFT). The chrome light fixture (BELOW RIGHT) was ordered from a standard movie-theater lighting catalog. The print is by Miró.

Pure white tiles and fixtures combine with chrome detailing to give the downstairs powder room a pristine look.

he used them in ways different from anything I had done before. . . . Many afternoons we sat for a couple of hours on a sawhorse talking over the house changes as I did not always agree with his ideas. Many times he was right and I was wrong.

The master bedroom is another complex space. The bedroom area itself is quite small, with just enough room for a bed and two side tables. Yet a narrow, seventeen-foot-long ribbon window expands the space visually and a dressing area separated from the bedroom by a glass partition enlarges it physically. These two areas flow into each other but are far more functional than a single room of the same size.

The house has many pieces of furniture that were handmade in the workshops of the Dessau Bauhaus for the Gropius home there. Marcel Breuer headed the Bauhaus shop that produced these furnishings, and many of the designs are his, including the dining room table and chairs, the living room daybed, the study desk, and the beds in the master and guest bedrooms.

Breuer and Gropius had long been colleagues, and Breuer followed Gropius to teach at the Harvard School of Design. His own home, of equally avant-garde design, was built only a hundred yards down the road from the Gropius House, on which he had collaborated. At Harvard, as at the Bauhaus, Gropius recruited many talented designers, and their collective influence began to spread throughout the United States just as the Bauhaus designers' had in Europe. Collaborative efforts, machine-made parts, elimination of decoration, and functional spaces all became the hallmarks of American design through the 1950s and 1960s, and this influence is still strongly felt today.

The Gropiuses adopted a limited color palette—white and gray for the exterior of the house and black, white, brown, and gray with an occasional touch of red for the interior. Wall-to-wall floor coverings helped unite the small spaces and make them appear larger. Cork flooring was used in the hall and on the staircase. Black linoleum covered the pantry and kitchen floors, while walnut-brown wool carpet was used for the living room, dining room, and study. All interior walls were white, which produced a most pleasing effect in combination with the large window areas.

The landscaping of the Gropius House is quite simple: several red oaks and pine trees, a few large vines strategically placed on the house, and a single planting bed outside the screened porch. There is no "lawn" in the usual sense, that is, no culture of one grass variety—watered, fertilized, and mown short. Rather there is a meadow of old mixed grasses and wildflowers—a look that many gardeners strive for today but that Gropius favored a half-century ago. He may have merely admired its natural simplicity, but perhaps his humane vision extended to the natural environment as well. For whatever reason, the meadow, tidily clipped only in the area immediately around the house, provides a perfect setting for the house. Just as the living room was furnished for day-to-day living, the garden was left as a place where many kinds of wildlife could flourish.

It is difficult today to realize how startlingly revolutionary the Gropius House was when built. Our eyes have become accustomed to the many Bauhaus principles incorporated into designs built from the 1950s on. This is truly a house in which the design grew out of functional concerns—the bedroom–dressing area combination and the study–living room arrangement, for example. Care was also given to the relation of the house to its environment—the thoughtfully placed windows and porch, the unique central drain for the roof, the sun visor on the south side, and the exterior blind on the west wall. The colors were kept muted so that individual works of art, and their human observers, could take center stage. Each element in the house is spare but carefully considered. The result is a calm, almost ascetic, atmosphere in which to live and work. In short, the house is an admirable summary of the design philosophy of Gropius and his Bauhaus colleagues. The Society for the Preservation of New England Antiquities, which owns and operates thirty-four historic properties, is to be praised for its foresight in preserving this rare landmark for future generations to study and enjoy.

LEFT *The master bedroom and dressing room are separated by a clear glass wall with a suspended mirror that makes each room seem much larger. This unusual design created two different heat zones— a cool one for sleeping and a warm one for dressing and grooming. A cantilevered lab bench, ordered from a catalog, serves as a long dressing table.*

RIGHT *The master bath is in the Gropiuses' preferred palette of black, white, gray, and brown.*

International Style
(1925–1940 AND LATER)

In the years between the two world wars, European and American architectural fashion diverged sharply. Avant-garde European designers became fascinated with starkly modern buildings that discarded all hints of the architectural past, while American architects favored historical revival architecture based on models from Colonial America, medieval England and France, and Renaissance Italy.

By the early 1930s there were distinguished practitioners of modern design in several European countries. Among the most notable were Le Corbusier in France, Pier Luigi Nervi in Italy, J.J.P. Oud in Holland, and Walter Gropius and his Bauhaus associates in Germany. As the Nazis gained power, many members of the Bauhaus fled Europe; those who came to the United States were responsible for introducing the new International style to this country.

Gropius left Europe in 1934 and in 1938 became chairman of the Department of Architecture at Harvard University. In 1937 Gropius's successor as Bauhaus director, Ludwig Mies van der Rohe, also left Germany to be-come dean of the School of Architecture at Chicago's Illinois Institute of Technology. American acceptance of the radical designs of these pioneer modernists was cautious at first. Only a sprinkling of International-style houses and public buildings were commissioned in the 1930s. With their unornamented walls (usually of smooth white stucco), flat roofs, and lack of decorative detailing, they are often found in the midst of, and are strikingly different from, their historically based Eclectic-era neighbors. Among the most important of the early International-style houses is the landmark dwelling that Gropius built for himself near Boston in 1938. (Ironically, Gropius disliked stylistic labels and never accepted the term *International style* for the movement he helped to found.)

By 1950 Gropius, Mies, and their associates had trained a generation of American students in Bauhaus principles, which have since become central to American design. Although never a widely popular style for house design, International-style public and commercial buildings dominated American cities for several decades.

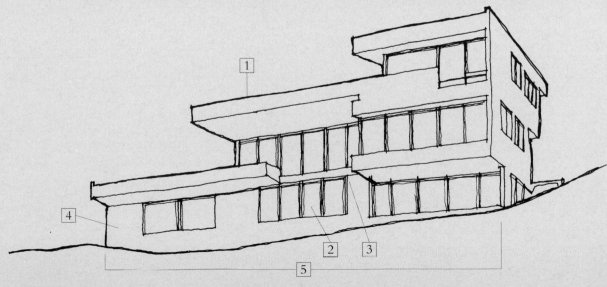

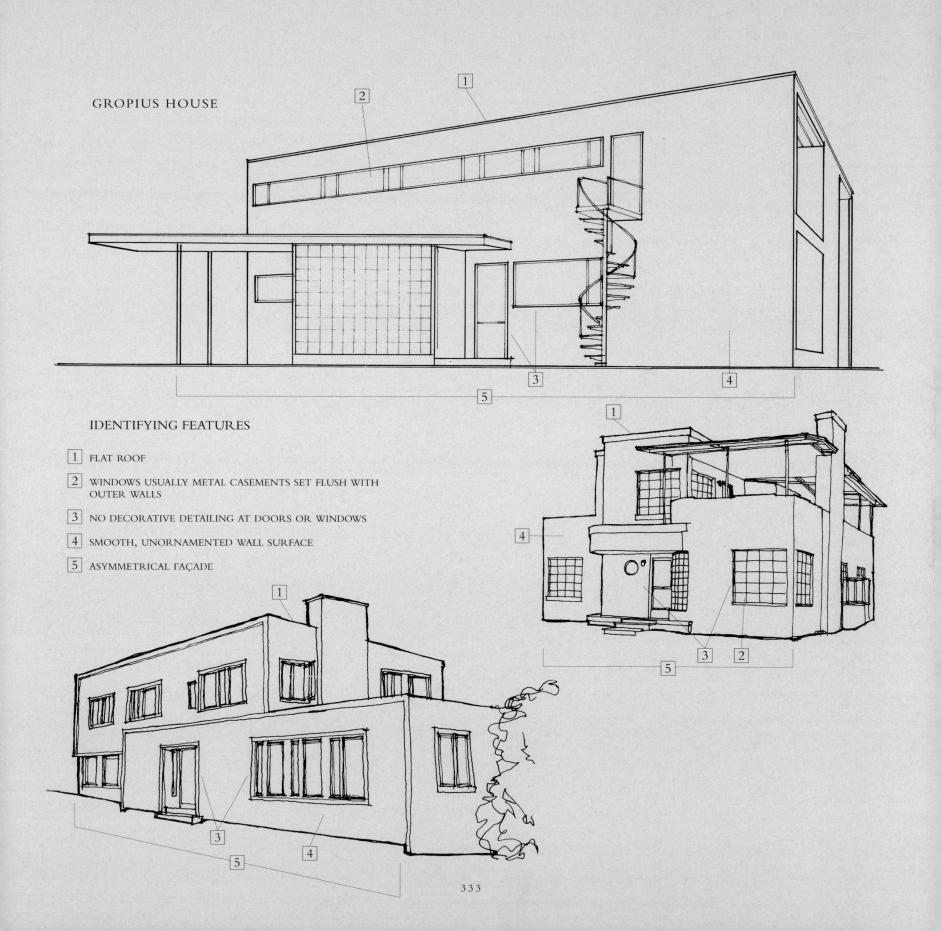

GROPIUS HOUSE

IDENTIFYING FEATURES

1　FLAT ROOF

2　WINDOWS USUALLY METAL CASEMENTS SET FLUSH WITH
　OUTER WALLS

3　NO DECORATIVE DETAILING AT DOORS OR WINDOWS

4　SMOOTH, UNORNAMENTED WALL SURFACE

5　ASYMMETRICAL FAÇADE

333

Visiting the Houses

All of the houses in this book are open to the public except Casa del Herrero (Santa Barbara, California), whose owners have recently transferred the property to a private foundation that plans to permit public access on a limited basis in the future.

Most of the houses charge an entry fee in the $3–8 range. An exception is Biltmore (Asheville, North Carolina), whose current fee of $23 permits a full day of visiting the house, on a self-guided basis, as well as the extensive gardens and grounds, winery, restaurants, and shops.

Several of the houses in New England and on New York's Long Island are open only for the summer season, which usually includes part of the late spring and early fall. We have indicated these as "open seasonally." The remainder of the houses are open throughout the year. A few are open every day, but most are closed one or more days each week.

Our advice for planning a visit to a historic house-museum is to call ahead to confirm when it will be open. We have refrained from including visiting days and hours because these frequently change and it is no fun to schedule a visit only to find that the hours have changed or that the house is closed to visitors because of a special event that day.

Most houses offer visitors guide-accompanied tours that typically last about an hour. A few offer self-guided tours that let you walk through the house at your leisure.

House-museums list closing times in two different ways. Some state the time they actually shut the doors and go home. Others list the last moment you can enter the house for a guided or self-guided tour. The crucial questions to ask are: "When does the last tour start?" or "What is the latest time I can enter the house for a self-guided tour?"

Opening times are similarly confusing. The listed time may be the moment the ticket desk is unlocked, which can precede the first tour by as much as an hour. Again, ask when the first tour begins, or, in the case of self-guided tours, what is the earliest time one may enter the house.

Biltmore
U.S. 25, 3 blocks north of Interstate 40
Asheville, North Carolina
Telephone: (800) 543-2961
Administered by: The Biltmore Company
(Mailing address: One North Pack
Square, Asheville, NC 28801)

Casa del Herrero
To be administered by a private foundation
established by the Steedmans' heirs.
(Not yet open to the public)

Château-sur-Mer
Bellevue Avenue
P.O. Box 510
Newport, Rhode Island 02840
Telephone: (401) 847-1000
Administered by: Preservation Society of
Newport County

Dana-Thomas House
301 E. Lawrence Avenue
Springfield, Illinois 62703
Telephone: (217) 782-6776
Administered by: Illinois Historic
Preservation Agency

Falaise
Sands Point Preserve
95 Middleneck Road
Port Washington, New York 11050
Telephone: (516) 883-1612
Administered by: Nassau County Department
of Recreation and Parks
(Open seasonally)

Gamble House
4 Westmoreland Place
Pasadena, California 91103
Telephone: (818) 793-3334
Administered by: University of Southern
California School of Architecture in
cooperation with the City of Pasadena,
which owns the house

Glenmont
Main Street and Lakeside Avenue
(go to Visitor Center for Edison National
Historic Site)
West Orange, New Jersey 07052
Telephone: (201) 736-0550
Administered by: U.S. National Park Service

Glessner House
1800 Prairie Avenue
Chicago, Illinois 60616
Telephone: (312) 326-1393
Administered by: Chicago Architecture
Foundation

Gropius House
68 Baker Bridge Road
Lincoln, Massachusetts 01773
Telephone: (617) 227-3956
Administered by: Society for the Preservation
of New England Antiquities
(Open seasonally; very limited hours rest
of year)

Iron Works House

244 Central Street
Saugus, Massachusetts 01906
Telephone: (617) 233-0050
Administered by: U.S. National Park Service
(Open seasonally)

Lee House

161 Washington Street
Marblehead, Massachusetts 01945
Telephone: (617) 631-1069
Administered by: Marblehead Historical
    Society
(Open seasonally)

Lyndhurst

635 South Broadway
Tarrytown, New York 10591
Telephone: (914) 631-0046
Administered by: National Trust for Historic
    Preservation

Mark Twain House

351 Farmington Avenue
Hartford, Connecticut 06105
Telephone: (203) 247-0998
Administered by: Mark Twain Memorial

Melrose

Melrose-Montebello Parkway
Natchez, Mississippi 39120
Telephone: (800) 647-6742
Administered by: U.S. National Park Service

Monticello

Route 20 South at Interstate 64
    (Visitor's Center)
P.O. Box 316
Charlottesville, Virginia 22902
Telephone: (804) 295-8181
Administered by: Thomas Jefferson
    Memorial Foundation

Morse-Libby House

(also known as Victoria Mansion)
109 Danforth Street
Portland, Maine 04101
Telephone: (207) 772-4841
Administered by: Victoria Society of Maine
(Open seasonally)

Naumkeag

Prospect Hill Road
P.O. Box 792
Stockbridge, Massachusetts 01262
Telephone: (413) 298-3239
Administered by: Trustees of Reservations
(Open seasonally)

Parlange

8211 False River Road
New Roads, Louisiana 70760
Telephone: (504) 638-8410
Home of Mr. and Mrs. Walter C. Parlange;
    visitors welcome

Russell House

51 Meeting Street
Charleston, South Carolina 29401
Telephone: (803) 724-8481
Administered by: Historic Charleston
    Foundation

Spanish Governor's Palace

105 Plaza de Armas
San Antonio, Texas 78205
Telephone: (210) 224-0601
Administered by: San Antonio Park and
    Recreation Department

Stan Hywet Hall

714 North Portage Path
Akron, Ohio 44303
Telephone: (216) 836-5533
Administered by: Stan Hywet Hall
    Foundation
(Closed for several weeks in January)

Vanderbilt House

Albany Post Road/U.S. 9
Hyde Park, New York 12538
Telephone: (914) 229-9115
Administered by: U.S. National Park Service
(Located just north of the town of Hyde Park)

Vizcaya

3251 South Miami Avenue
Miami, Florida 33129
Telephone: (305) 579-2813
Administered by: Metro-Dade Parks and
    Recreation Department

Westbury House

71 Old Westbury Road
P.O. Box 430
Old Westbury, New York 11568
Telephone: (516) 333-0048
Administered by: Old Westbury Gardens
(Open seasonally)

Whitehall

Cocoanut Row
P.O. Box 969
Palm Beach, Florida 33480
Telephone: (407) 655-2833
Administered by: The Henry Morrison
    Flagler Museum

Bibliography

GENERAL WORKS

Clark, Clifford Edward, Jr. *The American Family Home, 1800–1960*. Chapel Hill, N.C.: University of North Carolina Press, 1986.

Davidson, Marshall B. *Notable American Houses*. New York: American Heritage Publishing Co., 1971.

Handlin, David P. *The American Home*. Boston: Little, Brown and Co., 1979.

McAlester, Virginia, and Lee McAlester. *A Field Guide to American Houses*. New York: Alfred A. Knopf, 1984.

Mayhew, Edgar DeN., and Minor Meyers, Jr. *A Documentary History of American Furnishings to 1915*. New York: Scribners, 1980.

Moss, Roger W. *The American Country House*. New York: Henry Holt and Co., 1990.

COLONIAL HOUSES

Adams, William Howard. *Jefferson's Monticello*. New York: Abbeville Press, 1983.

Cummings, Abbott Lowell. *The Framed Houses of Massachusetts Bay, 1625–1725*. Cambridge, Mass.: Harvard University Press, 1979. The definitive treatment of the First-Period English style.

McLaughlin, Jack. *Jefferson and Monticello*. New York: Henry Holt and Co., 1988.

Morrison, Hugh. *Early American Architecture*. New York: Oxford University Press, 1952.

Pierson, William H., Jr. *American Buildings and Their Architects: The Colonial and Neoclassical Styles*. Garden City, N.Y.: Doubleday and Co., 1970.

Stein, Susan R. *The Worlds of Thomas Jefferson at Monticello*. New York: Harry N. Abrams (in association with the Thomas Jefferson Memorial Foundation), 1993.

ROMANTIC HOUSES

Downing, A. J. *Cottage Residences*. 1842. Reprint. Watkins Glen, N.Y.: American Life Foundation, 1967. The first popular house pattern book.

Kennedy, Roger G. *Greek Revival America*. New York: Stewart, Tabori & Chang, 1989.

Pierson, William H., Jr. *American Buildings and Their Architects: Technology and the Picturesque—The Corporate and Early Gothic Styles*. Garden City, N.Y.: Doubleday and Co., 1978. Includes comprehensive chapters on Lyndhurst and its architect, A. J. Davis.

VICTORIAN HOUSES

Baker, Paul R. *Richard Morris Hunt*. Cambridge, Mass.: MIT Press, 1980. Biography of the Stick-style innovator and architect of the Château-sur-Mer remodeling and of Biltmore.

———. *Stanny: The Gilded Life of Stanford White*. New York: Free Press, 1989. Biography of the architect of Naumkeag and collaborator on the Vanderbilt House.

Faude, Wilson H. *The Renaissance of Mark Twain's House*. Larchmont, N.Y.: Queens House, 1978.

Glessner, John J. *The Story of a House: H. H. Richardson's Glessner House*. Chicago: Chicago Architecture Foundation, 1992.

Holly, H. Hudson. *Modern Dwellings*. New York: Harper & Brothers, 1878. Architectural manifesto by the influential advocate of the Queen Anne style and designer of Glenmont.

Landau, Sarah Bradford. *Edward T. and William A. Potter: American Victorian Architects*. New York: Garland Publishing, 1979. Biography of the architect of the Mark Twain House.

O'Gorman, James F. *H. H. Richardson*. Chicago: University of Chicago Press, 1987. The most recent biography of the architect of the Glessner House.

Scully, Vincent J., Jr. *The Shingle Style and the Stick Style*. Rev. ed. New Haven, Conn.: Yale University Press, 1971.

Wilson, Richard Guy. *McKim, Mead & White, Architects*. New York: Rizzoli, 1983. This summary of the work of the partnership includes early photographs of Naumkeag.

Winkler, Gail Caskey, and Roger W. Moss. *Victorian Interior Decoration*. New York: Henry Holt and Co., 1986.

ECLECTIC HOUSES

Aslet, Clive. *The American Country House.* New Haven, Conn.: Yale University Press, 1990.

Boegner, Peggie Phipps, and Richard Gachot. *Halcyon Days.* Old Westbury, N.Y.: Old Westbury Gardens, 1986. Lavishly illustrated memoir of life at Westbury House.

Gebhard, David. "George Washington Smith." In *Santa Barbara Architecture,* by Herb Andree and Noel Young, pp. 83–93. 2d ed. Santa Barbara, Calif.: Capra Press, 1980. Biographical essay on the architect of Casa del Herrero.

Ginaven, Marlene. *Not for Us Alone.* Akron, Ohio: Stan Hywet Hall Foundation, 1985. Memoir of life at Stan Hywet Hall.

Gropius, Ise. *Gropius House: A History.* Boston: Society for the Preservation of New England Antiquities, 1977.

Harwood, Kathryn Chapman. *The Lives of Vizcaya.* Miami: Banyan Books, 1985.

Hewitt, Mark Alan. *The Architect & the American Country House, 1890–1940.* New Haven, Conn.: Yale University Press, 1990.

Jordy, William H. *American Buildings and Their Architects: Progressive and Academic Ideals at the Turn of the Twentieth Century.* Garden City, N.Y.: Doubleday and Co., 1972. Includes a chapter on the Gamble House.

King, Robert B. *The Vanderbilt Homes.* New York: Rizzoli, 1989. Includes chapters on Biltmore and the (Frederick) Vanderbilt House.

Makinson, Randell L. *Greene & Greene.* Salt Lake City: Peregrine Smith, 1977. Biography of the architects of the Gamble House.

Twombly, Robert C. *Frank Lloyd Wright.* New York: Harper & Row, 1973. Biography of the architect of the Dana-Thomas House.

Wright, Frank Lloyd. *The Early Work.* New York: Horizon Press, 1968. Reprint of *Ausgefürte Bauten.* Berlin: Ernst Wasmuth, 1911. The original edition of this illustrated monograph helped popularize Wright's modernism in Europe. Includes early photographs of the Dana-Thomas House.

Acknowledgments

Many people have helped to make this book possible. On a personal level, the advice and counsel of our friend Tom Wittenbraker smoothed the way for the project from its inception. He and his assistant Sharri Prosser then provided invaluable support throughout the entire preparation process.

Our agent, Angela Miller of the Miller Agency, has not only gracefully performed an agent's usual functions but has also gone far beyond the call of duty. This included supervising many of the photo shoots, for one of which she had to abandon two dozen house guests!

We feel very lucky that Alex McLean agreed to be the book's photographer. Before moving to New York Alex lived in France for thirty years and studied photography in Paris. One of his specialties is taking interior photographs using mostly natural light. Not only is this approach less disruptive to the historic houses, but it also gives the reader a clearer idea of how each house actually looks. The shooting was done on a very tight schedule requiring fast footwork and careful timing to follow the light as the sun moved all too quickly around each house. Amazingly, Alex maintained his temper and sense of humor throughout this marathon.

Larry Boerder, a Dallas architect who specializes in designing new houses, did the delightful sketches of each landmark as well as those of the smaller, more typical neighborhood examples. Among other skills this required intuiting what was hidden behind obscuring trees, bushes or walls in many of the photographs we provided. Larry's sister, Carol Boerder-Snyder, who is also an architect, patiently and meticulously drew the floor plans—in many cases from vague and hard-to-read copies of original drawings.

The endpaper map was drawn by Jerry Guthrie, a Dallas graphic artist who is both intuitive and enthusiastic about cartography.

Our editor at Abbeville Press, Jackie Decter, has seen the book through production with great skill and dedication. We have much appreciated her calm consideration of each new challenge and her consistently insightful suggestions. The book's designer, Nai Chang, not only turned our rough ideas into a splendidly polished whole but also managed to closely coordinate text with illustrations throughout. Finally, we must thank Bob Abrams, president of Abbeville, for his belief in and support of the project.

We are also much indebted to all of the following for their generous cooperation:

Biltmore

The Biltmore Company
William A. V. Cecil, owner of Biltmore
   and a founder of the Historic House
   Association of America, a program of the
   National Trust for Historic Preservation
Travis Ledford, Public Relations Officer
Kelly Simpson, Communications Assistant
Julia Weede, Communications Coordinator
Diana C. Pickering, Vice President

Casa del Herrero

George Bass
Claudia Lane
Jane and Ildo Marra

Château-sur-Mer

Preservation Society of Newport County
Monique Panaggio (Mrs. Leonard J.), Public
   Relations Director

Dana-Thomas House

The Illinois Historic Preservation Agency
   (State of Illinois)
Frank Lloyd Wright's Dana-Thomas House
   State Historic Site
Dr. Donald P. Hallmark, Site Manager

Falaise

Nassau County Department of Recreation
   and Parks
Nassau County Museum, Sands Point Preserve
Ronald J. Wyatt, Supervisor, Museum
   Collections
Glen Sitterly, Curator of Decorative Arts
Phyllis Braff, former Curator of Fine Art

Gamble House

University of Southern California School of
   Architecture
The City of Pasadena
Ted Bosley, Director
Randell L. Makinson, former Director

Glenmont

Edison National Historic Site: U.S. National Park Service

Theresa Flynn Jung, Chief of Visitor Services and Resource Protection

Kristen Herron, Curator of Glenmont

Leah Burt, former Curator of Glenmont

Doug Tarr, Assistant Archivist

Camille Agricola for information from her unpublished 1980 Columbia University master's thesis on the interior finishes of Glenmont

The Oral History Research Office, Columbia University, for permission to use excerpts from pages 32, 47, and 160 of "The Reminiscences of Theodore Edison," recorded in July 1970, on pages 162–63.

Glessner House

Chicago Architectural Foundation

Janice Griffin, Curator

Michael McDonough, former Curator

Carol Callahan, former Curator

Lisa Philips, Curatorial Assistant

Susan Mastro, Public Programs Coordinator

Charles Flaggs, Caretaker

Gropius House

Society for the Preservation of New England Antiquities

Nancy Curtis, Public Relations Officer

Peter Gittleman, Manager of Property Interpretation

Iron Works House

Saugus Iron Works National Historic Site: U.S. National Park Service

Carl R. Salmons, Chief, Division of Museum Services

Janet Regan, Museum Technician

Phil Lupsiewicz, Supervising Park Ranger

Reed Johnson, Superintendent

Lee House

The Marblehead Historical Society

Betty Hunt (Mrs. John P., Jr.), Executive Secretary

Judy Anderson

Lyndhurst

The National Trust for Historic Preservation

Henry Duffy, Curator

Mark Twain House

Mark Twain Memorial

Marianne J. Curling, Curator

Walter Schwinn for information from his unpublished history of the house

Dr. Robert H. Hirst and the Mark Twain Project at the Bancroft Library, University of California at Berkeley, for permission to publish the excerpt of a letter quoted on page 143 and the Tiffany contract on page 144.

Melrose

Natchez Historic Park: U.S. National Park Service

Thom Rosenblum, Museum Curator

Kathleen Jenkins, Museum Technician

Stuart K. Johnson, former Superintendent

Monticello

Thomas Jefferson Memorial Foundation

Libby Fosso, Communications Officer

Daniel P. Jordan, Executive Director

Robert C. Lautman for his generosity in permitting us to use seven of his photographs of Monticello's interiors taken during the exhibition "The Worlds of Thomas Jefferson at Monticello," which commemorated the 250th anniversary of Jefferson's birth.

Jack McLaughlin, author of *Jefferson and Monticello: The Biography of a Builder.* Much of the Monticello chapter was inspired by his insight.

Morse-Libby House

Victoria Society of Maine

Bruce T. Sherwood, Director

Glenn Uminowicz, former Director

Naumkeag

The Trustees of Reservations

Mark Bauer, Historic House Administrator

Lindy Green, Administrative Assistant

Parlange Plantation

Mr. and Mrs. Walter C. Parlange, Jr.

Russell House

Historic Charleston Foundation
J. Thomas Savage, Jr., Curator
Robert Leath, Assistant Curator

Spanish Governor's Palace

San Antonio Park and Recreation Department
Nora Ward, Museum Assistant
Jeanette Bradfield, Recreation Services
    Supervisor
Gilbert Lopez, Museum Aide
Jeffe Rico, Custodian
Ronnie Burkholder, Service Administrator

Stan Hywet Hall

Stan Hywet Hall Foundation
Margaret A. Tramontine, Curator of
    Collections

Vanderbilt House

Roosevelt-Vanderbilt National Historic Sites:
    U.S. National Park Service
Duane Pearson, former Superintendent
Frank Mares
Margaret Partridge, Management Assistant

Vizcaya

Vizcaya Museum and Gardens
Metro-Dade Parks and Recreation
    Department
Doris B. Littlefield, Chief Museum Curator
Holly Blount, Public Relations Director

Westbury

Old Westbury Gardens
Susan Tripp, Director
Laura Carpenter-Correa, Archivist
Monica Reissman
Jethro Meriwether Hurt III, former Director

Whitehall

The Henry Morrison Flagler Museum
Kay Graham, Public Relations
Joan Runkel, Curator
Tom Prestegard, Assistant Director

Other

David J. Brown, Executive Director,
    Preservation Alliance of Virginia
Al Cox, Preservation Planner, City of
    Alexandria, Virginia, Planning and
    Community Development Department
Abbott Lowell Cummings, Professor of Art
    History, Yale University
David Gebhard, Curator of the Architectural
    Drawing Collection, University of
    California at Santa Barbara
Joseph B. Going of Middletown, Rhode
    Island
James Z. Kypprianos of the Ipswich
    Historical Society
Mrs. E. M. Smith of Newport, Rhode Island

Index

Photography Credits

All photographs courtesy of Alex McLean, with the exception of the following:

Avery Library, Columbia University in the City of New York: p. 100 (Drawings and Archives), p. 248 top (McKim, Mead & White Collection).

Biltmore Estate, Asheville, North Carolina: p. 234.

Charles R. Clark, courtesy Chicago Historical Society, Chicago, Illinois: p. 180.

The Dana-Thomas House, Illinois Historic Preservation Agency, Springfield, Illinois: pp. 190, 296.

The Henry M. Flagler Museum, Palm Beach, Florida: p. 208.

The Institute of Texan Cultures, University of Texas, San Antonio, Texas; The San Antonio Light Collection: p. 74.

Robert C. Lautman, courtesy Monticello/Thomas Jefferson Memorial Foundation, Inc., Charlottesville, Virginia: pp. 50 right, 51, 52, 53 bottom, 54, 55 top and bottom.

Library of Congress, Washington, D.C.; Manuscript Division: pp. 34 right, 173 (Fletcher Steele Collection).

Los Angeles Public Library, Los Angeles, California; Security Pacific Collection: p. 311 top and bottom.

Louisiana and Lower Mississippi Valley Collection, LSU Libraries, Louisiana State University, Baton Rouge, Louisiana; Edward Turner and Family Papers: pp. 88, 89.

The Metropolitan Museum of Art, New York; Harris Brisbane Dick Fund, 1924: pp. 84, 163 top left.

Monticello/Thomas Jefferson Memorial Foundation, Inc., Charlottesville, Virginia: pp. 8, 53 top (H. Andrew Johnson); p. 53 center (Edward Owen).

Collection of The Newport Historical Society, Newport, Rhode Island: p. 128.

Newsday photograph, c. 1960s, Copyright © 1994 Newsday, New York City: p. 265.

Office of the Custodian of Notarial Records for the Parish of Orleans, Louisiana: p. 62.

Old Westbury Gardens, Old Westbury, New York: p. 194.

Roosevelt-Vanderbilt National Historic Sites, Hyde Park, New York: p. 255 top and bottom.

Society for the Preservation of New England Antiquities, Boston, Massachusetts: p. 13 (Sullivan L. Holman); p. 325.

Stan Hywet Hall & Gardens, Inc., Akron, Ohio: p. 225.

David Stansbury, Wadsworth Atheneum, Hartford, Connecticut; The Ella Gallup Sumner and Mary Catlin Sumner Collection Fund: p. 28 left.

Mark Twain Memorial, Hartford, Connecticut: pp. 124, 148, 149.

Collection of The Victoria Society, Portland, Maine: p. 114 top.

Vizcaya Museum and Gardens, Miami, Florida: p. 270 top and bottom.

U.S. Department of the Interior, National Park Service, Edison National Historic Site, West Orange, New Jersey: p. 154.

Frank Lloyd Wright Home and Studio Foundation: p. 305 right.